WORDS THAT TRANSFORM

Preaching as a Catalyst for Renewal

James T. Flynn

University Press of America,® Inc.
Lanham · Boulder · New York · Toronto · Plymouth, UK

Copyright © 2010 by
University Press of America,® Inc.
4501 Forbes Boulevard
Suite 200
Lanham, Maryland 20706
UPA Acquisitions Department (301) 459-3366

Estover Road
Plymouth PL6 7PY
United Kingdom

Library of Congress Control Number: 2010927820
ISBN: 978-0-7618-5237-7 (paperback : alk. paper)
eISBN: 978-0-7618-5238-4

To Monica, the love of my life.
Your companionship has taught me what it
means to be faithful. Your life as an artist
never ceases to inspire me. Your support has
made my life and ministry possible.

To Mom and Dad.
Your faith in me and constant support
have been a constant inspiration to me and have
made this work possible.

To Stephen, Rachel, Heather, and Benji.
You are my legacy. You have walked
with me through many difficult times.
Now rejoice with me—my fruit is
your fruit.

Contents

Foreword

Dr. James Flynn has been a colleague and friend of mine for many years. I have known him as a most capable student, professor, and administrator at the Regent University School of Divinity. At one time, he served as my administrative dean as well as the first dean of the Regent University School of Undergraduate Studies. He currently serves as associate professor of practical theology and director of the Doctor of Ministry Program here at Regent. Over the years, he has put a very positive stamp on all the students he has taught and mentored.

Before I met him, Flynn enjoyed many years of experience as a church planter and pastor in Pittsburgh, Pennsylvania. In 1976, at the height of the Charismatic Renewal, he helped to plant a church that grew from a living-room Bible study to a thriving congregation of twelve hundred members. From 1990 to 1999, he served as senior pastor of the church. All this pastoral experience has served him well as he has taught and mentored a new generation of pastor here at Regent. He refers to his current work as teaching the "pastoral arts" to his students, who come to him from many denominations in the U.S. and other nations.

In addition to all of these accomplishments, Flynn has been a prolific writer of articles and books. His previous book, *A Well-Furnished Heart: Restoring the Spirit's Place in the Leadership Classroom* (2002), was done in cooperation with Russell . West and Wie L. Tjiong, two colleagues at Regent. This work prepared the way for this book, *Words That Transform: Preaching as a Catalyst for Renewal* (2010).

Some observers feel that preaching has become a lost art in the present-day churches. Although many churches have great worship and dynamic music ministries, they often have pastors who give sermons that could be termed "theology lite" with little scriptural content and often with conversational blather meant to soothe and comfort but not to challenge believers to a deeper understanding of the Bible and the great issues of the day.

In *Words That Transform*, Flynn calls for what he calls "incarnational preaching and teaching" through a four-part process centered on the Scriptures. The four parts are: (1) conception of the word, (2) growth of the word, (3) maturing of the word, and (4) delivery of the word. He calls for "imagination, creativity, stories, and testimonies" that will bring forth "transformational" preaching, which will challenge and ultimately transform the hearers.

What makes the book so important is that Flynn writes from his many years as a pastor of a large urban church. Although *Words That Transform* was written by a man with a charismatic background, his insights will be helpful and inspirational to pastors and teachers from any church tradition. This book walks a fine line between popular and academic theology. Although it is well researched and documented with thorough footnotes and a wonderful bibliography, it reads in a very interesting and popular style. In the end, Flynn recognizes the crucial role of the Holy Spirit in effective preaching. Without the "anointing" of the Spirit, even the best-constructed and well-delivered sermons will have little lasting effect on the faithful.

I am grateful that Jim Flynn is sharing his rich store of learning and experiences, not only with his students in the classroom, but also with the thousands of hardworking and sincere pastors who can learn much from this wonderful book.

Vinson Synan
Dean Emeritus
Regent University School of Divinity
January 2010

Preface

Preaching is one of the highest callings any man or woman can receive. This year marks thirty-five years since I received that calling. The most rewarding part of these years has been seeing lives changed by God through my preaching ministry. As I sit here writing, I can still see many of the faces of those whose lives were transformed. I see the couple who came to my church with their marriage hanging by a thread, only to become marriage counselors themselves in the years that followed. I see the face of a dear woman who was a recovering alcoholic—she not only put her life back together but also established a ministry to the poor in her community. I can still see the faces of some of the young lions who sat listening to my words and who made the choice to go live those words out: Mike is in India with his wife and family as a missionary planting churches and exceeding anything I will ever accomplish in my own ministry. Greg is in Asia planting churches and Christian schools in places I will never go. David is in youth ministry, touching his generation with God's Word. I look back over these thirty-five years and ask myself, "What could be better than this?" The power of God's Word to transform and empower those with open hearts seems limitless. The effects of preaching ripple down through years and multiply themselves in and through the lives of faithful servants who have answered their own calling to preach.

In many ways, this book is a trust of wisdom passed on to those called into preaching ministry. It captures the wisdom I have learned over the past three decades, and my hope is that it will inspire others to new levels of effectiveness in their preaching ministries. From the start of my ministry, I learned that transformational sermons do not happen by accident. There is a significant price to be paid by anyone who answers God's calling to preach. There are long nights without sleep, the burden that souls hang in the balance, and the grind of weekly sermon preparation. Over time we find our rhythm and learn what works and what does not. Much of what we learn is by trial and error, and many times it is

by "error" that we learn the most. We learn that preaching is a partnership between God and human beings, one in which God gives us His Word and we give
Him our lives. It is at the mingling point of God's Word and our humanity that
transformational sermons are born. God's Word invades the preacher's life and
something new is born in the womb of the heart. We nurture His Word until it
becomes our word, taking upon itself flesh in our own lives in a way that mirrors
the incarnation of the Son of God Himself. His word begins to live within my
heart, and it changes me. My thoughts, beliefs, attitudes, and, ultimately, my
actions are changed as the transformational power of God's Word has its way in
my heart. When we have been changed by God's Word, something alive with
transformation is birthed in our hearts—that word grows, matures, and takes on
a life of its own. At the right time, it can be delivered to others with the same
transformational effect. Sermons birthed in this way have the power to transform
both the preacher and those that hear us preach.

Life is so very short and the Scriptures remind us that we are but a vapor.
Each moment we are given is a precious gift that quickly fades. It is my prayer
that as you read through this book, you will see yourself in its pages and gain
new hope and encouragement as a preacher. Perhaps the words written here will
answer some questions that have puzzled you or will provide some keys to unlock greater effectiveness in your preaching ministry. Maybe the book will provide you with a whole new way of looking at preaching ministry or stir fresh
creativity and imagination in your heart. I release this book like a rock thrown
into a vast ocean, trusting God to make whatever ripples He desires in the hearts
of those who read its words. Read with an open heart and mind. Determine, if
nothing else, to allow the words that follow to draw you closer to your Lord. If
this book and its words save you a few sleepless nights, then its purpose has
been fulfilled. If this book and its words help you and encourage a few hopeless
souls then my joy will be made complete. Take away what you can, but by all
means give away everything you learn.

Carpe diem!

Soli Deo gloria!

James T. Flynn
Associate Professor of Practical Theology
Regent University School of Divinity
Virginia Beach, Virginia
January 2010

Acknowledgments

No individual can take credit for a book. Each book is a wonderful tapestry, woven together by a competent people who each contribute his or her time and talents to make it possible. This book is no different—it is the result of the nurture, friendship, and deposits left by many in my life. My wife, Monica, has been a source of endless inspiration that I find woven into each page of this book. Monica, you have taught me how to see beyond the shadows of everyday life and to experience the beauty of God in creation that I would otherwise have missed. My eye for metaphor and word pictures have come from being married to an artist whose joy for life and eye for God's beauty have made me who I am today.

Stacy Mattingly is an accomplished writer and author, and her specific coaching and editing on this book have been a golden opportunity to be schooled in the art of writing. Her wisdom, encouragement, and wealth of professional advice can be found on every page of this manuscript. The professors and administration in the School of Divinity at Regent University have been an amazing source of support, wisdom, and encouragement. Dean Emeritus H. Vinson Synan, a legend in the world of Renewal history, has always been present to guide and encourage. Deans Michael Palmer, Randall Pannell, Donald Tucker, and Joy Brathwaite are responsible for making sure I had the time necessary to compile this manuscript and have been a consistent source of encouragement in its completion. My colleagues at Regent are a constant source of inspiration with their spiritual and academic excellence, and their input has been essential in shaping this book.

Finally, there is my legacy—my seed. I think of my children Stephen, Rachel, Heather, and Benjamin. Your world is complicated and presents a new set of challenges that my generation has not faced. Your love, sacrifice, and support over the years have made me a rich man, and my hope is to pass on some of the things I have learned so that you will be more effective in reaching this world for Christ. My fruit is your fruit and you are my legacy. You will impact the world long after I am gone. Run well and run straight. I am what your grandparents James and Gretchen have sown into me. They built the foundation upon which I stand, and this work is dedicated to them as it is you. Run well, and run straight.

Chapter 1
Can These Bones Live?

The hour is very late—or is that "very early"? The clock reads 4:00 a.m., as the first hints of dawn shine over the horizon, and the ground below my farmhouse window becomes faintly visible. In another three and a half hours, the "man of God" will meet with his beloved intercessors to pray over the Sunday service and the morning's message. Afterward, about four hours from now, five or six hundred souls will gather, eager to worship God and hear another "word from heaven," otherwise known as my sermon.

Preachers live and die by their sermons. Other kinds of professionals can point to the tangible work of their hands with pride. A contractor can take you on a tour of a new house and show you the floors, let you touch the smooth, freshly painted walls, and ask you to examine the new counters. An automobile salesman might sit you in the soft leather seat of a new car so you can put your hands on the wheel and play with the knobs on the dash board as you smell that seducing, new-car smell. Preachers have only words and the lives we influence. Changed lives are largely up to God—our part as preachers is to pray, study, and learn what we can in order to cooperate with Him in the process of transforming others.

I have not slept all night. The heavens seem to be like brass, as the Bible says—shut up tightly with God nowhere to be found. God and I have been wrestling all night over this sermon—not to mention the week I've already struggled with it—and unlike my biblical counterpart Jacob, I have not prevailed, I have no new name, and I have bigger problems than Jacob's limp. I am paralyzed.

I am a preacher. I love God with all my heart. I am committed to serving God with all my strength. Like everyone else, I sin; I fall short. But calling urges me onward to serve God's people. One of my primary responsibilities is to serve those people a hot, nourishing, spiritual meal a couple of times a week. Sometimes folk complain about the dinner. Other times they say nothing and just spit it out on the floor for me to clean up. Occasionally, they actually enjoy the food and tell me so—that feels good! Right now, though, I don't even know what's on the menu, and meal time is just a few hours away. The cook doesn't even know what to prepare! Fleeting thoughts of failure run through my mind—what will it be like to walk into the pulpit this morning and admit I have nothing to say? Should I "fake it," pull some leftovers out of the file cabinet, and warm them up? A lukewarm meal is better than nothing to eat, right? Then comes the ultimate question: Am I really called to preach, and if I am, where are you, Lord? I wonder if selling used cars would be an easier way to make a living than wrestling with words.

My last ounce of faith in God and my calling urge me onward. We walk by faith, not by sight or feelings. I start to make bargains with God—have you ever done that? No more time to feel bad for myself—I have a job to do, and God's people are counting on me. *Lord, I need a word for your people. I'm tired, desperate, and lonely for you. Can you come through for me one more time? Not for me, but for your people? They're hungry and thirsty. Souls who don't know you will be at church this morning. Marriages are hanging by a thread, and someone who is giving up on life may be there. Prodigal sons and daughters will be in the congregation, needing a pathway back to their loving Father. Someone is about to run out of unemployment with no job, and a battered wife is trying to hang on for just one more day. My God, I don't have the words to meet their needs, but you do. You encourage them, give them strength for another day, and transform their world. Lord, give me—the one who so desperately needs your transformational word—a word to strengthen and encourage your people.*

I pray and nod off to sleep. I awaken to the voice of an angel calling my name, only to find it's my wife. "What are you doing sleeping on the floor, and why I didn't you come to bed last night?" She gently reminds me that it is 6:00 a.m. and we are running late for church. I beg a few more minutes, scribble down some notes, and get a fifteen-minute shower. We are soon out the door, praying with the intercessors, and then the morning service begins. The sermon actually goes pretty well. Where in the world did those thoughts come from? Somehow God helped me to draw on some of the deep things He was doing in my own life and then tie those examples to the Scripture passages I was wrestling over. I have no idea how it all came together.

People respond to the altar call and are weeping as the elders pray for them. Afterward, there are people to greet and words of praise for the sermon. I just shake my head and wonder at God's goodness. My last thoughts as I arrive at home, fall on the bed, and drift into sweet unconsciousness that afternoon affirm the amazing faithfulness of God and the power of His Word to transform the lives of those who hear it.

Life in the Valley of Dry Bones

Is it just me, or can you identify with the long nights that can occur before you preach? In spite of our best efforts to prepare throughout the week for Sunday's message, there may be those weeks when we still find ourselves up on Saturday, wringing our hands, sweating, and pleading with God. Preaching is one of the most remarkable undertakings any man or woman aspires to in life. Preaching has the power to transform a valley of dry bones into a mighty army. Over the last three decades, I have been privileged to preach in local churches, classrooms, and seminars around the world. I have yet to experience a ministry that is more exhilarating, challenging, or fruitful than preaching. Preaching can change lives, alter destinies, and renew minds. It can bring hope to the hopeless, encouragement to the broken, and light to people who live in darkness. Preaching has the potential to change this generation and to send a legacy into the next. But the call to preach comes with a great personal price tag.

Ezekiel was a man quite familiar with ministry's price tag. His audience was a lot more challenging than mine has ever been. Ezekiel's calling to ministry was also just a bit more dramatic than mine (see Ezekiel 1). My congregation was not always the easiest to get along with, but the house of Israel put the "funk" in dysfunctional. Their ancestors dwelt in a foreign land as slaves and captives, only to be delivered by a cascade of miracles. Those miracles culminated in the splitting of the Red Sea and the spectacular destruction of their enemies before their very eyes. Because of rebellion and unbelief, the house of Israel ended up wandering in a desert for a generation, but God remained faithful, sending His Word—commandments written in stone with His very finger while the Israelites were down on the plain below, busy breaking most of those laws. God led the people with a cloud by day and a pillar of holy fire by night, yet they murmured. When Israel's sons and daughters were brought into a land overflowing with milk and honey, they soon forgot about their God, serving other gods. Endless cycles of sin followed, as did repentance, judges, good kings, not-so-good kings, and really bad kings. There were also the prophets. Some, like Isaiah, were sawn in two. Others, like Ezekiel, the people kept alive to torment. But despite the pain and hardship Ezekiel suffered, God had a purpose for His prophet.

When Israel's iniquity got so bad it burst the floodgates of judgment, Ezekiel and his people were taken captive by the Chaldeans. Israel was scattered abroad in a strange and foreign land. The land of the Chaldeans became the grave of the nation of Israel. Ezekiel's heart was broken I can imagine his thoughts: *Spiritual dryness, death, broken dreams, and destruction are all around us. Should we continue to hope? Has God abandoned us forever—we certainly deserve that! Is there a word in the land, or has God now departed from us forever? As I cried out these words to God in my despair, then . . .*

The hand of the LORD was upon me, and He brought me out by the Spirit of the LORD and set me down in the middle of the valley; and it was full of bones. [2] He caused me to pass among them round about, and behold, *there were* very many on the surface of the valley; and lo, *they were* very dry. [3] He said to me, "Son of man, can these bones live?" And I answered, "O Lord GOD, You know." [4] Again He said to me, "Prophesy over these bones and say to them, 'O dry bones, hear the word of the LORD.' [5] "Thus says the Lord GOD to these bones, 'Behold, I will cause breath to enter you that you may come to life. [6] 'I will put sinews on you, make flesh grow back on you, cover you with skin and put breath in you that you may come alive; and you will know that I am the LORD.'" [7] So I prophesied as I was commanded; and as I prophesied, there was a noise, and behold, a rattling; and the bones came together, bone to its bone. [8] And I looked, and behold, sinews were on them, and flesh grew and skin covered them; but there was no breath in them. [9] Then He said to me, "Prophesy to the breath, prophesy, son of man, and say to the breath, 'Thus says the Lord GOD, "Come from the four winds, O breath, and breathe on these slain, that they come to life."'" [10] So I prophesied as He commanded me, and the breath came into them, and they came to life and stood on their feet, an exceedingly great army.[1]

A preacher named Ezekiel and a people who had become like dead men's bones. People who were exiled in the lonely valley of a foreign land that had become their grave. No hope, only a once great army now reduced to a pile of sun-baked bones. What is the answer? *Speak to the bones, Ezekiel. Prophesy to them. Preach to them, saying, "O dry bones, hear the word of the Lord."*

The solution was not a new program to try to stir things up. It was not time to call an emergency deacon's meeting or to call the prayer chain. It was time to preach. "Prophesy over these bones, and say to them, 'O dry bones, hear the word of the LORD.'" Preaching has the power to make dry bones come to life. It has the power to put new sinew and flesh on people's dead, dry bones and then to cover them with new skin. More importantly, preaching has the power to put breath in people and to cause them to come alive. Preaching can cause the broken and dead in spirit to come back to life and stand on their feet "an exceedingly great army." A slain army lies motionless in the dust. Dead men's bones devoid of flesh and life lie dry in the valley. But when words that transform are spoken by God's servant, a great army rises from the dust as God breathes new life into those bones and they obey the irresistible the word of God. This is transformative preaching at its best. I have determined that I will settle for noth-

---

[1] Ezek. 37:1-10. All quotes from the Scriptures, unless otherwise specified, are from *The New American Standard Bible* (La Habra, CA, 1995). For the Hebrew and Greek words used in this book, I have tried to note the simplest noun, verb, or other part of speech without regard to the grammatical form actually found in the passage, unless otherwise noted. My motive is to introduce readers at all levels of language proficiency to the richness of the meanings of some of the original Greek and Hebrew words in the Old and New Testaments in the simplest manner possible to encourage further study.

ing less in my preaching ministry, because transformation is one of the primary purposes of preaching, and God's people deserve nothing less than God's very breath in my sermon's words.

I Will Cause Breath to Enter You

The concepts of *life* and *transformation*, when used in the context of preaching, are difficult to define. I recognize a handsome man or a beautiful woman when I see one, but how do I define *beauty*? So it is with life and transformation—they often defy explanation, but I know them when I see them. Life and transformation are often best understood using contrast. When Frank is breathing, talking, and walking around, he is probably alive. When Frank is lying in a casket with no pulse and looking rather pale, he is probably dead. When Frank's life is a world-class mess and it seems as if he is beyond hope, and then he is miraculously changed into a fruitful, successful man serving God, he has been transformed. We know life and transformation when we see them. If we want further definition, the Scriptures can help.

What is *life*? The Bible makes it very clear that life issues from the very heart of God Himself—it is His animating force. In Gen. 2:7, God breathes the breath of life into an inanimate lump of clay, and that pile of dirt becomes a living soul named Adam. The "Second Adam," Jesus Christ, was called the "Bread of Life," the "Light of Life," and "the Resurrection and the Life" (John 6:35; 6:63; 8:12; 11:25). Life defines who Jesus is, and life is the animating force behind all His actions and words. No wonder Jesus is "the way, the truth, and the life" and came that we might "have life and life more abundantly" (John 14:6; 10:10). Life is who He is.

The result of His presence is life and renewal. When life comes near, it is contagious. The sheer vitality of the life of God causes transformation—God's life changes everything it touches for the good. When His life touches us at salvation, we are transformed from death to life and our inner person is born again (John 3:3; 2 Cor. 5:17). Simply coming to know Him and drawing near to Him is so transformative that it imparts eternal life (John 17:3). God and life are inseparable. Life is what animates Him at the very core of His being. God's life and transformation are intertwined—the life of God renews everything with which it comes in contact. When we encounter God, we encounter life, and that life produces transformative change in us. That is where preaching and words enter the picture.

When God creates, He speaks. His spoken words contain the power to create something from nothing as He did at creation.[2] As Jesus put it so well, "It

---

[2] The term used by theologians to describe God creating everything from nothing is *ex nihilo*, literally "out of nothing." The act of creating everything from nothing is an expression of the very nature of God. He is so full of life that His life finds its expression in

is the Spirit who gives life. The flesh profits nothing; the words I have spoken to you are spirit and are life" (John 6:63). When Jesus spoke, people who were lame from their mother's womb walked and Lazarus rose from the dead. That is transformation. When He speaks today through His Word, that same "spirit and life" can be released to raise people who are spiritually dead and to impart eternal life to them. God's transformative word, when directed to those who are spiritually lame and broken, has the power to renew them and make them whole. Spirit and life are the essence of transformation and are the only things that can make piles of dead men's bones come back to life. Spirit and life are also basic to transformative preaching.

Fred was a pile of dead men's bones.[3] He struggled with serious personal pain, but he began going to church and listening to what the preacher had to say. Was there any hope his life could change? He sat in the center back row and said nothing for weeks, just staring at me as I preached. Quite honestly, his disheveled long hair and empty eyes scared me. His eyes had such a far-off look to them.

At first, I had no interaction with him other than from afar while preaching, because he would come in after service began and leave before it was finished. Uncertain about his intentions, the ushers kept an eye on him throughout the service. Week after week he came back and listened. Then one Sunday, Fred came forward after my message, looked straight into my eyes, and as I remember, said only these words: "Pastor, pray for me." I prayed for him, perhaps a bit more out of fear than faith. Over the next few months, we had little personal interaction, but he continued to listen.

Fred's appearance began to change slowly over the next several months. I could see a spark of life in his eyes. One Sunday he confided in me after service about his struggles—he had been suicidal for some time. I remember the day when Fred told me those struggles were over. He went on to grow in our church and served faithfully.

Fred is the reason I keep preaching, even if I have those sleepless nights and things aren't flowing well. In fact, Fred was there in church on that Sunday morning after the long night I described at the beginning of this chapter. Fred is what transformation looks like. He reminds me to this day of the power of God's spoken word when we are obedient to preach. The power of a sermon infused with God's transformative life brings renewal. It is hard to miss the sound of dry

---

being utterly creative and pregnant with the ability to create and to recreate. This creative process is accomplished by His word, which is pregnant with His life to create or transform.

[3] The name of this individual and of others whom I have had the privilege to minister to over the years have been changed to protect their identities. They are just a few of the individuals I have seen miraculously transformed by the preaching of God's word. They are forever in my heart as examples of the power of God's spoken word to transform.

bones snapping together and shiny new flesh covering a redeemed life once lying so profoundly dry in the valley.

Shall I go on about the prostitutes who heard God's word in our church and were saved? These women certainly raised a few eyebrows when they came to visit, but we overlooked their attire and outer appearance, rejoicing in the hope of transformation and renewal.

And yet, while preaching is the key to transformational life in any ministry, often the preacher is the one who feels dry, parched, and as if his or her bones are those scattered across the valley floor. Preachers too are in desperate need of transformational life, and if we are going to impart that life to others, we must have ongoing encounters with it ourselves.

Physician, Heal Thyself

I am burdened for preachers. If the ministry of God's word can be so pregnant with transformational power, then why does that power sometimes seem absent in my own life? Why do I struggle with message preparation? Why does transformation seem to be lacking sometimes in the people to whom I preach? I am convinced that the answers to these questions lie partly in the approach I take to preaching. If I treat preaching as a purely external task—another ministry item to check off my to-do list—it will soon lose its transformational power. The message does not have its full opportunity to breathe life into my own soul on its way to the congregation. My own personal transformation suffers, and as the preacher goes, so goes the message and, eventually, the church. My personal life, messages, and church are soon found lacking in transformational life.

When a lack of transformational life reaches critical mass in the churches of any nation, we see the kinds of problems that are present in the Western church today. The church loses its vitality and starts to plateau or decline. God's people lack inward transformation and renewal, so their actions and attitudes begin to more closely resemble those of non-Christians. Fred no longer comes to church, because he needs not words but transformational power. Prostitutes never leave the street, because there is little transformational power present in church to persuade them to change.

The Western church as a whole lacks vitality. In America, we have been blessed beyond measure over the last several centuries, just as the nation of Israel was blessed before their terrible captivity. We have sent missionaries to other nations, contributing to the extraordinary spiritual renewal occurring today in Asia and Africa, but for the first time in our history, other nations are now sending more missionaries to America than we are sending abroad. Church growth is now largely flat in America and has not kept up with population growth over the last fifteen years.[4] We need God to breathe new life and vitality into the Western church, as is confirmed by the following statistics about the American church in particular:

- The percentage of Americans who attended a Christian church on any given weekend declined from 20.4% in 1990 to 17.5% in 2005.[5]
- If the American church was to continue on the same trajectory, the number of people who attend church on any given weekend would drop to 14.7% by 2020.[6]
- There was no state in the United States where church growth kept up with population growth from 1990–2006.[7]
- From 1999–2005, 52% of American churches were in decline, 17% had plateaued or were stable, and only 31% were growing.[8]
- From 2000–2005, an estimated 4,000 new churches were started each year, but 3,700 churches closed their doors—a net gain of only 300 new churches per year, when a net gain of at least 2,900 new churches per year would be needed just to keep the same church-to-people ratio in the United States.[9]

Like the people of Israel, the people of America have dwelt in a land overflowing with milk and honey but have been sidetracked for decades by wealth, politics, and self-interest. There is dryness in the land, and what was once a formidable army looks a bit more like a valley of dry bones. Our churches and nation are lying in the valley, just waiting for God's word to breathe new life into them once again. But where is the preacher with words that transform?

Individual Christians in the Western church also exhibit a lack of transformational power at work in their lives, as illustrated by their actions and attitudes. Some time ago, George Barna documented the difference between the lifestyles of Christians and non-Christians in America. The results of the survey showed a distinct lack of transformation in Christians when their behaviors and attitudes were contrasted with those of non-Christians:[10]

---

[4] David T. Olson, *The American Church in Crisis* (Grand Rapids: Zondervan, 2008), 36. Olson points out that while the population of America has grown by 52 million from 1990–2004, the percentage of the population going to church has declined from 20.4% in 1990 to 17.5% in 2005.

[5] Ibid., 36.

[6] Ibid., 175.

[7] Ibid., 37.

[8] Ibid., 132.

[9] Ibid., 145-46.

[10] George Barna, *The Second Coming of the Church* (Nashville: Word, 1998), 5-7. The data was from OmniPoll and was taken in a series of surveys in 1996 and 1997 with a sample volume of over a 1,000 people in each case. This data is now over ten years old

	Christian	Non-Christian
• People who were divorced	27%	23%
• People who bought a lottery ticket (past week)	23%	27%
• People who gave money to the poor (past year)	24%	34%
• People who had time with a professional counselor (past year)	15%	15%
• People who filed a lawsuit (past year)	3%	4%
• People who took prescription drugs for depression (past year)	7%	8%
• People who watched a PG-13 or R-rated movie (past three months)	76%	87%
• People who watched an X-rated movie (past three months)	9%	16%

These numbers paint a picture of a church that lacks the power to transform even its own members' lives. Everything that God's life touches experiences transformation. God does not expect Christians to act differently by their own strength and will power—that would amount to mere human effort to create a façade. Rather, these statistics suggest a lack of the kind of deep, inward transformation that eventually creates outer changes in people's lives, observable through their everyday choices and actions. There is no substitute for inner transformative power—my own works and righteousness are like filthy rags and cannot save me or change me to be more like God.[11] Only the transformative work of the Holy Spirit can produce the internal change necessary to make me more like Christ—transformation is a work of grace based on the transformative power of God's word.

The Western church is waiting for preachers to rise up with transformative words for this hour, but preachers cannot give what they do not first possess. A transformative word must have its way in the preacher's own heart and life before it can have a truly transformative effect on the lives of others. The key to transformative life in the church depends on the ongoing transformative work of God in the preacher's own heart. Certainly, God can get through to people in spite of the condition of the preacher, but if the preacher's heart is not right, it

---

and nothing convinces me that it has gotten any better—if we look around at the Western church today, we see more similarity rather than less.

[11] In Isa.64:6 it is said that all of our righteousness is like a "filthy garment." The Hebrew construction used here, "וּכְבֶגֶד עִדִּים" (u'k'beged iddim), is much more blatant and should be translated "unclean menstrual rags." The word picture makes it very clear just how inadequate any work we could ever do to try to change ourselves would be. Transformation is not a result of our works but of the work of God in our lives as He changes us.

can hinder or stop the flow of transformational life in a sermon . Ezekiel can't speak life to a valley of dry bones if he does not have the breath of life resident in his own heart.

Work done by Dr. Richard J. Krejcir at the Francis Schaeffer Institute of Church Leadership Development (FASICD) indicates a clear lack of transformative life and vitality in the lives of American preachers today. Krejcir's work in the area of ministerial health began at The Fuller Institute as early as 1989 and continued as the project was transferred to FASICD in 1998.[12] Some other similar studies are aging, such as those done by David Goetz (1992), but clearly show the start of the kinds of problems ministers are experiencing today.[13]

Krejcir did two separate studies at separate pastors conferences in Orange County, California, in 2005 and 2006, involving a combined total of 1,050 pastors; the studies aimed to gauge the pastors' health and vitality. Some of the results of the surveys taken by these two groups of pastors show how badly preachers themselves need renewal:[14]

- 100% of the pastors surveyed stated that they had a close associate or friend from seminary who had left the ministry due to burnout, conflict in the church, or moral failure;
- 90% stated that they were frequently worn out on a daily or weekly basis;
- 89% had considered leaving the ministry, and 57% said they would leave the ministry if they had a better place to go, including secular work;
- 77% said they felt they did not have a good marriage;
- 72% stated that they only study the Bible when they are preparing for sermons or lessons;
- 38% had been divorced or were in the process of getting a divorce;
- 30% admitted to having an ongoing affair or sexual encounter with a parishioner;
- 26% had regular devotions and felt adequately fed spiritually;
- 23% felt happy or content with who they are in Christ, at church, and at home.

---

[12] The Francis Schaeffer Institute exists to provide biblical resources for the church. It specializes in providing research for insight and application for church leaders and pastors. Its research findings are often made public at http://www.intothyword.org/pages.asp?pageid=56972 . Dr. Krejcir is co-founder of FASICD.

[13] David Goetz, "Is the Pastor's Family Safe at Home?" *Leadership: A Practical Journal for Church Leaders* 13:4 (Fall 1992), 39.

[14] Richard J. Krejcir, "Statistics on Pastors," The Francis Schaeffer Institute (FASICD), http://www.intothyword.org/apps/articles/default.asp?articleid=36562&columnid=3958 (accessed July 2, 2009).

Krejcir also conducted a metadata survey, distilling data over a period of years from other studies on ministerial health and wellbeing. Some of the sources for metadata included studies conducted by Barna, Focus on the Family, and Fuller Seminary, and from prior work with a church consulting firm. The data seems to back up Krejcir's own survey findings. Here is what he concluded, having compiled the data from other sources and having reviewed his own past surveys:[15]

- 1,500 pastors left the ministry each month due to moral failure, spiritual burnout, or contention in their churches;
- 70% of the pastors did not have anyone they would consider to be a friend, and almost none had anyone they would consider to be a close friend;
- 70% of the pastors continually fought depression;
- 60% to 80% of those entering ministry would not be in ministry ten years later, with only a fraction involved in lifetime ministry.

Recently, some of the research data just presented has been criticized for a lack of tight scientific design. Some of the surveys, it is contended, may have been designed improperly with questions that were potentially biased. There may have also been a lack of representative sampling that would include diversity of gender, ethnicity, and polity.[16] But even if this data were off by a factor of two and pastors' struggles only half as bad as the data reports, the information would still represent an enormous gap between what is preached from the pulpit and preachers' personal lives. The need for personal transformation in preachers' lives is obvious.

What do all these numbers mean? The statistics point to a pattern of ministry that must be broken in the Western church and in its ministers. We need transformative change in the heart and soul of God's people, beginning with their shepherds. Look at the statistics—preachers are struggling with ministry to the point where they get worn out, burn out, or flame out, with some desperately looking for any way out possible. Along the way, marriage vows are broken, and ministers and their families crash and burn. These are but symptoms of a need for personal renewal. The state of the personal devotional lives of ministers is more telling. The preacher's personal relationship with Christ is the essence of a transformational Christian experience. These statistics suggest that many of us are going through the motions without any deep transformational power at work in our prayer lives. A lack of intimacy with God in our prayer lives eventually impacts the lives of those to whom we preach and then the church as a whole.

---

[15] Ibid.

[16] Anne Jackson, "Info-porn: Don't Spread the Bad Stats," FlowerDust.net, http://www.flowerdust.net/2007/12/26/christians-like-info-porn-don't-believe-the-stats/ (accessed July 2, 2009).

How ironic that preachers hold the very source of God's transformational life in their hands each week yet often lack transformational power in their own lives. This paradox suggests we need to re-envision our approach to preaching to restore its transformational impact in our lives first. Physician, heal thyself. The transformation of those who hear us will follow.

When our lives don't match our words, it is a matter of character deficit, demonstrating our need for deep personal transformation in order to build an inner life that will sustain the weight of our calling. God does not use people— He *partners* with them in ministry. His desire is to do a deep transformative work in preachers' lives so we can model what we preach and so our lives can withstand the pressures and rigors of ministry. Personal transformation leads to transformative preaching. What can we do to restore transformative life to our sermon preparation? How can preachers be personally transformed as they preach? What will cause our personal transformation by the Word to spill over in our preaching ministry to those who hear? The answer to these questions has to do with the way we conceive of preaching, and that goes back to the way God designed us to learn.

Learning through Comparison

Humans have a marvelous built-in capacity to learn through comparison— to understand things by understanding what they are "like." Abstractions are made concrete in our minds when we compare them with things we already understand. God designed us to learn this way—indeed, He communicates with us this way. When God shaped creation, He left His marvelous fingerprint on it so we could see what *He* is like (Rom. 1:20). If I want to understand what God's power is like, I can look at the ocean with its vastness and waves. If I want to understand His faithfulness, I can rejoice in the sunrise and sunset of each new day. I constantly build metaphoric bridges between the unknown and what I already know in order to learn and gain new insight.

Take time, for instance. Time is an abstract concept, but I understand it if I consider what it is like. Time is like money. I can spend it, invest it, waste it, or squander it. My metaphoric understanding shapes the way I relate to time, and my thinking about time ultimately shapes my actions. We all relate to the world by means of comparison—by understanding what something is like. These bridges of comparison are often visual, giving us images or pictures on which peg our understanding. Figures of speech like metaphor, analogy, and simile help us to see. Changing human behavior often comes down to changing the images that hang on the walls of people's hearts, giving people new images to understand with or swapping old, worn out images for new, useful ones.

Jesus was an expert at giving people new images—He was constantly telling people what the kingdom of God was like. The kingdom is like a field of wheat and tares—don't pluck the weeds or you will uproot the good plants. The kingdom is like a dragnet that catches fish of every kind—don't be surprised when you see some strange ones in the net, and don't try to sort them out yourselves; leave it to God. The kingdom is like a field so valuable that even if the purchase requires the life of His Son, the owner is willing to pay the price. These word pictures in Matthew 13 illustrate the art of making something abstract come to life by using the power of comparison. I can't relate to an abstract "kingdom of God" except by knowing what it is like. The people of Jesus' day needed to construct a new understanding of the kingdom, so Jesus gave them new images. These new images radically changed their understanding, expectations, and ultimately their actions.

Now let's consider the ways we think about preaching. How do we conceive of preaching? What do we think of it as being like? What images might we have hanging in our hearts in the "preaching" section? Is preaching a lecture that is a monologue for instruction? Is it an argument that offers an apology for the truth? Is it a platform for social activism? A bludgeon through which I dispense God's anger? The images and bridges of comparison we reference when we think about preaching frame our understanding of what we do at both conscious and unconscious levels—those images and concepts strongly influence how we preach and prepare a message. If we want to change the results of our preaching, then we have to radically change the way we conceive of it, and that directly relates to the images of preaching that we have hanging in our hearts. Transformative preaching requires a transformative set of images for preaching, and we can find those transformative images in Scripture when we consider perhaps the most powerful metaphor that can be drawn from history—the incarnation.

Incarnation: The Pathway to Transformation

The incarnation of God as man in Jesus Christ has captivated me for the last twenty-five years. Some truths from Scripture seem to overtake you and never leave you alone again. I stand amazed at the willingness of God to clothe His only Son with human flesh in order to bring salvation to the world. I am in awe that God's plan involved a young, unmarried woman by the name of Mary from a little town on a hill in a country no bigger than the state of New Jersey. I marvel that God was unwilling to send just words but that He sent the Word Himself—a person.

When preaching is viewed through the lens of the incarnation, our understanding of what preaching is and how it should be approached is radically altered. What if message preparation starts not as an item on my ministry to-do list but with God overshadowing me so I can conceive His living word in my heart? What would happen to the preacher's life and spiritual condition if he or she was willing to join Mary in saying, ". . . may it be done to me according to your word," (Luke 1:38) allowing the word to become a transformational foundation for preaching to others? What if the preacher's focus became learning to facilitate the growth and maturity of God's word in the womb of his or her heart? The result would be a message alive with transformational power for the benefit of others, because God would have been given the opportunity to breathe His life into the preacher's heart first—before that preacher went and delivered the message to other people.

If I could see preaching ministry as being like the incarnation, and if I could act in accordance with that understanding, cooperating intimately with God in message preparation, then the potential for my own personal transformation and for my ability to deliver words that transform in my preaching ministry would be multiplied. Message preparation would help me to connect with God. Both my words and my very life would become communication tools potent with transformative life. This was true in the ministry of Jesus—He both spoke and demonstrated with His life what God was like. Should it be any different in my preaching ministry?

Do you see what I'm getting at? When we let God overshadow us and birth something in our hearts that we can deliver to others, we ourselves are changed. We then have a word *and* a changed life to offer others. We can both speak and show others what God wants to communicate, just as Jesus did. God could have sent just words, but He sent a person so we could see, touch, hear, and experience Him for ourselves:

> What was from the beginning, what we have *heard*, what we have *seen* with our eyes, what we have *looked at* and *touched* with our hands, concerning the Word of Life— [2] and the life was *manifested*, and *we have seen* and testify and proclaim to you the eternal life, which was with the Father and was *manifested* to us— [3] what *we have seen* and *heard* we proclaim to you also, so that you too may have fellowship with us; and indeed our fellowship is with the Father, and with His Son Jesus Christ (1 John 1:1-3; emphasis added).

God communicated by covering His Son with flesh. Jesus Himself is the Word, sent so we could experience Him—hear, see, and touch the Word—in order to know what God is like.

When the Word is clothed with flesh you have incarnation. When the word takes upon itself flesh in the preacher's life you have incarnational ministry. When the preacher's life is changed by the word and personal transformation becomes the foundation for his or her preaching, you have incarnational preaching. As He did through Jesus, God communicates through a person's life—not just through that person's spoken words. Incarnational communication happens when God is able to communicate through a transformed life overflowing with His transformative power. An encounter with words can be entertaining. An encounter with the person of Jesus Christ as seen in a life can be transformational. Dry bones respond when they encounter God and He breathes on them.

Incarnational preaching starts with an intimate encounter with the God of the Word so we can become pregnant with the word of God. Think about the implications of incarnational preaching. A sermon is no longer a separate event—it is a part of my life. In fact, it is merely an extension of what God is already at work doing in my life, and in the lives of the listeners who hear my words. The people I preach to do not just hear words, they see a transformed life. They see what the words I speak have done in my life. They can see, hear, and touch the effect of those words as we interact. There is alignment and congruency—my words and my life preach. God tabernacles among us, but not in a tent. He takes upon Himself flesh.

In order to preach an incarnational word, a deep work of God must occur in the preacher's heart long before any words are publicly spoken. I am convinced that preaching and teaching is seventy-five percent internal and twenty-five percent external. I am also convinced that the paradigm of the incarnation is a pattern given to help us release the transformative power needed so badly today. There is nothing shallow about an incarnational approach to preaching and teaching—the price paid by the communicator is quite high, personally speaking. Yet the price is worth paying, because it builds the spiritual foundation necessary to minister the word of God with transformative power. An incarnational approach to preaching allows me to say to my hearers, "Be imitators of me, just as I am also of Christ" (1 Cor. 11:1). The world does not need more words—it needs transformed people to minster transformational life to others. Incarnation is the road to transformation. Are you up for the journey?

Words That Transform

The incarnation as a metaphor or word picture for transformational preaching will guide this book's journey. Like the story of the incarnation itself, this book is a tender call toward intimacy with God in order to recapture the transformative power of preaching. If transformation flows from a person rather than from mere words, then the only solution for preachers today is to reconnect with that person as a foundation for transformative life. The preparation of transformational messages does not begin in the study but in the bedroom. It may involve books, but it is grounded in intimacy. Intimacy does not take place from across the room but face-to-face. Intimacy results in conception, and when the word is conceived, transformation has begun.

Chapter 2

What If God Were One of Us?
Preaching That Lives and Breathes

Preachers usually remember their first sermon. Many of our audiences won't forget them, either. For those of us called to preach, our first sermon is like our first kiss—we remember the place, time, sights, sounds, and even the smell. I gave my first sermon in 1975 in a small church a few miles from my house. I was a gangly teenager and had just made a commitment to Jesus Christ six months before. I grew up in a denominational setting that grounded me in my faith, but I had become restless and left the church to try other religions. Hinduism didn't seem to work for me. I liked Buddhism a lot more and enjoyed transcendental meditation, but I always had a gnawing feeling deep inside my heart that something was missing in my life.

By age sixteen, I was desperately trying to figure things out, reading through the Bhagavad Gita; the Koran; the writings of Gautama Buddha, Lao Tze, Confucius; and just about any other religious book I could get my hands on. I was also reading the Christian Bible and was struck when I came across John 14:7. Jesus claimed to be *the* way, the truth, and the life and said no man could come to the Father but through Him. Those words shook me up, so I kept reading intently though the Gospel of John, Acts, and into Romans. In March 1975, I read the words of Rom. 10:9,10 while alone in my bedroom. I confessed Jesus Christ as my Lord and told Him that I believed He rose from the dead. At that moment, my life was changed forever.

My transformation was not the result of a mental encounter with words on a page. It happened because I met a person at that moment for the first time. The Scriptures guided my way, but the simple prayer in my bedroom allowed me to encounter the Word Himself. I did not need more words—I had already read thousands of them in those various religious books written by sages. I already had contact with the spirit world through my meditation. I needed an encounter with the Spirit of God. My encounter with the God of the Christian Scriptures transformed my life. His presence was pure, loving, and holy—different than I had ever experienced before in any spiritual encounter and quite overwhelming. At that moment, I dedicated my life to finding out who this Christian God was and how I could serve Him. I began to devour the Scriptures each day, setting aside the other religious books and sacred writings. My encounter with God soon convinced me that I had a calling in my life to preach and teach, but I had no idea what to do with that calling. How should I prepare? How could I answer this newfound calling to preach?

I decided to visit that small church on the corner to check things out and see if the people there were crazy, as others had told me. I figured I had nothing to lose. My parents already thought I was crazy as a sixteen-year-old to be studying the Bible so much instead of partying with my friends like a "normal" teenager. Besides, the pastor's daughter was cute, and the pastor was known for stirring things up with his unorthodox style of preaching. If nothing else, the visit would be entertaining, and who knew if I might get a date with the pastor's daughter?

I don't know what that pastor saw in me, but he immediately took me under his wing. I shadowed him, watching his every move in church. I saw how he studied the Scriptures. I watched and listened closely when he prayed. He seemed to connect with my newfound God in an intimate, personal way. When he prayed, it seemed like God was actually listening to him, and even answering back sometimes. I marveled at the words he spoke when he preached, because they seemed to burn in my heart—they were pregnant with life and were trans-forming my faith, my thinking, and my daily life. Thirty-five years later, my first experience with transformative preaching is seared into my consciousness. I had to find a way to preach like this man preached.

As I mentioned, the pastor was known for his edgy sermons, which I loved but others hated. He preached exactly what he thought the church needed, and a few months after I got there, the congregation decided it was time to look for a new pastor. Preaching can be funny like that—doing a great job can get you into a world of trouble. The time for my pastor's last sermon was about a week away. I got a call from him and asked him about that last sermon. He said he had already preached it. I asked him, "What about Wednesday night?" and he simply replied, "Well, you are going to preach that one." I remember being stunned. "Me? Preach a sermon? On the last big night of your pastoral ministry in the church?" I had been a Christian less than a year. I thought I had no business say-ing anything. I had no training to preach. To this day, I am amazed at the risk my pastor took and at the faith he had in me. He must have seen the raw calling to preach in my life. Before my mind could say no, my mouth said yes.

I had never prepared a message before, but I had watched my pastor at work. He would pour himself into the Scriptures and spend time praying to seek

God's mind on a particular word to preach to the congregation. He would go to sleep at night and often wake up a few hours later with a message flowing from his soul. He let the words of Scripture speak directly to him first—to teach, train, correct, and even rebuke him—before a word ever left his mouth from the pulpit. He tried to live the word before ever preaching that word. I think that is what enraged the congregation the most about him. The words he preached were the words he lived by, and because people could find no hypocrisy in his life to discredit his words, they were forced to confront their own need to change. The word seemed to come alive in my pastor's life before he ever shared it from the pulpit, and that could be unnerving to anyone looking for a nice, quiet Sunday service. That's just how I wanted to preach, and I determined that was how my sermon would be on Wednesday.

I poured myself into the Scriptures and prayed, seeking God for a word especially designed for the occasion. Pastor was leaving us, and my heart was broken. Many were hurt in the church. There seemed to be so much division stirring. One faction wanted the pastor to leave, and the others resented them for it. Was this the way church was supposed to be? If so, I thought, maybe I would go back to Buddhism and transcendental meditation. I was angry with the people who wanted to toss my mentor out the door, and I found it hard to pray about the message. As I studied, I realized I needed to forgive the people who wanted to harm my pastor; my own resentment was hardening my heart. I remember the words of Eph. 4:32 jumping off the page as I studied, coming to life in my heart: "And be kind to one another, tender-hearted, forgiving each other, just as God in Christ also has forgiven you." I wept in my room as I read that verse. It melted my heart. I experienced release from my unforgiveness and a refreshing peace as the Holy Spirit's presence moved in my heart. I realized I had found my text for Wednesday night. There needed to be forgiveness in God's house before the pastor departed. Those words had cleansed me, and now I felt more able to preach them to others.

I thank God I was too ignorant to know what I was getting myself into that night. A teenager preaching his first sermon to a crowd of adults, half of whom hated the pastor and the other half hating them for hating him. A great crowd for the first time! All I knew was that I was pregnant with something God had birthed in my heart. Perhaps I would not have described my feelings that way, but that was what I experienced.

Before my salvation, one of my greatest fears was speaking in front of people. Public speaking made me ill, and I had always hidden from it. I had even developed a stuttering problem when I spoke publicly, because of my terror. But preaching—or, to that point, sharing about God—was different. I felt confidence when I spoke to others about God. I felt God's pleasure. God's Word and its work in my heart gave me boldness, and I remember the confidence I had as I stepped behind the pulpit that Wednesday night to deliver my first sermon.

The notes from that first sermon have long since yellowed and disinte-grated. I really don't remember all the passages of Scripture I shared, but I will never forget the people's reaction. As I preached, the soft sound of sobbing could be heard. Was I that bad? The sound got louder, and people began to openly weep as they responded to the Scripture passages being preached. I told the people of my need to forgive them for what they had done to my pastor. As I progressed, people began to put their hands over their faces and bend over cry-ing with emotion. The word of God was melting hearts, and the Holy Spirit was actively at work convicting the hearts of people who needed to forgive. People began to stand up and confess aloud their hardness of heart and their need to repent. They were publicly asking others to forgive them and crying out to God. So much for my carefully prepared sermon! At some point, the pastor walked up behind me and whispered in my ear, "Keep it up—keep it going!" I thought to myself, "Keep what up? I really don't even know what's going on here."

People began to come up to the altar and weep. Some were standing up and publicly confessing their unforgiveness. They were hugging one another and asking the pastor to forgive them. Some sat in the pews with their arms folded, and a few left. The night ended with a commissioning prayer for the pastor and one stunned teenager. I had just preached my first sermon, and I had had an en-counter with transformational power. I had seen what could happen when calling meets opportunity and need. I had watched while God breathed new life into a valley of very dry bones. That was it—I knew the rest of my life would be de-voted to preaching and to the quest for words that transform.

Picture This

Hundreds of thousands of sermons are preached every Sunday morning, but as I've shared, many lack transformational power. I am convinced many ser-mons lack transformational power because we preachers neglect the internal preparation necessary to give substance to our sermon's words. Our inclination to emphasize the external part of sermon preparation is evident in preaching literature. Books advocate different kinds of rhetorical method, different rules for textual treatment and exegesis, various ways to contextualize the sermon for specific cultures, and a plethora of other approaches to honing the sermon's ex-ternal attributes. These external aspects should be given due attention and ser-mons tweaked for greater effectiveness in the pulpit. But while important, the emphasis on the externals of a sermon's preparation leads me to believe that many of us start at the end of what should be the sermon preparation process rather than at the beginning. The beginning of sermon preparation is always in-ternal—in the heart of the preacher. This internal work is foundational for preachers who aim to deliver words that transform and renew lives.

As we touched on in our initial look at the incarnation in the last chapter, the reason internal work in the heart of the preacher is so important is because

God's truth was designed to be given flesh. God gave flesh to the dry bones in the valley when the word was spoken to them by Ezekiel, and God did the same thing by sending His Son. As we read in John 1:14, ". . . the Word became flesh and dwelt among us. . . ." By themselves, God and His word are abstractions to all who live on this side of heaven. Creation bears the mark of its Creator and gives us a beautiful glimpse of His invisible attributes, His eternal power, and His divine nature—creation was made to "give flesh" to God's internal attributes so we can see what He is like (Rom 1:20).[1] God has always meant for His word to take upon itself flesh in the lives of humans so that other people can see and experience His character, attitudes, values, and actions through our transformed lives. I found that out with my very first sermon. If I had not personally forgiven some of the people I preached to that night, I would not have preached a sermon with the kind of transformational results we witnessed. The word needed to do its internal work in my heart first—I had to forgive first in order to give "forgiveness" flesh when I preached it.

Transformation is the way "Christ is formed in you" and how one becomes a living witness of the truth for all to see, giving flesh to truth in a way that mirrors the incarnation of Jesus Christ Himself (Gal. 4:19).[2] Do you see how powerful an incarnational approach to preaching can be? Incarnational preaching is the result of the movement of the Holy Spirit in the heart of an open vessel as truth is illuminated in a new way. The sermon comes from insight as the Holy Spirit births new understanding of truth deep in my heart. That truth takes form and substance as it is applied to my own life and lived out, changing me, before a sermon is ever constructed.

---

[1] John Calvin called nature "God's Theater." An artist's creation takes on the characteristics of the creator, and God's creation has in it the characteristics of the Master Artist. Rom. 1:20 gives us warrant to look at creation to see what God is like. It is no wonder that Jesus made constant use of things in creation as divinely appointed images to explain abstract spiritual truth. What better way to explain God's heart than to reference a shepherd, or His people than to reference sheep? How much we can understand from a reference to a simple seed as a metaphoric image for the Word of God.

[2] In Gal. 4:19, Paul uses the root word "μορφόω" (*morphoo*) in the Greek text to express the fact that he was in labor until Christ be "formed" in them. This is also the same root word used in Rom. 12:2 where Paul urges his readers not to be conformed (Gr. "συσχημά τίζω" (*suschematizo*) with the verb *schema* as root) but rather to be transformed (Gr. "μεταμορφόω" (*metamorphoo*) with *morphoo* as root). The *schema* root is associated with the outer form of something (e.g., in English, "schematic"), whereas the *morphoo* root seems to be associated with inner transformation. Christ is "formed" in us as the word internally transforms us from the inside out by the influence of His word in our lives. As His word takes root and does its work, it changes our inner person to become more like Him, and our very character changes. This process is Christ formed in us and is the definition of inner transformation. If this process is active in our lives, it can be imparted to others effectively.

When preaching is understood this way—as incarnational—none of the classical concepts of the sermon, such as lecture, apology, or speech, seem adequate to represent the preaching task. But why does it matter that we view preaching through the lens of the incarnation or of any other metaphor or image, for that matter? What does the way we understand preaching have to do with the transformational outcome so badly needed in the church today? Why even care about things like metaphor and image with regard to what we believe preaching to be? Simply put, the way we view preaching is important because as we've discussed, images are at the very foundation of human comprehension and understanding, and the way we think affects what we do.

Our eyes are marvelous creations, containing more than one hundred million light receptors linked directly to the brain through the optic nerves—we are fearfully and wonderfully made (Ps. 139:14). Our eyes act as gateways for vast quantities of raw information that blast the human brain with images to be processed, interpreted, and stored, in many cases for a lifetime.[3] Vision and image are so central to human understanding and comprehension that many scientists think of the eyes as part of the brain or, better yet, the brain as part of the eyes.[4] The human mind is like a divinely created picture gallery, weaving images and their associated thought connections into our perceptions and constructs of reality. No wonder the author of Proverbs cautions, "Watch over your heart with all diligence, for from it flow the springs of life" (Prov. 4:23).[5] The images that we allow into our hearts, and the thought connections we build upon

---

[3] The science of neurophysiology has advanced considerably over the past several decades as scientists have begun to understand how the human brain works. They have found that image is at the forefront of thought, comprehension, and understanding. The human brain is divided up into two separate hemispheres—the left brain, which is the center for logical, sequential, and analytical thought; and the right brain, which is the metaphoric mind that invents, creates, and visualizes. The two hemispheres are connected by a large nerve bundle called the corpus callosum, which acts as a trunk line for communication between the metaphoric right and logical left brains. Dual coding theory for cognition holds that when the eye passes raw visual information to the brain, an "imagen" of that image information is formed as a basic representational unit in the nonverbal system of the brain. Through associative processing, an imagen is linked with "logogens," which are basic representational units in the verbal system (the associative process is called dual processing). This is the way humans make sense of their world. Through this process, raw image is associated with abstract words and concepts to weave meaning—image leads in the dance of understanding. For fascinating reading, see *The Metaphoric Mind* by Bob Samples (1976).

[4] Bob Samples, *The Metaphoric Mind* (Menlo Park: Addison-Wesley, 1976), 17-26. Developmentally speaking, the human eyes form first in the womb, and the brain grows out from them, illustrating the importance of vision and image to human beings.

[5] In Prov. 4:23, the word "heart" from "לֵב" (*leb*) in the Hebrew refers to the inner person. Further, the word "תּוֹצָאֹה" (*totsa'ah*) has the meaning of source, border, or outgoing. What we put into the heart gives border to our sense of reality and truth.

those images, literally frame our understanding of truth and reality, for better or for worse.

The way we conceive of something—the image we use to frame it and thereby understand it—can be a source of tremendous power or of debilitating limitation. A man or woman's self image can make or break him or her. The way we conceive of God has tremendous impact on our lives. Is He judgmental and harsh or warm, tender, and loving? Through images and metaphoric bridges, human beings relate to the world around them in order to understand it, and that understanding affects our choices and actions. As Warren Wiersbe observes, a person and his or her actions can rise no higher than the beauty and quality of the images that hang in the picture gallery of his or her heart.[6] Can you see that, as preachers, the metaphors, images, and other bridges of comparison we use to understand our calling have power to influence the outworking of that calling in our lives?

I asked this question in the first chapter and want to ask it again here: what images hang in the picture gallery's "preaching and teaching" section of your heart? The answer to that question is vitally important because the way we think of preaching and message preparation dictates the way we approach them and strongly influences the results we obtain. Are your images of preaching the appropriate images suited for the needs of the church at this moment in time, or are they old, dusty, worn out, and failing us? Do we like the outcomes that these images have produced, or are we ready to hang some new pictures on the wall? If transformational preaching is at the core of renewal in the church and so badly needed by its people and its preachers, then what images for preaching and sermon preparation might best facilitate transformation?

The whole way we conceive of preaching and sermon preparation must radically change if we want to see transformational results. We need to reimage preaching and message preparation from a fresh biblical perspective that will foster the kinds of action necessary to produce transformational messages needed for renewal in the church. It is not enough to tweak our preparation techniques or perfect our delivery. Dead things do not produce life and call forth dead bones from dry valleys—living things do. The potential for transformation exists in something that is vibrant and alive. As we've been learning, the Scriptures give us the perfect, vibrant image to frame transformational preaching and message preparation—the incarnation. The question is if the solution is so simple, then how did we get where we are today, and how can the incarnation be used as a new metaphor or image for understanding preaching and sermon preparation in order to restore transformational power to the pulpit?

---

[6] Warren W. Wiersbe, *Preaching and Teaching with Imagination: The Quest for Biblical Ministry* (Grand Rapids: Baker, 1994), 62.

Read It and Weep

The printing press is arguably one of the most influential inventions of the last two thousand years. Movable clay typeset printing was available as early as 1041 in China, but the technology lacked the ability to produce quantities of printed matter at an affordable price for common people. When Johannes Gutenberg invented his printing press in 1450, he changed the world as it was known at that time.[7] Few people, and then only the rich, could hope to own a book before Gutenberg's invention, because books were hand scribed and costly to produce. Printing technology and the printed word transformed Western culture, its history, and even the way people perceived reality. The impact reverberates into our present day.

Before the advent of mass printing technology, the world and its cultures were largely oral in nature.[8] Orality relied upon the transmission of truth primarily through the spoken word. Orality permeated the cultures of Old and New Testament times. The spoken word also shaped church culture until the early 1500s. In a culture of orality, truth is something that is highly relational. Truth and the truth-giver are highly interconnected because communication by spoken words demands proximity. Teaching and the transmission of truth were done in the context of intimacy, discipleship, and through a mentor-apprenticeship relationship, which was the way of Jesus and Paul.[9] In the world of orality, truth was conveyed by a person, and that person was deeply associated with his or her words.

Orality is one of the reasons the New Testament Scriptures were not written down as we know them until decades after the events of the Gospels had transpired. Why would anyone care about written words on parchment when you could hear personally from people who were eyewitnesses to these events or, at least, eyewitnesses to the eyewitnesses? Our print-conditioned minds can scarcely believe how long it took to write things down in Bible times. In the world of orality, words spoken by a living person were real and concrete, and one could believe them to be true because of the speaker—a person who was one with his or her words.

---

[7] Gutenberg, a business man and inventor, actually began experimenting with printing technology in the late 1430s. In 1450, he was backed by German businessman Johannes Fust to establish a printing business with the Gutenberg Bible being the first book to be published in volume. His printing business, technology, and the availability from that time on of the Bible to common people led to the Reformation shortly thereafter.

[8] For an excellent and detailed treatment of this topic, see *The Millennium Matrix* by M. Rex Miller. When our medium of communication changes due to technology, it produces significant changes in the way we perceive reality and the basic assumptions we make about truth.

[9] M. Rex Miller, *The Millennium Matrix* (San Francisco: Jossey-Bass, 2004), 27-29.

Those assumptions changed when print culture displaced oral culture near 1500 in the Western world. Mass printing became the great equalizer as all classes of people for the first time in history had access in printed form to the same thoughts and ideas, a privilege once reserved only for kings and the wealthy.[10] The general availability of thoughts and ideas from ancient Greek philosophers and great church theologians spawned a cultural revolution that resulted in both the Reformation and the Renaissance in Europe. The church, society, and Western culture were changed forever by the invention of the printing press, and with it came a new set of assumptions that changed the way people perceived reality.

Print culture created a megashift in the way people perceived reality and in basic assumptions about what was true. The printed word disconnected the reader from the person who was speaking—words on a page were disembodied and without life.[11] Unlike in oral culture, the reader became disconnected from both the message and the messenger. The reader became more susceptible to introducing his or her own biases and assumptions into the message because no living dialogue with a person was available. Whereas the key sense in oral culture is hearing, the key sense in a print culture is seeing. In an oral culture, the ear tells the mind to harmonize and synthesize (e.g., music). In a print-dominated culture, the eye is trained to tell the mind to discern (mentally separate) and analyze (break up the whole into parts—e.g., the frames of a movie or television program).[12]

The way Western culture perceives reality was altered with a single invention more than five hundred years ago. We unconsciously adopted a reductionist mindset for discerning truth that disintegrates the whole, chopping it into bite-sized pieces in order to comprehend the truth. Being largely disassociated with a person, truth became something much more abstract. While a reductionist approach has merit in helping us understand complex things, it can be harmful to holistic thought, damaging our understanding of truth.[13] Preachers can begin to

---

[10] Ibid., 35-44.

[11] Ibid., 36.

[12] Ibid., 44.

[13] Reductionism has worked out well in scientific thought to break complex systems into understandable units that can be more easily understood (e.g., the human body, earth's ecosystems, etc.). The parts of complex systems are broken into parts for study and analysis. This same reductionistic approach has flowed into our theological approaches to the Scriptures and our understanding of God. While there is some merit to these approaches, breaking God and the Scriptures into bite-size pieces has resulted in increasingly specialized branches of theology that are so far removed from a holistic concept of God and His Word that they have potential to damage truth, our understanding of the Scriptures, and our understanding of God rather than facilitating it. This is also true for sermon preparation—exegesis seeks to draw out meaning by breaking the Scriptures into minute parts and pieces. Words are not spoken that way and life is not lived that way. A return to a

concentrate on the words in Scripture—their tense, voice, and mood—while forgetting the person they reveal.

Should we regret the invention of the printing press? Certainly not any more than we should regret the invention of television or the personal computer, both of which have created similar seismic shifts in the way Western (and now global) culture perceives reality.[14] The introduction of each new technology brings with it advantages and disadvantages. Rather, it is important to understand both how print culture has affected the way the Western mind thinks and the biases print culture has created. More importantly for the church and preaching ministry, these changes provide the clues we need to understand why preaching and sermon preparation have evolved into their current state, what is broken, and how to fix it.

When the printed word is king, we become conditioned to understand through analysis rather than dialogue, which was the means in a more oral culture. Jesus didn't do exegesis with his disciples or read theology. He applied Scripture to life's circumstances as they were encountered, told stories, and lived in relationship with people, using teachable moments to impart truth.[15] Print culture creates expectations for a rational linear world, often leaving no room for anything mystical, because mystical things are not very rational or linear. Theologians who are deeply conditioned by the printed word might approach theology in a more reductionistic manner and begin to question the miraculous and the supernatural, which were given facts in the oral world of the Bible. In a print-dominated world, abstraction and conceptual understanding became more highly valued, replacing a more relational orientation and experience as the primary currency of life. Pedagogy replaced mentoring. A conceptual understanding about God became more valued than a relationship with God. We can understand how the people in the pews came to be given a lecture rather than words that transform aimed at helping them encounter a person.

The way the Western church approaches preaching has changed significantly because of print culture. Our tendency toward abstraction and our distrust of experience has caused us to ground sermons in theory, often with little attention to practical application. Karl Barth in his legendary book *Homiletics* represents the epitome of print culture's conditioning when he goes so far as to suggest that sermons should have no introduction, conclusion, humor, word pictures, or thought of relevance added to them. As often as possible, Barth argues, the Bi-

---

more holistic approach to God and the Scriptures would balance out this reductionistic tendency and greatly affect sermon preparation for the better.

[14] One cannot underestimate the importance of shifts in technology and their corresponding effects on culture. I am indebted to M. Rex Miller and his book for succinctly spelling out the implications of technology in cultural transformation as a means of understanding contextualization of the gospel and its truth for today's world.

[15] Warren W. Wiersbe in his book *Preaching and Teaching with Imagination* does a fantastic job of illustrating these points.

ble's written words should be read alone with as little as possible added to them.[16] To me, this seems to confuse the written words on the pages of the Bible with the person of the Word, who is constantly illuminating the written words in the context of relationship. It is not the words themselves but the God of the Word who is the source of transformational power.

If we are not careful, because of print culture and its conditioning, in our minds the Word can cease to be the Logos of John 1:1—a person who is alive and available for personal encounter.[17] Instead, "it" can become more of a printed abstraction on a page to be subjected to exegesis and examination rather than encountered. A leaning toward abstraction can lead to a kind of Christianity that is cold and sterile, lacking in the power to transform and renew. The sermon itself can easily become an encounter with abstraction and theoretical truth, rather than with a person, the Living God, and His transformational presence. It is important to remember that the highest truths are not reached through analysis and the deepest appeals not made to the intellect but rather to the heart.[18] Sometimes the folks in the pews need more than words—they need to encounter a living person so they can sob, weep, hug one another, and forgive.

Should we then forsake our libraries, burn our books, and retreat to caves to spend more time with God? Should we dispense with printed words and return to an oral culture, leaving Hebrew and Greek exegesis behind? Of course not. There is no going back, only moving forward, capitalizing on the best of oral and print cultures. But moving forward also requires that we understand the weaknesses programmed into our culture so we can build bridges over those weak points. The incarnation is a perfect place to begin that journey.

Incarnation: An Encounter with the Word

Given the power and place of image in human comprehension, is it any wonder that God sent His very own Son to live among us for all to see and experience? God was not content with sending only words through prophets or even with having His Word recorded in printed form. God was determined to send a person as a living witness—His Son, who is the very image of God the Father Himself—to show us what truth and its transformative power look like (Col.

---

[16] Karl Barth, *Homiletics* (Louisville: John Knox, 1994), 8-10; 95.

[17] The Old Testament Hebrew word "דָּבָר" (*dabar*) is always associated with a personal encounter—the messenger and the word were one in the minds of the writers. When the "Word of the Lord" came, it (He) came as a person who spoke the word, and the Word was an experience for the hearer rather than an abstraction. "Word" was associated with a person, as is evidenced by the Greek choice of *Logos*, translated "Word," to represent Jesus Christ Himself.

[18] Hugh Black, *Listening to God* (New York: Revell, 1906), 17, quoted in Wiersbe, 223.

1:15).[19] What if the answer for how to restore transformational power to preaching has been staring us in the face the whole time, and we could not see it? Is God once again hiding the answers to a complex question in one of the most basic truths—the coming of Jesus?

Our Christian heritage begins with the story of a baby born in Bethlehem. A baby born to a virgin named Mary, who was visited by an angel announcing to her that she would bear God's Son in her womb. The passage in Luke 1:26-38 describes in several short verses the incarnation of the Son of God. It recounts Gabriel's personal visit to Mary, perhaps as young as thirteen or fourteen years of age, in a rather insignificant city in Israel called Nazareth. There is nothing extraordinary about the woman or her surroundings. What stands out is the extraordinary personal encounter this young woman had with God. She had found favor with God (Luke 1:30). This young woman was greeted by the affirmation, "The Lord is with you" (Luke 1:28).

The angel related to Mary a process that would take place, one that theologians have come to call the "incarnation." The Latin *carne* means "meat" or "flesh." It is the process by which God clothed His Son, the Word of God, with flesh. The Word Himself existed before creation (John 1:1).[20] The language in the Greek text found in John gives us a peek at what the Father, Son, and Holy Spirit were doing before creation—they were enjoying one another's fellowship and company. The Word Himself, Jesus Christ, was enjoying an intimate relationship with the Father and Holy Spirit. The Word had always existed as God, even before creation, but was now going to take upon Himself human flesh as He was conceived in Mary's womb so people could see Him, hear Him, touch Him, and experience God for themselves as they experienced Jesus, the very image of God the Father (1 John 1:1-3).[21] This was God's ultimate intent in the

---

[19] Here the Greek word "εἰκών"(*eikon*) is used and translates "image or representation." Jesus, the God-man, was sent to perfectly represent God to the world—our ideal "image" of what God is like—so all could experience and understand Him. The word's Latin root literally means "window"—when we see Jesus, He is the *ikon* or window through which we see the Father.

[20] The Word (Jesus) existed "πρὸς τὸν θεόν" (*pros tov theov*), translated "with God." The Greek allows for a more intimate translation, "facing toward or in fellowship with God," based on the Hebraic significance of the word "know." To "know" someone in the Hebraic sense can imply intimacy, even sexual intimacy, which can be one of the deepest and richest forms of knowing (Gen. 4:1). In the English, a phrase often used to convey sexual intercourse with someone is to "be with" him or her. The Greek construct in John 1:1 is meant to convey a sense of intimacy and fellowship within the Godhead before the time of creation, illustrating God's nature of fellowship and relationship.

[21] This passage is central to understanding incarnational theology. It was written by John to counteract heresy at the time, proving that Jesus was one hundred percent God but also one hundred percent human, representing God's desire to be known, seen, and experienced by humankind. God delights in revealing Himself to humanity, and Jesus represents the epitome of God's desire to know and to be known.

incarnation of His Son—to allow ordinary people to experience His presence
and glory as Jesus "tabernacled" among us in human flesh (John 1:14).[22]

The pattern of the incarnation has several notable stages, the first being surrender. After Gabriel's words to Mary, she surrendered herself to God and His
plan as she said, "Behold the bondslave of the Lord; may it be done to me according to your word" (Luke 1:38). Through Mary's surrender, the Holy Spirit
would be the source of conception—He would overshadow her, and she would
conceive in her womb (Luke 1:31,35). The offspring conceived in her womb
would be fully God and fully man. Jesus would grow in her womb, mature, and
be delivered nine months later. He would then develop for the next thirty years
and transform the destiny of humankind with three years of ministry, His death
on the cross, and resurrection.

Can you see the process at work here? The world's hope for transformation
began with a divine conception in the womb of a young woman. It continued
with the growth of the divine seed in her womb.[23] It proceeded as the seed matured and took shape, finally becoming manifest when the mature seed was delivered—the life of God come to transform the world. The incarnation was an
organic, living process beginning with a seed infused with the life of God
through the Holy Spirit Himself and setting in motion the transformation of the
world and its entire history.

Let's consider more closely the ways the incarnation can be a perfect image
or metaphor for describing the essential elements of transformational preaching
and message preparation. What if message preparation is more about intimacy
with God and the conception of a word in the womb of the preacher's heart than
about the mechanics of sermon preparation? What might act as a spiritual contraceptive preventing conception? If intimacy with God can result in conception,
then what factors make the word grow and mature in our hearts? How do I know
if the baby is growing and maturing properly? What about delivery of the sermon? Timing would be everything—if delivered before its due date, the sermon

---

[22] It is no accident that John 1:14 uses the Greek verb root "σκηνόω" (*skenoo*) to describe
the Son of God dwelling among humanity. The root word can be translated "tented" or
"tabernacled" among us, an obvious reference to the Old Testament tabernacle and the
glory of God's presence within it. In the incarnation, we have the glory of God Himself
among humanity in bodily form with that body being a New Testament tabernacle for His
presence, modeling the life intended for believers in whom the Holy Spirit would dwell.
This is the crux of the New Testament experience—that all would know Him, from the
least to the greatest (Jer. 31:34).

[23] Note that the seed metaphor is used extensively in the Scriptures for both the Word of
God and the Son of God. The seed of the woman (Eve) would bruise the head of the serpent (Gen. 3:15) in victory at the cross. It was Abraham's seed that would rule forever
(Gen. 22:17,18; Gal. 3:16,17). The seed is also the perfect image for understanding the
nature of God's Word, which is planted in our heart through the Holy Spirit's illumination.

would be like a premature baby struggling for its life. What labor pains signal the right time for delivery?

The pattern of the incarnation suggests a sermon is more like a God-given word conceived in the preacher's heart than a wrestling match to find my next sermon topic. Thinking about preaching and message preparation in an incarnational way leads to personal transformation as the word I will eventually preach is first formed in me,[24] and I become like that word, a living witness for others to see and experience.[25] That is exactly what happened with my first sermon when I encountered Eph. 4:32. I let the word transform my heart and actions first—I forgave before I stood behind the pulpit and asked others to forgive. The word must first be conceived and take upon itself flesh in my life before it can breathe its transforming breath into the lives of others through my sermons.

Incarnational Communication

Incarnational communication occurs when I preach from a heart that has been personally transformed by God's Word. This kind of communication assumes the preacher has had an intimate encounter with the person of the Word and has been personally transformed as a result so that the word has taken upon itself flesh in the preacher's life. When God has something important to say or do, He sends a person, not just words.[26] Examples of incarnational communication can be found throughout the Scriptures. Hosea married Gomer and was a

---

[24] As mentioned earlier in this chapter, this is the spirit of the phrase "Christ is formed in you" "μορφωθῇ Χριστὸς ἐν ὑμῖν" (*morphothe Christos en humin*) in Gal. 4:19. The root word for "formed" is "μορφόω" (*morphoo*), which speaks of an inner transformation of the heart—one's essence as opposed to that which is external. This contrast is made in Rom. 12:2, where we are exhorted not to be conformed (root word "σχηματίζω" *schematizo*—to shape one's outer person) to the world but transformed (root word "μεταμορφόω" *metamorphoo*—to be transformed in one's inner essence).

[25] The Greek word for "witness" is "μάρτυς" (*martus*), from which we get our English word martyr. Becoming a witness begins with a transformed life not with words. This is echoed in a quote attributed to Francis of Assisi, who in the thirteenth century said, "Preach the Gospel often, and if you must, use words." Christ is formed in me as His word is integrated into my own life and changes me. There is then integrity between the words that come out of my mouth when I preach and the life that I live between sermons. I become that word and give it flesh in an incarnational manner for others to see rather than just hear.

[26] This is precisely why God sent Jesus in flesh to us. John 1:1 clearly says that Jesus existed throughout eternity as the *Logos* (λόγος)—the very core expression of God and all that He is. The mission of redemption required a person in human flesh to *be* what the mission was all about so people could see, hear, handle, and experience the truths of redemption and God's love for themselves before the gospel message was ever preached or recorded in print.

living sermon to those who saw what faithfulness to a harlot looked like—the perfect image for the relationship between God and Israel at that time. Jeremiah wept while Israel was led into captivity lest they confuse how God felt about their judgment. Paul met the Jewish religious leaders and their stones with conviction and determination after they had rejected the Messiah. In each case, it was not just the words, but a life embodying the Word coupled with words that had transformational impact.

Preaching and the sermon preparation need to begin at the beginning rather than at the end. The sermon must begin as a work in the heart rather than with external work on words, rhetoric, diction, style, or form. As important as external considerations are, if they dominate the message preparation process, they can strip the message of its power. When we prepare a message for the listener, we are not just preparing words; we are also hopefully preparing our lives for the Word. We place ourselves in a position of favor as Mary did. We encounter the Living God—the Word Himself—as He overshadows us in intimacy. The Holy Spirit "overshadows us." The Word deposits His seed in our hearts. Something alive is conceived and begins to grow in us. A mirror image of the incarnation process occurs. We whisper, "May it be done to me according to your word." An incarnational journey of preaching has begun.

Incarnational sermon preparation is built upon living relationship with God rather than on techniques alone. Isn't relationship what God has been looking for all along and the very purpose for which humanity was created?[27] The words of God to fallen humanity echo down the years to preachers of today: "[Adam], [w]here are you?" (Gen. 3:9).[28] The preaching journey originates in everyday life as we walk and talk with God about the events of the day. Was Mary doing the laundry when Gabriel visited, or was she in her study? Incarnational preaching begins when God bursts into the ordinary and makes it extraordinary by His presence so that transformational words can be conceived.

---

[27] Back to John 1:1—the Word was in fellowship with God the Father and Holy Spirit from all eternity. Fellowship and intimacy are at the very core of who God is and therefore of what He seeks and does. This is reflected in the reason God created humanity to begin with—for fellowship and to walk with Him (Gen. 3:9,10). That is why intimacy and fellowship are so essential and basic to the preaching process; they reflect who God is and what He is about. To not begin here in the preaching process is to ignore these simple facts.

[28] How easy it is for the preacher to use sermon preparation and busyness as fig leaves to cover the nakedness of our inadequacy for the task of sermon preparation. Overcoming that inadequate feeling, if it can ever be done, is only accomplished by laying the busyness aside and walking with God "in the cool of the day" as a source for transformational sermons. This removes some of the human element and places the onus on God for the sermon (Gen. 3:8).

The Conception of the Word

It happens every day. The same words are repeated by wives to husbands and by daughters to their parents: "I think I'm pregnant." When a man and woman are joined in sexual intimacy, conception is the natural by-product. Only things like timing, an underlying health problem, or measures specifically taken to prevent pregnancy can stop the course of nature. Something miraculous has occurred—a new life has sprung into existence, and though hidden in the warmth and safety of the womb, that new life is already full of potential because of God's sovereign plan.[29]

Life doesn't begin at conception but much further back in the mind of God, according to His sovereign plan. Sermons too have their origins in God's mind. Might we dare believe that God has something to say to His people before we ever sit down to consider our sermon topic? I believe God is already at work in the sermon process before we are aware of it, shaping the lives of people, churches, and communities and preparing them for the moment His word is delivered.[30] Transformational sermons originate in the mind of God according to His plan for a specific place, people, and time. Many preachers innately understand what I am describing but may have never had the words—or had the images—to describe the experience.

As we are learning, incarnational sermons begin with something alive that is conceived in the preacher's heart. Conception occurs as God illuminates truth from His written Word or as He uses truth from the Scriptures to illuminate truth in our life circumstances.[31] In either case, illumination occurs as a result of an intimate connection with God. The metaphor of conception, lying at the heart of

---

[29] See Isa. 46:9,10, which describes God as the Master Architect who sees the end from the beginning. From the moment of conception, God begins to superintend over a human life in order to bring that life into conformity with His master plan so that it will reach His ultimate goals. While human life is a dance between God's plan and the human will, His Spirit is at work in the many details (Ps. 139:12-16) that will work out His good pleasure in our lives.

[30] This statement is very reminiscent of the theology of Henry Blackaby, who asserts that God is already at work among us and simply invites us to join Him in what He is already doing. See Henry Blackaby, *Experiencing God* (Nashville: Broadman & Holman, 1994).

[31] J. Rodman Williams, *Renewal Theology* (Grand Rapids: Zondervan, 1996), 1:29-45. Here Williams asserts the centrality of the knowledge of God—God wants to be known. God cannot be known by means other than revelation, because He is veiled to human perception. All knowledge is revealed and is particular, progressive, saving, verbal, and personal. He has revealed Himself through special revelation in the form of the Scriptures and through subordinate revelation within the Christian community by His Holy Spirit. Out of fear of diminishing special revelation and the integrity of the inerrancy of the Scriptures, we have often neglected or diminished the place of subordinate revelation in the life of the church.

incarnational communication, is part of human sexuality.[32] In some cultural settings, such a parallel may produce embarrassment or even shock. In many Western settings, the beauty of God-given sexuality has been warped by a hyper-sexualized culture. I want to assure the reader that I use the sexual metaphor with the utmost holiness in mind and with the deepest appreciation for what God has given humanity in sexuality.

Sexuality has the God-given potential to weld two people together for a lifetime. Sexuality is designed to bring a man and a woman into the closest of possible relationships on earth.[33] Nothing comes close to sexuality's wonder, power, or satisfaction on this side of heaven when enjoyed as our Creator intended—in the context of marriage. Two people become one in the covenant of marriage (Gen. 2:21-25). God views sexuality as holy and unstained unless human beings choose to bring stain upon it (Heb. 13:4).[34] Sexual imagery gives us the perfect word picture for the kind of intimate fellowship God shared in as the persons of the Trinity before creation (John 1:1).

Sexual imagery is also a perfect vehicle for understanding the kind of fellowship God desires to have with men and women for the rest of eternity. Rather than over-spiritualizing the Song of Solomon, we should rejoice with the bridegroom, his bride, and God in the act of sexual consummation as the bridegroom declares:

> I have come into my garden, my sister, *my* bride; I have gathered my myrrh along with my balsam. I have eaten my honeycomb and my honey; I have drunk my wine and my milk. Eat, friends; Drink and imbibe deeply, O lovers" (Song of Sol. 5:1).[35]

---

[32] I am very sensitive to the reader at this point for several reasons. In some cultures, sexuality is not openly spoken of, and the kinds of sexual imagery invoked to model incarnational communication may therefore seem too forward or inappropriate. For others, a negative experience with sexuality may skew understanding or biblical meaning. With this in mind, I ask the reader to revisit sexuality in its biblical context as something positive, holy, and life-giving.

[33] Let's remember who designed sex, sexuality, and the human body for the capacity for sexuality—God Himself. Rom. 1:20 and God's artistic hand as seen in creation give us warrant to understand sexuality as a reflection of His invisible attributes. God at His very core is someone who loves intimate fellowship and to reveal Himself. Sexuality in its pure and God-given form is a perfect image for understanding the kind of relationship we should have with Him in worship, prayer, and our daily walk as we are "naked and una-shamed" before Him and walk in unity with Him.

[34] Note that in this verse marriage itself is something honorable in God's sight ("τίμιος" (*timios*), meaning esteemed) and that sexuality (literally "ἡ κοίτη ἀμίαντος" (*he koite amiantos*) or "the marriage bed," a metaphor for sexuality) is undefiled in the sight of God. It already exists as pure in God's sight unless we choose to defile it.

[35] The garden in Middle Eastern imagery was often used as a symbol of sexuality. God's response to the consummation of the marriage between Solomon and his bride was "Drink and imbibe deeply, O lovers."

Many scholars contend the imagery in this passage is best applied to the church and Jesus Christ, representing the "consummation" of the ages, when Christ is united with His spotless bride forever (Eph. 5:21-31,32). Yet simple human sexuality is described here as well—the ecstasy of sexual union between a man and his wife on their wedding night. There is no embarrassment or shyness on God's part. He tells the lovers, "Eat, friends; Drink and imbibe deeply, O lovers." God issues the same call to preachers today.

As with Mary, the Holy Spirit has a primary role in the conception of the word. He is the Great Teacher who prunes, cultivates, and teaches.[36] Human beings are incapable of understanding God or truth unless God reveals that truth, because He is utterly different from us and lies beyond the veil of heaven. The word that we use to describe this characteristic is *holy*, which at its root means "set apart" or "utterly different."[37] Conception of the word occurs as the Holy Spirit illuminates truth in our hearts. Perhaps you can relate to the experience of a burst of personal understanding about a truth from Scripture or some God-given illumination on truth discovered in your personal life. Conception is the moment when "the lights come on," and you can see something that may have been right in front of your eyes, but suddenly it is new, connected, and makes sense. In that moment, your interaction with the Holy Spirit has changed you, because something has become real, alive, and apparent to you about God, life, His nature, or His Word—something new and alive is conceived.

Illumination of truth by the Holy Spirit is captured in the Greek word *apokalupsis*, which is best translated "revealing or uncovering."[38] The truth has been

---

[36] For the work of the Holy Spirit and His ministry, John 13–17 is unsurpassed, capturing Jesus' words at the Last Supper before His death, speaking of the Holy Spirit whom He would send to His disciples after His departure. The Holy Spirit would be sent to teach (John 14:26), prune (15:2), cultivate (15:8), and convict (16:68). All these things assume abiding and ongoing relationship with the person of the Holy Spirit.

[37] The Hebrew word "קֹדֶשׁ" (*kodesh*) and the Greek word "ἅγιος" (*hagios*) share the same sense of otherness or set apartness, describing God as being wholly other than us. If He is wholly other than us, then how can we know Him except by His willingness to reveal Himself, and then only through the shadow of metaphor by what has been created, describing what He is "like."

[38] It is critical to point out very early in our study how to correctly define the term *revelation* lest personal (general) revelation be confused with the kind of revelation (special) that made the Scriptures possible. The Bible makes it abundantly clear that all Scripture is inspired by God, using the word "θεόπνευστος" (*theoneustos*), which means "breathed out" as it is used in 2 Tim 3:16. This verse identifies the work of the Holy Spirit and the special revelation involved as the source for the Scriptures as He revealed and preserved them through their original authors. General revelation, which is a more general enlightenment of truth to an individual, is not on the same level as special revelation. General revelation is fallible because of the frailness of our humanity. For this reason, many theologians cautiously approach the idea of these two distinct kinds of revelation by referring to special revelation as "revelation" and general revelation as "illumination." In one

there all the time, but the Holy Spirit's work has opened our eyes to see it—interaction with Him has allowed a truth to be uncovered for our hearts to see. The Holy Spirit's illumination starts a journey of understanding that begins like conception—something new is alive in the womb of our hearts and begins to grow as relationship with the Holy Spirit brings further illumination. The truth God has revealed becomes alive in us, becomes rooted in the womb of our hearts, and begins to grow. Something holy has taken place.

Many times preachers rob the Holy Spirit of His rightful place in sermon preparation. In doing so, we limit the transformational potential of a sermon at its very origin. David Buttrick's classic book *Homiletic* makes my point by dismissing the immediacy of the Holy Spirit's work in sermon preparation. To Buttrick, God's presence in the process is ". . . Presence in Absence." Buttrick states,

> Obviously, preaching is not itself an immediate word from God. Whenever preachers attempt to push back prior to understanding and to speak from some immediate God-awareness, they produce either arrogance or glossolalia.
> . . .Whenever preachers speak, supposing some inner, subconscious dalliance with God, the result is usually a freaky language deserving the apostle Paul's sharp rebuke.[39]

Can you imagine a groom trying to describe to his new bride his "presence in absence?" There is no room for intimate presence or relationship in Buttrick's kind of sermon preparation process. The whole process becomes intellectual and human-centered in its approach. It is as if the references to the work of the Holy Spirit in John 13–17 don't exist.

Rather than "presence in absence," the phrase "absence of presence" comes to mind to describe the quality and content of many messages produced according to Buttrick's formula. Words can sound wonderful, but where is the presence of God in them and from where does the transformational power of that sermon come? Can one imagine Jesus or Paul talking about presence in absence? Jesus specifically said He would go away and send the Helper, who as the Spirit of truth would personally guide us into all truth (John 16:7-13). Can you imagine receiving a dinner invitation requesting your "presence in absence"? Buttrick's view of sermon preparation explains a lack of transformative power in many sermons today. The Holy Spirit has always been a gentleman, and if extended an invitation requesting His "presence in absence," though He may be grieved, He seems willing to comply.

---

sense, general revelation exists only because the "light" of specific revelation from God's Word "illuminates" general truth in our hearts. For an excellent discussion of the difference between revelation and illumination as just described, see Greg Heisler, *Spirit-Led Preaching* (Nashville: B&H Academic, 2007), 38-52.

[39] David Buttrick, *Homiletic* (Philadelphia: Fortress, 1987), 320.

It is time to get back to basics and to invite the Holy Spirit to join us and fulfill His role in sermon preparation. Maybe issuing the invitation is so intimidating because it places the direction and result of our preaching beyond our control and under the rightful lordship of the Holy Spirit. Perhaps the humility required to become like a child again is overwhelming. God bids us to come close, as He did the people of Israel in Moses day, but we are still afraid that coming close will cost us our lives (Exod. 20:18,19).[40] In a sense, that is right—it will cost us our lives if we come close enough for conception to take place.

Growth and Maturing of the Word

I remember getting the call at about nine-thirty in the evening as I was easing into a night at home with my family. I had done John and Sally's wedding a few years back. Several months earlier, we had gotten the wonderful news that they were expecting a baby. The voice on the other end of the phone this particular evening was John's mother—Sally had gone into labor unexpectedly and was at the hospital. John's mom sounded frantic. She asked if I would pray and come to the hospital and wait with them for the outcome. Sally's pregnancy was about twenty-five weeks along—past the point of viability but in a dangerous zone that meant this baby would be in for the battle of its tiny life. I rushed down to hospital, and the baby was born about three hours later. That night I was introduced to the wonders of neonatal medicine, the pediatric intensive care unit, and the world of trouble that can surround a premature birth.

When I first saw little Michael, I could barely make out his form because of all the wires, tubes, probes, heaters, and diagnostic equipment. Michael was so small he could have comfortably fit in the palm of my hand. Machines were helping his underdeveloped lungs breathe and were recording his every heartbeat. The family and I gathered around the incubator and committed little Michael to God, praying for his survival. God answered those prayers. Michael remained in the hospital for several months, at first barely clinging to life. His parents grew spiritually before my eyes as they loved that little baby toward health. I'll never forget the day his parents brought him home, or the day we dedicated Michael in church one Sunday morning. Michael beat the odds. Premature babies that are delivered that small are so very vulnerable and at risk; many do not survive.

Once something new and alive has been conceived, it is by no mean ready to be delivered. If a new life does not have sufficient time to grow and mature in the womb, its potential for viability is greatly diminished or lost. So it is with sermons. The core of a transformational sermon begins with truth illuminated by

---

[40] In this Old Testament passage, it is clear that God's will was for all the people of Israel to prepare themselves and come close to God in order to personally experience God and His presence. They backed out and sent Moses instead.

a work of the Holy Spirit in the preacher's heart. However, that truth is not yet ready to be shared with others—it must be nurtured like a growing baby in the womb so it can become viable life before its delivery.

What does viable mean when we're talking about a sermon? A word that is revealed to us must become very personal to us first—before it is shared with others. Balaam's jackass preached the word to Balaam without benefit of any inner transformation, but do we really want her to be our role model for preaching?[41] As the word that was conceived is nurtured, it begins to grow like a seed in our lives. Seeds are already programmed with all the instructions needed to produce a healthy plant, which produces more seeds and starts the cycle all over again.[42] Given time and the right nutrients to grow, the seed from an oak tree has the potential to create a forest. God's living word has the same potential in people's lives. The word works its way into a listener's heart. There the word is watered by the person and work of the Holy Spirit. Once watered, the word takes on a life of its own, producing in that individual the very characteristics programmed into its "genetic" code. The same thing happens when the Holy Spirit conceives a word in the preacher's heart. The word must grow and become integrated into the preacher's own life before delivery lest that delivery be premature and fail to take root in the lives of the listeners.

"Quickening" is the moment when a woman feels the new life in her womb for the first time. At quickening, the baby becomes more than a rational concept in her mind—she actually feels the tickle of a new life within her womb. The psychological impact of quickening is immense. When quickening occurs, a woman actually comes to grips with the reality of the new life in her womb and grows toward attachment. The moment of quickening is a moment of encounter that changes her life forever. As the baby grows and matures, its movements will become more pronounced. The same is true with the truth God illuminates in the preacher's heart. As that truth grows and we begin to feel its life and

---

[41] This curious story is related in Num. 22:16-35. Both Balaam and the jackass are examples of creatures that are used by God to speak His word. Both are also examples of vessels that are used by God but are lacking inner transformation. For the jackass, that was no shame, but for Balaam, who was destroyed by his greed and unrighteousness, it spelled disaster (2 Pet. 2:15; Jude 11).

[42] James D. Watson and Francis Crick earned the 1962 Nobel Prize for physiology and medicine for their work in understanding DNA, the molecular building block of genetic code transmission. DNA is the chemical basis for building genetic instruction in every one of the more than thirty trillion cells in the human body. The DNA code that is imprinted in the genes within the nucleus of each cell carries exact instructions for the shape, size, and function of the human body for a lifetime and is unique for each individual. Seeds carry this same potential—the instructions to produce a living plant and its seeds, which have the potential to become a forest automatically. This is the kind of "automatic growth" referred to in Mark 4:28 whereby the growth of the seed in its soil occurs "by itself," from the root "αὐτόματος" (automatos).

movement in our hearts, its movement transforms the way we look at the world and our relationships—and even our perception of reality. Excitement tempts the young preacher to create a sermon for delivery, but the word still lacks the transformational power that comes from a deeply changed life. If preached prematurely, the word may make intellectual sense to the hearers and sound good, but it often lacks life and depth. At worst, a premature sermon can be destructive if words spoken from the pulpit don't match the preacher's life.

God is always at work in the preacher's life, using circumstances to grow and mature the word. God's Spirit is constantly speaking. The question is do we have ears to hear and eyes to see?[43] The experienced preacher uses life as a living laboratory to experience the Word. God is very efficient and wastes nothing. As God illuminates truth's meaning through life circumstances, truth comes alive to us. It becomes experiential truth that can be given away to others—as Augustine of Hippo once said, "What I live by, I impart."[44] The word begins to tinker with my attitudes and motivations, exposing them for what they really are. I begin to see where I am wrong in my beliefs, perspectives, and in what I value. I am confronted with the need to change so that I can come into alignment with the word. When adequate time is given to the growth and maturing of the word, the preacher's thoughts, attitudes, values, and actions begin to change, and the word becomes flesh. What was abstract now becomes visible. The preacher is ready to preach the word, because his or her life is already preaching it.

Delivery of the Word

After many months of pregnancy, a woman becomes heavy with child. The anticipation of giving birth increases but so does the burden. Planning begins. She gains weight. The child's movement becomes relentless, and the womb has false labor contractions to practice for the big day. Breathing itself becomes difficult as the baby's size increases. The woman thinks, "I can't wait to deliver

---

[43] As mentioned earlier in this chapter, I believe the church is indebted to the work of Dr. Henry Blackaby. In his perspective-changing work *Experiencing God*, Blackaby aptly points out that God is already at work all around us each day and that He asks that we join Him in what He is already at work doing. This is in contrast to the Western model of approaching God—we usually ask Him to bless what we are already at work doing. Blackaby's work strikes at the central questions of lordship and who is in control—will it be God or I?

[44] Augustine of Hippo, quoted in David Larsen, *The Anatomy of Preaching* (Grand Rapids: Kregal, 1989), 49. Larsen quotes Augustine as evidence that God is the only one who can form a preacher and that formation of character and community are at the heart of this formation process. Spirituality is *persona non grata* in Western Protestant Christianity in many places, but it remains the bedrock of ministry in general and of preaching and teaching specifically.

this child," yet her maternal instincts urge her to wait so the baby will be healthy.

The same burden and anticipation is experienced with a sermon as it grows in the womb of the preacher's heart. As with a human birth, the number of days spent in the womb make a big difference in determining whether a sermon will thrive or arrive fighting for its life. When the time of growth and maturity is nearly complete, it is important for the preacher to be patient, even though the burden of the word increases as the time for its delivery approaches.

But once it is time, it is time. There is nothing on earth like the experience of seeing a new baby born into this world. The same can be said of preaching a God-birthed sermon. The thrill of giving birth to something vibrant that has been formed by the handiwork of God is like no other experience on this side of heaven. Granted, this is the "payoff" for a lot of hard work. The sermon is the visible part, the reward for many months of struggle and nurture. Further, the delivery of the word, as with the birth of a human baby, is fraught with danger, peril, and pain. The preacher is always one word away from infamy. Yet because of God's dealings in the preacher's heart, something alive issues forth from human lips—not mere words, but more than that: words filled with God's transformative life. The experience is one of the most rewarding in ministry.

In human life, a baby's delivery is just as important as the growth of that child in the womb. A lively, viable, healthy child can suffer great harm as the result of a poor or botched delivery. When things go badly in the delivery room, all the growth and potential formed over the pregnancy period is jeopardized. As for the incarnational preaching process, three-quarters of a sermon's development has been internal. Without the internal part, there is nothing viable or alive to deliver. Without conception, there is no life present in the womb. Without sufficient time for growth and maturing, the baby is not viable and at risk. Yet that one-quarter of the process that remains—the external and visible delivery is vital. If the delivery does not go well, then the prior nine months gestation is in vain.

The Word Became Flesh

Are there ways that I can facilitate the conception of the word in my heart? What "spiritual vitamins" are necessary to grow the word in the womb of my heart? How will the maturing of the word in my heart change me? How will I know when the time is right to deliver the word? What things can I do to deliver the word to ensure that the "baby" is healthy and viable? Let's continue our incarnational journey through the pages of this book.

Chapter 3 asks the question, "How's Your Love Life?" and concentrates on building or rebuilding intimacy with God as a context for transformational preaching. Chapter 4 examines strategies for grounding sermons in life experience to grow and mature the word. Chapter 5 provides a detailed look at heart-shaping and the role of the Holy Spirit in molding the preacher's inner being as a foundation for transformational preaching. Chapter 6 will focus specifically on sermon-shaping and an organic paradigm for sermon delivery. Chapter 7 describes the role of imagination and creativity in the sermon-shaping process. In chapter 8, I will share some of my favorite examples of the incarnational preaching process at work in my own life over the years.

My personal experience with preaching and research tells me that the incarnational approach to preaching just described is, indeed, a pathway back to the kind of transformational preaching that has the potential to produce renewal in the church. God saw humanity's need and the Word became flesh to meet that need. The result was transformational power to save all who call on His name. The answer for the church's need today is the same—transformational power is released when I allow the Word to take upon Himself flesh in my life so I can give birth to words that transform. Lord, may it be done to me according to your word.

Chapter 3
How's Your Love Life?
The Place of Intimacy in Sermon-shaping

[2] "May he kiss me with the kisses of his mouth! For your love is better than wine. [3] "Your oils have a pleasing fragrance, Your name is *like* purified oil; Therefore the maidens love you. [4] "Draw me after you *and* let us run *together*! The king has brought me into his chambers." "We will rejoice in you and be glad; We will extol your love more than wine. Rightly do they love you" (Song of Sol. 1:2-4).

The Song of Solomon reads more like a romance novel than it does a book of the Bible. Being one of the more sexually explicit parts of the Scriptures, it gives scholars fits,[1] Whether you put Song of Solomon through the literary blender, claiming it as highly symbolic, or otherwise parse the Hebrew, the book still stands out as a blatant description of human sexual love. I believe God intended it that way—to shock us back to reality. God is the creator of human sexuality, and sexuality is one of the most holy and precious gifts He created. God's creation is so full of wisdom that created things always have multiple dimen-

---

[1] Andrew E. Hill and John H. Walton, *A Survey of the Old Testament* (Grand Rapids: Zondervan, 2000), 376. As Hill and Walton note, "No single book of the Old Testament has proved more perplexing for biblical interpreters than the Song of Solomon. Centuries of careful study by scholars of various religious traditions and theological persuasions have produced very little interpretive consensus . . . the topic and the frank language of the Song have confused, shocked, and embarrassed both Jewish and Christian readers— so much so that for generations the rabbis and early church fathers debated the value of the book and its place in the Old Testament." The Song of Songs provides a divinely inspired reality check for us—sometimes life and theology are not best understood by the exegesis of words on a page but by opening the heart to a love novel and letting it touch our innermost being with its beauty!

sions of purpose—a multitude of interwoven purposes at work all at once. Human sexuality is like that. It serves a very practical human purpose, but it is also a wonderful metaphor for our relationship with God.

Sex has power. It can be a source of tremendous joy and blessing that fuses a couple together for a lifetime in the covenant of marriage.[2] If used improperly, it can kill, maim, and leave scars that do not heal. We each decide how to use the gift of sexuality—it is a God-given tool to allow two people to experience a small taste of the kind of intimacy God desires to have with His people. But it can easily go off like a bomb if not used according to its intended design.

Jesus did not die to establish a religion but rather to make a way back to a relationship with God that was broken at the fall of humanity. Because of Jesus, eternal life can begin right now as we come to know Him more intimately in relationship each day (John 17:3).[3] We experience this intimacy as we abide in relationship and discover for ourselves over time that His ". . . love is better than wine." May He kiss me with the kisses of His mouth! We learn the familiar "fragrance" of His presence in our daily walk. For some, there comes a time when calling is discerned and God bids us come: ". . . let us run together!" When preachers answer the call to run with God, we seem to have a special kind of access to the King's chambers. His chambers are the place of intimacy—the place where conception takes place. The King's chambers are where transformative sermons are born.

The Kisses of His Mouth

It is essential that preachers focus on the primary source of that transformative power—relationship with God. The power to change life resides in God alone. Ministers have a tendency to replace *being with* God with *doing for* God. When the balance between being and doing suffers, the flow of transformational power also suffers. Doing without being allows for depersonalization to slip into a preacher's consciousness, and intimacy begins to grow stale. We begin to see God as the "boss" we work for and not the friend or lover the Scriptures describe Him to be. As intimacy decreases, preachers start to go through the familiar motions and do out of a sense of duty rather than love. Jesus wished Martha

---

[2] Gen. 2:24,25 describes the effects of the "one flesh" experience of sexuality by saying that a man would "cleave"—"דָּבַק" (*dabaq*)—to his wife and they would become one flesh. The word describes the power of human sexuality—the power to "glue or weld" two people together as the two become one in the sexual act.

[3] In this verse of Scripture, John records the definition Jesus gave for eternal life (Gr. "ἡ αἰώνιος ζωή" (*he aionios zoe*))—it is to "know" God. This implies that knowing God intimately is the essence of what eternal life is all about and that this eternal life can be experienced right now on earth by knowing Him—again the emphasis is on relationship and intimacy.

would just come and sit with Mary and Him in conversation and fellowship rather than doing additional busywork (Luke 10:41,42). He told the sisters that there are only a few things necessary and that intimacy was at the top of His list. Preachers often abandon the simplicity of the gospel—the simplicity and purity of devotion to Christ—in favor of doing things in His name (2 Cor. 11:2,3). It's easy to lose perspective when buildings and board meetings demand our attention. People fuss, get married, need counseling, and die at unpredictable times. To be sure, there is no faith without works (James 2:18-24), but we can't forget that God yearns for our friendship. After all, love is who He is at the very core of His being.

The Word as Person

Western culture has been conditioned over the last five hundred years to think of the Word of God as words on a page. At times, we have embraced abstract theological ideas and propositions represented by the words in Scripture and neglected relationship with the person behind those words. When embracing abstract thought over personal relationship, we are thinking more like Greeks than Hebrews.[4] Hebrew thought is dynamic, vigorous, passionate, and very relationship-centered. Greek thought is much more static, peaceful, and harmonious with a greater emphasis on the idea or concept. [5]

Take, for example, the way the Hebrew culture conceptualizes the word for "word." For the Hebrew, true being is the "word" (Heb. *dabar*), which is used to signify being. The word *lo-dabar* in Hebrew translates "no being" or "nothing," but literally means "no word"—literally "a thing of nothing."[6] Can you see how closely the idea of "being" and "word" are tied together in the Hebrew mind? For the Hebrew, the word is our being—a person is his or her word. Hearing the word of a person is intimacy with that person. Thorlief Boman notes:

> All over the ancient Orient, in Assyria and Babylonia as well as in Egypt the word, particularly the word of God, was not only nor even primarily the expression of thought; it was a mighty and dynamic force . . . The Israelite-oriental conception of the word is formally the opposite of the Greek conception, as Bultmann also maintains. . . . in the Old Testament, the word of Jahveh is never a force of nature as in Assyria or Babylonia, but is always the function of a conscious and moral personality. . . . Jahveh's word belongs not to the physical but to the spiritual sphere; by it his will comes to expression.[7]

---

[4] A classic work comparing Hebrew and Greek thought is Thorlief Boman, *Hebrew Thought Compared with Greek* (London: SCM, 1960).
[5] Ibid., 30-31.
[6] Ibid., 56-57.
[7] Ibid., 58, 60, 65.

Boman also notes a decisive contrast between the way Hebrews thought of "word" and Greek thought:

> The basic meaning [of *logos*], which is so characteristic of the Greek mind, explains the three principle meanings of the concept which are so hard for us to reconcile: speak, reckon, and think . . . The term was generally used 'only with regard to the principle functions of a reasonable man.'[8]

For the Hebrews, then, the "word" is the person. For the Greeks, the "word" is the highest form of mental expression—the "idea." Both definitions are valid cultural constructs for understanding the truth, but we must be careful. We can easily fall in love with ideas presented in the Scriptures, carrying on a mental affair with abstract truths, and neglect to give due attention to the person to which those truths point. I can "kiss" a person but not an idea.

The apostle John perfectly captures the Hebrew ideal of the word as a person in John 1:1. Was this partly because John so highly prized intimacy with Jesus? The "disciple whom Jesus loved" (John 21:20) used the Greek word *logos* to describe Jesus as "God the Word".[9] John 1:1 leaves no doubt that "In the beginning of all material things, the Word (as a person already) was." The Word was already in existence as a person when material things were created. John's language also places the Word in dynamic relationship as a person with the other persons of the Godhead: ". . . and the word was facing towards (in fellowship with) God."[10] The verse equates the Word with God Himself by saying firmly and clearly, ". . . and the Word was God." So, the Word existed as a person before the creation of material things. We learn what God was doing before creation—He was in perfect fellowship with Himself and enjoying the splendor of that fellowship. The verse forever equates God and His Word as one and the same—the Word is God, a person, and at the core of His existence are fellowship, relationship, and intimacy.

---

[8] Ibid., 67-68.

[9] John 1:1 is written very clearly to equate God with the Word: "Ἐν ἀρχῇ ἦν ὁ λόγος, καὶ ὁ λόγος ἦν πρὸς τὸν θεόν, καὶ θεὸς ἦν ὁ λόγος." (*Ev arche en ho logos, kai ho logos en pros tov theon, kai theos en ho logos*). This Greek passage could easily be rendered: "Before the beginning of material things, the Word already was in existence, and the Word existed in fellowship with the other persons of the Godhead, and the Word Himself was also God." The language is pregnant with meaning as it equates God with the Word and places Him in fellowship with the other persons of the Godhead, giving us a clue as to Their nature and the centrality of fellowship to His nature.

[10] The Greek phrase "πρὸς τὸν θεόν" (*pros tov theov*) allows us the freedom to translate this passage as "the Word was facing toward God," which is a language construct denoting fellowship the way our English phrase "face-to-face" implies closeness and personal interaction.

John wrote his gospel to counteract many heresies in his time that deperso-nalized and dehumanized Jesus and, in some cases, stripped Him of His deity.[11] The early church grappled with these heresies in a series of council meetings to consider the issues surrounding the person and nature of Jesus Christ. Even so, are we honestly comfortable with the idea of the Word as a person? Is there room in the lives of busy preachers for relationship with a person rather than with a book of words? You can kiss a book, but it can't kiss back.

Relationship with God through His Spirit grants us access to the transforma-tive kiss preachers so badly need each day. This is the secret to transformative preaching—intimacy with the person to whom the book points so we can minis-ter His presence in our preaching. The Scriptures cannot kiss us with the kisses of their mouth, but they can point us toward the person who can.

Intimacy with the Word

Since time began, humanity has been searching for the answers to some very basic questions: "Why did God make me?" and "Why am I here?" Is it to fulfill a certain destiny with my job? Is it to work hard and to accumulate pos-sessions? Is it to have a family and launch the next generation? Is it to somehow please God by doing things that fulfill calling or destiny? Is it to win souls and preach good sermons? These questions evoke some of the reasons we are alive, but ultimately, as we are learning, the reason for our existence is not found in *doing* but in *being*—specifically being in a relationship with God. Without rela-tionship as the wellspring of our activities, they are shallow at best and quite possibly a waste of time. As we see in the book of Genesis, the answer to ques-tions about why we are here involves relationship and intimacy with God.

Humanity was made in God's own image and likeness (Gen. 1:26).[12] God made human beings to reflect His own nature with the capacity and need for

---

[11] For an excellent summary of the various heresies surrounding the person of Christ, see W. Graham Scroggie, *A Guide to the Gospels* (Old Tappen: Revell, n.d.), 525-546. Throughout the early church, there were many different heresies related to the nature of Christ. The Apollinarians denied His human nature. The Ebionites considered His divini-ty as defiled, making Him a mere man and not God. Arianism denied the deity of Christ, and Bishop Nestorius said that He was actually two people—God and man—while Ab-bott Eutyches said that He was of one nature with deity and humanity blended as one. The various church councils that were convened gradually defined an orthodox view of Jesus Christ and His nature. The Council of Chalcedon in 451, attended by 630 bishops, declared that the incarnation allowed for a true and whole human nature to enter into union with the divine personality of the Logos at the moment of conception as one indi-vidual life. As a result of the incarnation, Jesus becomes the "God-man"—one person who is at once wholly divine and wholly human.

[12] Here the Hebrew words are "צֶלֶם" (*tselem*) and "דְּמוּת" (*demuth*). The Aramaic root for *tselem* implies a copy—it is used in prohibitions against making idols (representations of

relationship. Once He made Adam, God made someone corresponding to him so that he would not be alone (Gen. 2:18).[13] God made us for relationship—because we are made in God's image, we are like God and yearn to relate. God was moving to restore relationship with us right after the fall. It was God who was seeking Adam and Eve, though they had just sinned (Gen. 3:8,9).[14] It was the man and his wife who hid themselves from the presence of God after they had sinned, because their relationship with God was broken. It was God who then immediately spoke of a way back to fellowship through the one who would bruise the head of the serpent with His redemptive sacrifice (Gen. 3:15). From Genesis 3 onward in the Scriptures to the end of Revelation, the abiding thread is the redemption of humanity through the blood of Jesus Christ to restore us to relationship and sweet fellowship with Him (2 Cor. 5:17-21). God has been pursuing a love relationship with us ever since the Fall, and it seems that if necessary, He will love us all the way to hell if that is our choice. His blood was shed so we could draw near with confidence (Heb. 10:19-22). We were created for relationship with God—to experience the daily kisses of His mouth and to learn the pleasing smell of His garments.

As He did with Adam and Eve, it is God who pursues preachers for their fellowship. Henry Blackaby in his book *Experiencing God* rightly observes that it is God who takes the initiative in this pursuit:

> God Himself pursues a love relationship with you. He is the One who takes the initiative to bring you into this kind of relationship. He created you for a love relationship with Himself. That is the very purpose of your life. This love relationship can and should be personal to you. . . . God always takes the initiative in this love relationship. God must take the initiative and come to us if we are to experience Him. This is the witness of the entire Bible. He came to Adam and Eve in the Garden of Eden. In love, He fellowshipped with them and they with Him. He came to Noah, Abraham, Moses, and the prophets. God took the initiative for each person in the Old Testament to experience Him in a personal fellowship of love. This is true for the New Testament as well.[15]

---

deity). The word *demuth* amplifies *tselem* in this verse, rendering the best translation a "likeness-image"—a human being is the visible representation of the invisible God. See R. Laird Harris, Gleason L. Archer, and Bruce K. Waltke, *The Theological Workbook of the Old Testament* (Chicago: Moody, 1980), 2:767-768 (*tselem*) and 1:473, 438 (*demuth*).

[13] It was not good that man should be "לְבַדּוֹ" (*lebaddo*), "only himself," but that "עֵזֶר כְּנֶגְדּוֹ" (*ezer kenegdo*), a "counterpart," be made for relationship.

[14] Theologians consider the appearance of the Lord God to be a "theophany"—a visible appearance of God to human beings. Since "No one has seen God at any time" (John 1:18), it is assumed that this was a pre-incarnate encounter with the Word of God Himself, who loved to relate to the man and woman that He had created.

[15] Blackaby (1994), 79, 85, 86.

He pursues us because relationship and intimacy are the central needs of our lives and the only source of the transformative power we so desperately need. To cut off intimacy is to cut off the "living waters" of transformation and to invite problems. Just like a flower cut off from the plant, we dry up and wither quickly.

Recent statistics on the health and wellness of ministers and their families show some of the effects of a lack of intimacy with God. Ellison Research recently did a study on pastors and their prayer habits with some interesting facts about the state of our relationship with God:[16]

- The average pastor prays 39 minutes per day;
- 21% of the pastors pray less than 15 minutes per day;
- The most satisfied with their prayer life spend almost an hour in prayer per day; those who are least satisfied with their prayer life spend an average of 21 minutes in prayer per day;
- The most satisfied spend less time making requests and more time being quiet and listening to God; those least satisfied spend a majority of their time making requests.

I am convinced the quality of relationship with God reported in this study had more to do with intimacy than it had to do with time. While intimacy cannot be rushed, the people who spent their time trying to get God to do things in prayer were less satisfied than the ones who enjoyed being with God. We need to spend more time kissing and less time giving Him the grocery list. This is the key to a transformative relationship with God.

"Be It Done to Me"

God's greatest gift to humanity was the gift of His Son, and the way that He gave His Son tells us so much about His nature. There are many ways God could have arranged to pay the price for our sins to counteract the fall, but He chose to do so by clothing His Son with human flesh. Luke 1:26-38 captures the miracle of the incarnation:

> [26] Now in the sixth month the angel Gabriel was sent from God to a city in Galilee, called Nazareth, [27] to a virgin engaged to a man whose name was Joseph, of the descendants of David; and the virgin's name was Mary. [28] And coming in, he said to her, "Hail, favored one! The Lord *is* with you." [29] But she was greatly troubled at *this* statement, and kept pondering what kind of salutation this might be. [30] And the angel said to her, "Do not be afraid, Mary; for you

---

[16] Ellison Research, "Study Shows Only 16% of Protestant Ministers Are Very Satisfied with Their Personal Prayer Lives," as reported by Anne Jackson, *Mad Church Disease* (Grand Rapids: Zondervan, 2009), 52.

have found favor with God. [31] "And behold, you will conceive in your womb, and bear a son, and you shall name Him Jesus. [32] "He will be great, and will be called the Son of the Most High; and the Lord God will give Him the throne of His father David; [33] and He will reign over the house of Jacob forever; and His kingdom will have no end." [34] And Mary said to the angel, "How can this be, since I am a virgin?" [35] And the angel answered and said to her, "The Holy Spirit will come upon you, and the power of the Most High will overshadow you; and for that reason the holy offspring shall be called the Son of God. [36] "And behold, even your relative Elizabeth has also conceived a son in her old age; and she who was called barren is now in her sixth month. [37] "For nothing will be impossible with God." [38] And Mary said, "Behold, the bond slave of the Lord; be it done to me according to your word." And the angel departed from her.[17]

This passage is pregnant with meaning. It opens by introducing us to Mary, who was engaged at the time to Joseph. Nazareth was a small town in the north central part of Israel, situated on the side of a five-hundred-foot hill rising from the plains below in Galilee.[18] Mary's age is not given, but it was not uncommon for a woman to be engaged at the age of thirteen or fourteen years old at that time. Joseph would have been older, perhaps in his late twenties, having established a household and income sufficient to be married and raise children. I am struck by the commonness of all this. The city where Mary and Joseph lived was not known for much of anything, as was echoed in the proverb "can any good thing come out of Nazareth?" (John 1:46). By the offering of two young turtledoves or pigeons, which Mary and Joseph presented at the dedication of Jesus after his birth, we can infer that the family did not have much wealth (Luke 2:23,24).[19] Mary and Joseph were both descendents of David, but other than

---

[17] Here I quote from: *The New American Standard Bible* (La Habra, CA, 1977), rather than from the 1995 translation, because the 1977 translation has a slightly more poetic feel to the verse, especially with Mary's response "Be it done to me according to your word."

[18] For an excellent description of the geography of this area and the town itself in biblical times, see Alfred Edersheim, *The Life and Times of Jesus the Messiah* (Peabody: Hendrickson, 2004), 105.

[19] Ibid., 105. When a child was born, the parents followed the law in Lev. 12:1-8, which gives provision for purification after childbirth. If the child was a male, there was a forty-day waiting period and if a female, eighty days. At the end of that time, the parents were to appear at the temple with their purification offering. If they had means, that offering could be a one-year-old lamb for the burnt offering and a young turtledove or pigeon for the sin offering (12:6). If the couple did not have the financial means to afford a lamb, then two turtledoves or pigeons could be offered—one for the burnt offering and one for the sin offering (12:8). This was the case for Joseph and Mary (Luke 2:24).

that, they had no particular pedigree.[20] And yet, with God, the very ordinary becomes extraordinary.

God was speaking to us loudly through these ordinary circumstances. God loves to give birth to the miraculous through the ordinary. For the miracle of the incarnation, He chose a small place called Israel in a small, no-name town called Nazareth; an unknown young woman; and an unknown carpenter to be her husband. When glitter and glamour are kept out of circumstances, God gets all the glory. Mary was a willing vessel. What stands out about her is not her circumstance, education, wealth, or status in life but how ordinary her life was—and how her heart was already prepared at the time of the angel's visitation.

When the angel greeted Mary, she was surprised that he would call her "favored"—literally "one upon whom grace is bestowed freely" (Luke 1:28).[21] She was unaware at that moment, but she was about to become pregnant with the Son of God. In saying, "be it done to me according to your word," she became a living example of an incarnational pattern that still reverberates through the heart and soul of any human being who will open his or her heart to God. Could it also be that Mary was laying down a pattern for intimacy meant to be embraced by those of us preaching the word today?

In a moment of intimacy, the Son of God was conceived in the womb of a willing young woman in an insignificant town in a small occupied nation. The angel told Mary ". . . The Holy Spirit will come upon you; and the power of the Most High will overshadow you; and for that reason the holy Child shall be called the Son of God" (Luke 1:35). Here we see the mingling of divinity and humanity. The Holy Spirit contributed the divine and Mary, because of her willingness, contributed what was human. The result was God Himself clothed in human flesh—the God-man, Jesus Christ. The divine had no beginning: He was the Word who took upon Himself flesh like the tabernacle of old so that God could once again dwell with humanity, not in a tent as in Old Testament times, but in human flesh (John 1:14).[22] God's Spirit overshadowed a human being and conceived something divine in her womb, the Word now clothed with flesh. God

---

[20] Ibid. Being a descendant of David on both Joseph's (step father) and Mary's (mother) side technically qualified Jesus to be the "Son of David," making him therefore eligible to the throne of Israel.

[21] The greeting used by Gabriel to Mary was "χαῖρε, κεχαριτωμένη"(kaire kechairitomene)—"rejoice, one upon whom grace is bestowed freely."

[22] This is a very important point and must once again be repeated for emphasis. In John 1:14, John deliberately uses the Greek word "ἐσκήνωσεν" (eskenosiv), which can be translated "dwelt," but the Greek root is from the word for "tent." It is much more accurate to translate this rich construction as the Word became flesh and "tented" or "tabernacled" among us. It is a reference back to the Old Testament tabernacle where God dwelt with the Israelites in a portable tent, built to His specifications, called the tabernacle. Jesus was doing the same thing through the incarnation, but in His case, the tent was human flesh.

was demonstrating an incarnational pattern that anyone could experience if willing to say, "be it done to me according to your word."

I am convinced that this incarnational pattern, among other things, is a meant to be a wonderful word picture or metaphor for the preacher's intimacy with God and resulting conception, as the preacher becomes "pregnant" with His word. The incarnation perfectly pictures how God wants to be known and how He wants to make truth known. He does not want to make truth known exclusively in written form but also through lives so that truth can be seen, heard, handled, and touched. God places value on the experience of Himself in and through the lives of people. Let's look at this passage from 1 John again:

> What was from the beginning, what we have *heard*, what we have *seen* with our eyes, what we have *looked at* and *touched* with our hands, concerning the Word of Life-- [2] and the life was *manifested,* and *we have seen* and testify and proclaim to you the eternal life, which was with the Father and was *manifested* to us-- [3] what *we have seen* and *heard* we proclaim to you also, so that you too may have fellowship with us; and indeed our fellowship is with the Father, and with His Son Jesus Christ (1 John 1:1-3; emphasis added).

God is willing to visit all who have open hearts and to impart "grace bestowed freely," overshadowing them with the Holy Spirit's presence in order to give birth to something new and transformational in their lives. The incarnational pattern gives us a perfect way to picture how sermons can be birthed in any preacher's heart if we are willing to be intimate with the Holy Spirit and allow Him to overshadow us. We must make ourselves available to "the kisses of His mouth" and say like Mary, "be it done to me according to your word."

"I Have Come into My Garden"

Perhaps the most beautiful passage in the Song of Solomon records the joy of the bride and groom at the consummation of their marriage:

> [12] "A garden locked is my sister, *my* bride, A rock garden locked, a spring sealed up. [13] "Your shoots are an orchard of pomegranates With choice fruits, henna with nard plants, [14] Nard and saffron, calamus and cinnamon, With all the trees of frankincense, Myrrh and aloes, along with all the finest spices. [15] "*You are* a garden spring, A well of fresh water, And streams *flowing* from Lebanon." [16] "Awake, O north *wind*, And come, *wind of* the south; Make my garden breathe out *fragrance*, Let its spices be wafted abroad. May my beloved come into his garden And eat its choice fruits!" [5:1] "I have come into my garden, my sister, *my* bride; I have gathered my myrrh along with my balsam. I have eaten my honeycomb and my honey; I have drunk my wine and my milk. Eat, friends; Drink and imbibe deeply, O lovers" (Song of Sol. 4:12-5:1).

This passage is intensely sexual and describes the heights of sexual desire the groom has for his new bride and that desire's fulfillment. The garden is often used in Oriental culture as a symbol of sexuality. The garden is locked—the bride is a virgin, and no one has ever entered her garden before and eaten of its fruit. The bride invites the groom to enter her garden, a place of intimacy where only two lovers can go. God says to them, "Eat, friends; Drink and imbibe deeply, O lovers."

When I said at the beginning of this chapter that the Song of Solomon has given scholars fits because it reads more like a romance novel than Scripture, this was certainly one of the passages I was talking about. The very frank description of sexual love between a groom and his bride on the wedding night forces us to come to grips with the very heart and nature of God. He simply loves relationship and intimacy. Sexuality was His idea. He created sexual love to be the highest and most wonderful thing that a man and woman could experience on this side of heaven. In it, the two become one in the covenant of marriage, and a wonderful word picture is given to us for the kind of relationship God desires to have with His people.

The metaphor of sexual fusion and passionate love as two people become one constitutes one of the greatest descriptions of how God feels about His church and His people. Paul uses this same romantic imagery in Eph. 5:22-32 to describe the relationship that Christ has with the church—as a groom to his bride. In Matt. 25:1-13, Jesus describes Himself as the bridegroom coming for His bride and longing for that consummation. In the last chapter of the last book of the New Testament, we read, ". . . the Spirit and the bride say 'come'" (Rev. 22:17). We have biblical and historical precedent for seeing sexual love as a living word picture for the way God feels about His people and His church. Sexual love helps us understand how intensely God loves us, and it gives us a picture of the intensity and passion that should encompass our intimate relationship with Him.

When the imagery used to express God's love for us is combined with the beautiful imagery of the incarnation of Jesus Christ, a new way of looking at our lives emerges. An incarnational life is one lived in intimate relationship with God—one in which, because of grace freely bestowed on us, God's Spirit overshadows our lives and gives birth to His destiny and will each day. Incarnational witness does not involve only spoken words but a life lived in intimacy with God, allowing us to give birth to truth that others may hear from our mouths, see in our actions, and touch as it impacts their lives too. An incarnational relationship is one in which my heart is constantly saying, "be it done to me according to your word." The garden of my heart is always open for the King to enter.

An incarnational sermon is a result of intimate contact with the Holy Spirit and the conception in the womb of my heart of a word to be delivered to God's people once it has grown in me to full term. It doesn't happen to just the rich, the well known, or the best educated—it also happens to ordinary preachers from ordinary towns in ordinary countries and those who only have a turtledove or a few pigeons to spare.

Let Me Hear Your Voice

Hearing the voice of the one you love is one of the greatest joys of any relationship. When you love someone, communication literally determines what you possess together.[23] People will go to great lengths just to hear a few words from the one they love, because words are the way human beings connect and share what is in the depth of our hearts. In Song of Solomon, the bride longs to hear the voice of her groom: "O my dove, in the clefts of the rock, In the secret place of the steep pathway, Let me see your form, Let me hear your voice; For your voice is sweet, And your form is lovely" (Song of Sol. 2:14).

We are made in God's image, and God loves to communicate. He has communicated by His written word in the Scriptures. He has communicated through the life of His Son (Heb. 1:1,2). He also desires to communicate daily as we walk in fellowship with Him. The Scriptures are the foundation of His communication to us; His life is our model; and His living voice is our compass. His written Word, His life, and His living voice comprise the key ways we experience intimacy with God, but it is the nature of His words that make them transformative.

The Scriptures are clear that God's words carry with them life. Heb. 4:12 describes the Word of God as "living and active."[24] His Word, whether written, spoken, or lived, cannot help but carry life with it, because that is who He is (John 14:7). Because God is life, when people touched Jesus, they were healed. Because God's words carry life, people like the Samaritan woman and Zaccheus

---

[23] The word *communication* itself comes from the Latin word *communicare*, which can be translated "possessing together." Shared communication literally determines what we possess together in relationship with someone else. Sounds and words are unique—they arise in the heart and soul of someone and are taken inside the heart and soul of the hearer. As such, they are extraordinarily intimate when spoken, because what was inside me is now inside you when you hear me. The other senses do not function as hearing does—what we see, taste, touch, and smell are external-to-internal in transmission and our experience. The spoken word is internal-to-internal. That is why the proximity of the spoken word has such power to create intimacy between people or from the pulpit.

[24] Scholars have debated for centuries as to whether the "word" in Heb. 4:12—"λόγος τοῦ θεοῦ" (*logos tou theu*)—refers to the written Word of God in the Scriptures, the person of the Word ("λόγος") Himself, or in general to any word that God speaks. I believe these arguments to be irrelevant because just as God is truth, God is Life itself (John 14:7). When God speaks in the form of His written Word, His Son's life, or words communicated to us in intimacy, they are full of life because that is who He is. For an excellent summary of the debate over what is meant in this verse, see Adam Clarke, *Clarke's Commentary* (Nashville, Abingdon, n.d.), vol. 5, New Testament (Hebrews), 711-13.

could hear Jesus' words and be transformed in a moment. No altar call—simply His words of life (John 4:5-29; Luke 19:1-10).

Because of the life God's words contain, they are literally pregnant with transformation when heard by receptive and prepared hearers. The Scriptures use the symbol of the seed as a word picture for understanding the nature of God's Word. The Word of God is alive and can produce automatic and trans-formative growth in a person's heart when it is received, as noted in Mark's gospel (Mark 4:26-29).[25] One of the Greek words for "seed" is *sperma* from which we get our English word sperm.[26] Do you see how the Scriptures are rich in layers of meaning when it comes to the metaphor of intimacy? As the original language helps us understand, when the Word of God, the seed, encounters the human heart, a spiritual conception takes place in the womb of the heart. Once it impregnates us, the living Word possesses the proper "DNA" to replicate itself as a living and vital agent in our hearts.[27]

What a perfect way to understand sermons and sermon preparation! As we are seeing, the preacher must "get pregnant" with a word from God and allow that word to grow in the womb of his or her heart. The words are alive and will be "delivered" later in order to impregnate others with their life and vitality. As we are learning, this process of conception, growth, maturity, and delivery de-scribes the different phases of incarnational teaching and preaching, and it all begins with God's word—His "seed."

The idea of incarnation through conception is also used in other passages of the Scriptures, sometimes in a negative sense. In Psalm 7, we see the description of a wicked man whom God will judge if he does not change his ways. That wicked man is said to "travail with wickedness" and "conceive" mischief in his heart (Ps. 7:14).[28] Likewise, Job says of the godless, "They conceive mischief

---

[25] This parable chronicles the automatic growth of the seed as a word picture to describe the Word of God. The word used in Mark 4:28 to say that the seed grows "by itself" in the Greek is "αὐτόματος" (*automatos*), from which we get the word "automatic." Living things grow all by themselves because that is a property of life.

[26] The Greek word used in the Mark 4:24-29 passage is actually "σπόρος" (*sporos*), from which comes the English word "spore." In other places the word for seed is "σπέρμα" (*sperma*).

[27] DNA (deoxyribonucleic acid) is the basic genetic building block of living organisms. It is the chemical that is the organic code or recipe built into each cell of the body as the master control system for growth and development. Each person's DNA is unique and contains a unique set of encoded instructions to generate the form, shape, and characteris-tics of the human body automatically according to these instructions. The Word of God seems to function the same way.

[28] Here the Hebrew text uses the word root "הָרָה" (*harah*) to describe the evil that is "con-ceived" in the heart of a wicked man. The word can be translated "conceived, become pregnant, or be with child." When we are intimate with sin and decide to know it perso-nally, something is conceived in our heart and we ultimately become pregnant with that sin until it is given birth through our actions.

and bring forth iniquity. . ." (Job 15:34,35). James also makes it clear that sin is something that is conceived in our heart and that then gives birth to its "babies" through our actions if we are willing to bring it to birth:[29]

> [13] Let no one say when he is tempted, "I am being tempted by God"; for God cannot be tempted by evil, and He Himself does not tempt anyone. [14] But each one is tempted when he is carried away and enticed by his own lust. [15] Then when lust has conceived, it gives birth to sin; and when sin is accomplished, it brings forth death. [16] Do not be deceived, my beloved brethren (James 1:13-16).

This passage gives us a peek at the workings of sin in the human soul when we choose to be intimate with it. James reminds us that the ultimate action of sin starts in the heart when we choose intimacy with that sin. He tells us not to blame the baby on God—God does not tempt. Rather, sin is the illegitimate bastard child of adulterous intimacy with something else—in this case, lust. When we are intimate with our own lust, something is conceived in the womb of our hearts. We can take the thoughts captive to the obedience of Christ with His Word, or we can let them grow in the womb of our hearts ever larger until we give birth to sin (2 Cor. 10:3-5). Why are we then surprised when we "deliver the baby" and act out what we have allowed to grow in our hearts? Any action is committed twice—once in the heart and once in the real world.

We see the "birth" of sin at the fall of Adam and Eve. The tree itself was not the problem; the tree of the knowledge of good and evil didn't have little "good and evil" fruits growing on it. The problem for Adam and Eve was coming to know evil intimately. Humanity was never designed for intimacy with sin. Adam and Eve heard God's command not to touch the fruit, but in their minds, they played with the thought of touching the fruit. Temptation came, and they acted on their thoughts. The results of intimacy (knowing) with evil were corruption and, ultimately, death. The death birthed from the wombs of their hearts was the seed of destruction for us all. We were designed by God with the capacity to know only good intimately.[30] Adam and Eve gave birth to the fruit of

---

[29] In this verse, the Greek root for the word translated "conceive" is "συλλαμβάνω" (*sullambano*), which can be translated "to take part with, become pregnant, or conceive." Here the "spirit" is not the Holy Spirit but lust.

[30] One can see the James 1:13-16 pattern of conception unfold in the lives of Adam and Eve. They were told they could have fruit from any tree but one particular tree. This shows the hopelessness of human beings trying to be saved through the law—they could not even keep one commandment, let alone ten. The tree became the tree of the knowledge of good and evil when they decided to taste the forbidden fruit—they came for the first time to know evil intimately through experience as they disobeyed God. This disobedience started with lust in the mind—God said not to eat it (Gen. 2:16,17), but Eve said that God told them not to "eat or touch it" (Gen. 3:2,3). It is clear that she had been

knowing evil, and we all died with them. They gave sin flesh and "became death," and we in them.

If sin can work in an incarnational way, should we be surprised that God's truth works in this way? When we are intimate with God, His Spirit conceives His truth in the wombs of our hearts, and something living is born.[31] The Holy Spirit is the person of God who specializes in the conception and birth of His word. The Spirit did so at creation as He hovered over the face of the deep, waiting for God's word (Gen. 1:2). He does so now in the hearts of willing vessels who take the time to be intimate with Him. God conceives His word in our hearts in two primary ways—through His written Word and through His "spoken" word to us in the midst of life. Let's first examine the conception process by way of His written Word.

The Scriptures and Conception

The words on the Bible's pages are indescribably rich, but the illumination of those words by the Holy Spirit is the primary pathway for the conception of the word in the preacher's heart. The illumination of God's Word is one of the primary ministries of the Holy Spirit. Jesus said when He left the disciples, ". . . the Helper, the Holy Spirit, whom the Father will send in my name, He will teach you all things, and bring to your remembrance all that I said to you."(John 14:26).[32] This passage highlights the Holy Spirit's intimate role in the disclosure of truth to believers.

Note that the Holy Spirit's disclosure is predicated on what follows in John 15—abiding in Him. The pathway to disclosure is abiding in intimate relationship. When friends come to know one another over time, they start to talk alike, act alike, and think alike. People who have been married for a while often think the same thing at the same time and even complete one another's sentences. Intimate knowing produces transformation as two become one. Preachers are transformed in the same way, as we let the Holy Spirit draw us to Himself and as we begin to "run with Him" (Song of Sol. 1:2). As we run with God in inti-

---

thinking about touching it, because God only said not to eat it. The lust to touch and eat, when conceived in the heart, grew to fruition and sin was born.

[31] Another rich word picture for understanding this occurs in Gen. 1:2: "The earth was formless and void, and darkness was over the surface of the deep, and the Spirit of God was moving over the surface of the waters." In the Hebrew text, the phrase "מְרַחֶפֶת" (m'raheft), which is translated "was moving," does not do the Hebrew justice. The words convey the action of a mother hen who has laid eggs and is sitting on them to hatch them—this is called brooding. The words are better translated "brooding" because the Holy Spirit was waiting to give birth (hatch) to God's word.

[32] In this role, the Holy Spirit is called "the Helper," which in the Greek is "παράκλητος" (parakletos), translated "one called alongside (to help)." Even the name suggests intimacy and friendship, which is the context for the disclosure of truth to the believer.

mate relationship, we start to see truth, think true thoughts, and act according to the truth, because He is the "Spirit of Truth" (John 16:13).

Conception occurs when the Holy Spirit takes God's written Word and uses it to illuminate specific truth in the preacher's heart. The New Testament text itself is very clear about the nature of the written Word of God and claims "inspiration" for itself: "All Scripture is inspired by God and profitable for teaching, for reproof, for correction, for training in righteousness; that the man of God may be adequate, equipped for every good work" (2 Tim. 3:16,17). The Greek word used in this passage, *theopneustos*, is translated "inspired" but might be better translated as "God-breathed."[33] The "spiration" processes have to do with breath. We can "respire," as with the term *respiration*, when we breathe. We can "expire" when we die and breath leaves our body. We can also "inspire" someone when we breathe the breath of encouragement and life into his or her heart with our words. God breathed on the dry bones in the valley, and they became alive. God "breathed the breath of life" into Adam, and he became a living soul (Gen. 2:7).[34] The second Adam breathed on His disciples after His resurrection, telling them to "receive the Holy Spirit" (John 20:22). God breathed His breath of life into the Scriptures, setting them apart as unique words. Systematic theologians call this the doctrine of inspiration.

Peter described the inspiration process as, not an act of human will, but God's movement in people to write His words down (2 Pet. 1:20,21): "But know this first of all, that no prophecy of Scripture is *a matter* of one's own interpretation, for no prophecy was ever made by an act of human will, but men moved by the Holy Spirit spoke from God."[35] Wayne Grudem notes the term *inspired* used to describe the Scriptures has lost its meaning because the popular use of the word has weakened it. We use inspire to describe what we do when we give encouragement to other people. [36] Still, inspiration sets the Scriptures apart as something unique, unlike any other kind of communication, and as the basis for authoritative belief and proclamation.[37] The preacher can literally inhale fresh life from the Scriptures because of the life God has breathed into them.

---

[33] The Greek word "θεόπνευστος" (*theopneustos*) is translated "inspired."

[34] Here the Hebrew word "נִשְׁמָה" (*neshamah*) is used and is translated "breath of life" but is also the word for soul. It seems that God breathed His animating life force into the dust of man's body, and he became a living soul as a result.

[35] This verse uses the word "φέρω" (*phero*) to describe the process of the Holy Spirit's inspiration of the written Word (Scripture) as God moved the authors. The word translates "to carry or to bear" and illustrates a cooperative effort as the Spirit moved men to write under His guidance and as He carried them along with His guidance.

[36] Wayne Grudem, *Systematic Theology* (Grand Rapids: Zondervan, 2000), 75.

[37] Theologians use the terms *general revelation* and *special revelation* to describe the special place that the Scriptures as our guide for understanding truth. General revelation describes how God is revealed in creation and life as He has left His fingerprints on what has been created. We see signs of God in the way He created things (Rom. 1:20) because

Attitude is all important when approaching the Scriptures in sermon preparation. Proper respect for the Scriptures and their place in the preaching process is vital to presenting a transformative word from the pulpit. Respect does not mean worship of the Scriptures. The cry of the Reformation was *sola scriptura* (by Scripture alone) as the church emerged from centuries of darkness and corruption. The Reformers believed the Scriptures alone were the infallible and inerrant authority for the Christian faith; by the Scriptures alone one discerned truth. The generations that followed the Reformers fell in love with the written Word. Then they fell deeply in love with the written Word. As noted earlier, it is possible to fall too deeply in love with words on the page and forget the person to which those words point.

As M. Rex Miller notes, written words can disconnect the reader from the person speaking—words are written in a linear fashion and in themselves are without life.[38] We come back to the effects of the print culture—the reader disconnects the message from the messenger. Disconnection happens because reading and interpreting words demand that the reader break the text up into tiny parts in order to understand it. The eye tells the mind to discern (mentally separate) and analyze (break up the whole into parts). This process creates a very linear and rational relationship with truth and tends to leave what is mystical behind in the dust. The process creates a very abstract and structured culture and a world that has no room for the supernatural.[39]

In the time following the Reformation, a print mindset developed that conditioned theologians and the general culture to embrace what was rational, logical, and orderly as they built their concept of reality. What began as the restoration of the authority of the Scriptures evolved for many into a systematic theology built of abstracted, linear, and orderly "God boxes" that purported to explain Him. Reason, analysis, systematic thinking, and rational explanation were reintroduced to the pursuit of truth during the Reformation and became the rule of the day, gradually crowding out the role of experiencing God and communion with Him as an accepted source for understanding truth. M. Rex Miller notes that the preacher's emphasis on experiencing the Word of God through the sacraments (and preaching) was replaced by retelling the story of the gospel in preaching.[40] The tidiness, rationality, and orderliness of the times following the Reformation left little room for preaching a messy, transformative word that might disrupt the new sense of reality. In the end, within several generations, the

---

an artist leaves something of himself in everything he creates. Special revelation describes the way God moved men to record the Scriptures. The way God moved on men through the Holy Spirit to record the Scriptures sets them apart a unique and invaluable guide in our quest to know truth. For an excellent discussion on special and general revelation, see J. Rodman Williams, *Renewal Theology*, 1: 32-45.

[38] M. Rex Miller, 36.

[39] Ibid., 36, 44.

[40] Ibid., 45.

world saw a gradual rejection of the idea of divine inspiration of Scripture and with it, a rejection of Scripture as an overarching source of authority in preaching.

Today we suffer from the effects of this rejection. Certainly, systematic theology and analytical approaches to the Word have value in preaching, as long as they are used to unlock the breath of God in the Scriptures. But if we surrender the idea of inspiration, then where does the breath of God that we and our listeners so badly need come from? What breathes transformative life into our lives, our sermons, and our daily walk? If we abandon the belief that the Scriptures are inspired, then from what does preaching draw its power to transform? Certainly not from the elegance of our own words or the clever stories we tell. As David Larsen notes, we face a crisis of authoritative preaching today with little power to transform that is directly related to the issue of inspiration:

> Carl F. H. Henry rightly observes, "Nowhere does the crisis of modern theology find a more critical center than in the controversy over the reality and nature of divine disclosure." Some go so far as to question whether there is objective truth and whether truth, if it exists, can be known. So strong is the aversion to the objectivity of revealed truth in some circles that there is virtually a total withdrawal to non-rational categories. The historic faith of the church is clear in these matters, holding the Bible is the only infallible guide to faith doctrine, and practice. Emil Brunner noted that the fate of the Bible is the fate of Christianity. The principle of the Reformation was *Sola Scriptura*. The only authority is the Bible. Ramm is correct in asserting, "The Holy Spirit speaking in the Scriptures, which are the product of the Spirit's revelatory and inspiring action, is the principle of authority for the Christian Church.[41]

Theology and our faith literally spin out of control unless the Scriptures and a high view of inspiration are at their center. Sermons lose their way without the written Word and its authority to guide them. They also lose their ability to transform without that center, because all that is left are the feeble fallen thoughts of human beings to hold the message together, rather than the breath of God's life.

As Larsen notes, trying to build an authoritative base for the proclamation of the Word based on human thought, natural data, the physical universe, human consciousness, or even religious experience leaves us without authority and quickly becomes a hopeless endeavor that only a Ph.D. could sort out.[42] Intimacy with God thrives when His inspired Word breathes out new life into our hearts—that is when conception of a transformational word can take place.

---

[41] Carl F. H. Henry, *God, Revelation and Authority* (Waco: Word, 1976), 1:7, and Bernard L. Ramm, *The Pattern of Religious Authority* (Grand Rapids: Eerdmans, 1957), 10, quoted in Larsen, 23. Larsen quotes from both sources in this passage.
[42] Ibid., 24.

The New Testament church continued in God's Word daily (Acts 6:4). The word of God was increasing in their midst (12:24) and spread widely, growing in power (19:20). People of influence became mighty in the Scriptures (18:24). Might we also once again embrace the Scriptures as a source of devotion and life so that we also can have the impact of the New Testament church?

It is the job of the preacher to wrestle with each text of Scripture until it gives up its life-changing, transformative power. This is what some German theologians used to call the *winkel* of the passage. They considered it their job to wrestle with a passage until they saw the angle or slant (*winkel*) in that passage, and the life-changing power in it was disclosed.[43] This was the kind of wrestling I was engaged in during my all-night marathon described earlier in the book, and it is the hardest part of preaching a transformative sermon:

> . . . I hear the voices of preachers of every age saying, "You lie. You know it never gets any easier." I hear the complaints of those who have found the spoken word to be an intolerably heavy burden. I hear old Martin Luther, fed up with Wittenburg and Wittenbergers, complain, "I would rather carry stones than preach one sermon." I hear poor John Bunyan confessing that he sometimes feels like shouting obscenities at his congregation! I hear young Richard Niebuhr worrying to his diary that if he doesn't get his act together the weekly sermon will become a "terrible chore." I hear a tired Martin Luther King Jr. describe the "calling to speak" as the "vocation of agony."[44]

Wrestling invites the Holy Spirit's illumination of the passage and allows Him to perform His role as Helper and teacher, as Jesus said He would be. Let's invite mystery back to the table. Let's learn to dine with the Holy Spirit and get comfortable with His role in disclosing truth directly to our hearts, based on the written Word (Rev. 3:20). What stood out about Jesus was His ability to preach the word of God as "thus saith the Lord," as one with authority, because He knew what the written word of God said, who He Himself was, and what the Holy Spirit was saying to Him at any given moment (Matt. 7:29). As Larsen notes, truth does not often give us a polite tap on the shoulder and does not often say "excuse me" when it invades our soul.[45]

---

[43] Richard Lischer, *The End of Words* (Grand Rapids: Eerdmans, 2005), 63. In this part of the book, Lischer talks about a terminally ill friend who read the Bible differently than he did—she "clung to it and seemed to claim it as her personal prize" (56). Our perspective and attitude as we come to the Scriptures is all important to the conception of the word in our hearts.

[44] Ibid., 19-20.

[45] Larsen, 26.

Illumination and Conception

Preaching is a partnership between God and human beings that, as we are seeing, mirrors incarnation. I have heard many preachers pray something to this effect: "Lord, let this be all of You and none of me. Let these be Your words and not mine." What a well-meaning humble prayer—but it is not a request that God will fulfill.

As in the incarnation, God wants to give flesh to His word through intimacy with the preacher. Conception takes place as the preacher is intimate with the Holy Spirit and the Spirit reveals new truth. God's Spirit shines new light on God's written Word—He "illuminates" truth for the preacher to personally see, experience, and understand. The Holy Spirit's role in the illumination of truth is central to the conception of the word in the preacher's heart and the ultimate wellspring of transformative power in the preacher's life and sermons.

God's written Word is the starting place, but it only releases its transformative life as the Holy Spirit "broods over the face of the deep" and gives life to those words by incubating them like a mother hen until they hatch in our hearts (Gen. 1:2).[46] As the word *illumination* implies, it occurs when the Holy Spirit shines the "light" of understanding upon the Word of God. At the Last Supper, when it was just about time for Him to depart, Jesus uttered these words:

> [12] "I have many more things to say to you, but you cannot bear *them* now. [13] "But when He, the Spirit of truth, comes, He will guide you into all the truth; for He will not speak on His own initiative, but whatever He hears, He will speak; and He will disclose to you what is to come. [14] "He will glorify Me; for He will take of Mine, and will disclose *it* to you. [15] "All things that the Father has are Mine; therefore I said, that He takes of Mine and will disclose *it* to you (John 16:12-15).

Greg Heisler defines the illumination process as God's giving us new eyes to contemplate heavenly things that cannot be understood by pure reason or empirically proven.[47] Heisler's definition of illumination and the words of John 16:12-15 underscore the importance of the present-day work of the Holy Spirit in illumination. Jesus plainly said that He had much more to say to the disciples but no time left to say it. He then taught the disciples about the role of the Holy Spirit, whom He would send to them. The Holy Spirit's role would be one of guidance by illumination of the truth, because He is the Spirit of Truth. His role was de-

---

[46] As mentioned earlier, the word "hover" in Gen. 1:2 "מְרַחֶפֶת" (*m'rachefet*), could easily be translated "brooding," the way a mother hen sits on eggs until they are hatched. This is what the Holy Spirit did at creation as He waited over the "face of the deep" until God spoke His word, and the Spirit then gave birth to creation.

[47] Heisler, 38-39.

fined as one of disclosure or annunciation—not coincidently, the precise words that describe authoritative and transformational preaching and teaching.[48]

What is the difference between inspiration and illumination? Inspiration occurred when God "breathed" His life into the words written by men "moved by the Spirit" in Old and New Testament times. This "special revelation" resulted in a set of Scriptures that are inspired (2 Tim. 3:16) and trustworthy (2 Pet. 1:20,21) and that can be used for doctrine, training, reproof, and correction as a standard for what is true. The Scriptures stand, therefore, as a unique kind of God-breathed revelation. Rightly, it makes many nervous today when individuals, too, claim to have "revelation." The use of the term *revelation* is often (but not always) innocent—meaning, there is often no intent to place a personal revelation received by an individual on par with the special revelation seen in the process of generating the Scriptures. Still, when we hear the term revelation used by an individual, red flags may go up, for we tend to associate revelation with Scripture, and, thus, distrust the speaker. For our purposes in this book, to overcome any confusion, we are using the word illumination in place of revelation when referencing the process of understanding generated by the Holy Spirit in the life of the preacher.

Inspiration occurred when God breathed revelation into the words of the Scriptures; that inspiration was fixed and complete at a point in time.[49] Illumination is an ongoing work of the Holy Spirit and should be an ongoing pattern in the life of any believer. Because illumination is ongoing and continuous, it is subject to fallibility. Any illumination we might receive needs to be subject to the judgment of the Scriptures, which are revealed, authoritative, and complete. As Heisler points out, inspiration was the "inscripturation process" whereby God insured that the original texts of the Scriptures would be completely true, without error, and expressed faithfully within the culture of that day. "Illumination is when the Holy Spirit so impresses, convinces, and convicts the believer as to the truthfulness and significance of the author's intended meaning in the text that a change in action, attitude, or belief occurs, resulting in a more transformed, Spirit-filled life."[50]

The illumination process assumes that God wants to be known. God cannot be completely known through material things—He is "other" and veiled to human perception. All knowledge of truth is hidden to us and must be revealed. In the case of the Scriptures, that revelation was special, particular, progressive,

---

[48] In this text, the Greek word "ἀναγγέλλω" (*anangello*) was translated "disclose." The root suggested a better translation would be "announce."

[49] Thomas H. Troeger, *Ten Strategies for Preaching in a Multimedia Culture* (Nashville: Abingdon, 1996), 23.

[50] Robert Stein, *A Basic Guide to Interpreting the Bible* (Grand Rapids: Baker, 1994), 43, quoted in Heisler, 43-44. The part of the quote concerning illumination is Heisler quoting Stein.

saving, verbal, and personal.[51] In the case of illumination, the Holy Spirit continues to illuminate truth at the direction of the Father and the Son to open-hearted men and women today, because He is a living God. To be sure, this disclosure or illumination is a kind of revelation, as articulated in Paul's prayer in Eph. 1:17,18:[52]

> [17] that the God of our Lord Jesus Christ, the Father of glory, may give to you a spirit of wisdom and of revelation in the knowledge of Him. [18] *I pray that* the eyes of your heart may be enlightened, so that you may know what is the hope of His calling, what are the riches of the glory of His inheritance in the saints . . . .

In other words, illumination *is* revelation, but it is the work of the Holy Spirit's revelation in the heart of a believer today. The process of illumination is further defined in a passage found in 1 Cor. 2:4-14:

> [4] and my message and my preaching were not in persuasive words of wisdom, but in demonstration of the Spirit and of power, [5] so that your faith would not rest on the wisdom of men, but on the power of God. [6] Yet we do speak wisdom among those who are mature; a wisdom, however, not of this age nor of the rulers of this age, who are passing away; [7] but we speak God's wisdom in a mystery, the hidden *wisdom* which God predestined before the ages to our glory; [8] *the wisdom* which none of the rulers of this age has understood; for if they had understood it they would not have crucified the Lord of glory; [9] but just as it is written, "things which eye has not seen and ear has not heard, and which have not entered the heart of man, all that God has prepared for those who love Him." [10] For to us God revealed *them* through the Spirit; for the Spirit searches all things, even the depths of God. [11] For who among men knows the *thoughts* of a man except the spirit of the man which is in him? Even so the *thoughts* of God no one knows except the Spirit of God. [12] Now we have received, not the spirit of the world, but the Spirit who is from God, so that we may know the things freely given to us by God, [13] which things we also speak, not in words taught by human wisdom, but in those taught by the Spirit, combining spiritual *thoughts* with spiritual *words*. [14] But a natural man does not accept the things of the Spirit of God, for they are foolishness to him; and he cannot understand them, because they are spiritually appraised.

---

[51] Williams, 1:30-32. In this treatment of the concept of revelation and the knowledge of God, Williams gives an excellent explanation and contrasts different kinds of revelation and how they work.

[52] In these verses, Paul uses the Greek word "ἀποκάλυψις" (*apokalupsis*), which is the proper word used in the Scriptures for revelation, meaning "uncovering or unveiling." He then prays for the eyes of their hearts to be "enlightened," ("φωτίζω" (*photizo*), which is translated "illuminated."

Paul assumed in this passage that his own preaching was not based on the power of his own literary or communicative skills but rather on the power of God. Paul's preaching was based on "Things which eye has not seen and ear has not heard, and which have not entered into the heart of man. . . ." He was not talking about revealed Scripture in this passage but truth revealed to the believer by the Holy Spirit in the form of illumination (vv. 4,12).

Paul describes the Holy Spirit's illumination of truth to the believer. God has things prepared for those who love Him, and He wants to disclose those things to His people (v. 9). The Holy Spirit knows the mind of God and is constantly searching its depths (v. 10). He knows the thoughts in the mind of God at any given time and takes these thoughts and illuminates them in the hearts of believers at the direction of the Father and Son (John 16:13-15). Through the process of illumination, the Holy Spirit also helps the preacher to combine "spiritual thoughts" with "spiritual words" as these thoughts are conceived in the womb of our hearts through illumination.

To be sure, the process of illumination is fragile, because human flesh is involved. But fragility does not justify taking a position that ignores or does away with the present work of the Holy Spirit in the life of the believer. Walking with God and hearing His voice has always been a risky business fraught with error and humanity, but then again, human fragility is what makes the stories in the Scriptures so interesting. When human flesh meets God, things can get messy. But the illumination process is critical to the conception of the word and a nonnegotiable part of transformational preaching.

Daily immersion in God's Word is critical for anyone preaching and teaching. The Word itself has the power to transform from the inside out. It changes our thinking, beliefs, and values over time, eventually manifesting results in our right actions and attitudes (Rom. 12:2). Our daily immersion in the Word is essential for personal renewal. The renewing of our minds is something too big to happen all at once—who could bear it? The transformational effects of a day-by-day relationship with God through His Word can be maximized if we approach the Word with an open heart by laying down our agenda and "letting the Word read us."

Approaching the Word this way is called an *inductive* approach. I do not come to the Scriptures simply to "get a sermon." I do not come to the Scriptures to prove a point or enforce what I believe. I come to the Scriptures to learn God's mind. Instead of a proof text for my ideas, the Scriptures become a place where I find God—His thoughts, His illumination, and an opportunity for Him to share with me what is on *His* mind. His Spirit becomes active. He begins to lead and guide me to key portions of the Scriptures and to tie them together. He begins to apply them to my life and to the lives of those I serve. Illumination becomes a living dance—a partnership between God and His child—that yields inner transformation in our own lives, a little here and a little there, day by day as He leads. Holy conception takes place in the womb of our hearts in such times of intimacy. But in order to facilitate that process, the heart of the preacher must be unencumbered so that barriers to conception of the word are minimized.

Catch the Little Foxes

Right in the middle of a beautiful love story, there is an interruption. It seems very out of place at first glance. The bride contemplates the sound of her lover's voice. It is sweet, and He sure looks good. One of the most beautiful tributes to love ever written comes two verses later—"My beloved is mine and I am his," restated more famously in Song of Sol. 6:3, where we read, "I am my beloved's and he is mine."[53] In between admiration and the bride's declaration, though, is that interruption. Here is the passage from Song of Sol. 2:14-16:

> [14] "O my dove, in the clefts of the rock, In the secret place of the steep pathway, Let me see your form, Let me hear your voice; For your voice is sweet, And your form is lovely." [15] "Catch the foxes for us, The little foxes that are ruining the vineyards, While our vineyards are in blossom." [16] "My beloved is mine, and I am his; He pastures *his flock* among the lilies.

Do you see it? Right in the middle of the bride's unfolding monologue of love and commitment, we encounter some little foxes. How did they get in there? This is the same question that needs to be asked by every preacher who is serious about the conception of the word in his or her heart. How did those foxes get in there?

We have already begun to understand the importance of our relationship with God and His intended outcome of our intimacy—the conception of the word in our hearts. We have briefly explored the place of the inspired written Word, the Scriptures, in that conception process and the Holy Spirit's illumination of the Word as the source of conception. But sometimes in our walk with God, conception fails and there is no life in the preacher's womb—no sermon anywhere in sight. When that happens, what is wrong?

There is never a problem with the seed—the Word is living truth, and it never changes (Heb. 13:8). The Word is alive and powerful, waiting to do its God-appointed transformative work (Heb. 4:12). If there is a problem in the conception process, we can look to two possible hindering issues—the heart of the preacher or unprepared hearts among those who listen. Each soul is responsible for his or her own heart, so here we will concentrate on the preacher's heart. I can do something about my own heart condition.

---

[53] One of the most famous love sayings in the Hebrew Scriptures is "אֲנִי לְדוֹדִי וְדוֹדִי לִי" (*ani l'dodi v'dodi li*). Because of its sweet and gentle directness, this phrase appears inscribed on many Hebrew wedding bands, including the one I wear on my finger right now.

Just like a woman's womb, the preacher's heart must be prepared to receive the conceived word, or the word will not take root and grow. The Scriptures make it abundantly clear that the condition of the heart is of the utmost importance in conception, for without a ready heart, the conceived word withers or even dies before it can take root, grow, and do its transformative work. The trick is to catch the little foxes before they spoil the vineyard and its precious blossoms—if the foxes can kill the vine while in blossom, then there will be no fruit.

In Prov. 4:23 we are told, "Watch over your heart with all diligence, For from it *flow* the springs of life." As is often the case, the English text does not yield the powerful meaning of the more emotional words of the Hebrew text. The words of Prov. 4:23 conjure up the image of a watchtower of guards guarding the heart like they would a secure prison. The reason? Because from the inner person flow "the goings out of lives."[54] Just as the human heart physically pumps blood to every cell in the body, so the inner person is the source of life for us, and for those to whom we preach. When anything interferes with the flow of life-giving blood to a part of our body, that area is six minutes away from death, gangrene, and possible amputation. Life works the same way in the human spirit. If something interferes with the life flow from our inner being, we begin to feel numbness. If the numbness continues, we start to feel nothing. This is the warning sign that life has been cut off like a limb first going numb, and then going to sleep.

Numbness is extremely serious for preachers. We are called to maintain a spiritual life that not only nourishes our own soul but brings life to others as well. When the "goings out of lives" is hindered or interrupted, it is a matter of life and death for those who depend on us for spiritual nourishment, the source of transformative life. Let's face it—many in the church "hire the preacher" to do their Bible reading for them. Most in the audience would never eat just one meal a week, but this is many people's approach to church and Bible study. The sermon is so very important, because it is, sadly, a meal offered to starving people who eat nothing else the rest of the week. Can you see why for the

---

[54] As with many of the Proverbs, the Hebrew text is pregnant with very forceful and deeply emotional words. The text in the Hebrew is "מִכָּל־מִשְׁמָר נְצֹר לִבֶּךָ כִּי־מִמֶּנּוּ תּוֹצְאוֹת חַיִּים". The word "מִשְׁמָר" (*mishmar*) is used, and its original meaning is a place of confinement, jail, or prison, used in later Hebrew to mean "guard" or "watch." The word "נְצֹר" (*natsar*) is the word for keeping watch like those in a tower of watchmen would guard that prison. Here the analogy is powerful—we are to watch over our inner being with the same diligence of a tower of watchman watching over a jail. Why? Because from the heart are the "תּוֹצְאוֹת חַיִּים" (*totseoth chayyim*)—the going forth of lives. Clarke (vol. 3, 713) observes that there is an obvious analogy between the natural heart with its blood vessels that reach the remote parts of the body with the life-giving blood they supply (Lev. 17:11, the life of the flesh is in the blood) and the human spirit. Life flows out from our spirit to every part of our being and, in the case of preachers, to others who will receive nourishment through the preached word.

preacher it is vital to watch over our own hearts like a tower of watchman would watch over a maximum security prison? The stakes are very high.

Ears to Hear and Eyes to See

When couples want to wait to have children, they often decide to use some form of contraception as a means of birth control. This is not anything new— birth control has been practiced in one form or another since the dawn of time with methods that are as varied as they are strange. Physical barriers have been used to block conception, preventing the seed from reaching its destination. Chemicals such as tree resins or herbal mixtures have acted as contraceptives and have even caused the abortion of the growing child after conception.

Similarly, a kind of spiritual birth control can be applied to the human heart. If barriers or poisons are introduced to the womb of our heart, they can have a contraceptive effect or even abort something already conceived. These spiritual contraceptives prevent, kill, injure, or immobilize the seed from doing its life-producing work. Or they render the heart unable to sustain what has been conceived.

Jesus' parable of the sower (Matt. 13:1-23) shows how delicate the process of conception and growth of the word in our hearts can be. In this parable, the sower sows the same seed on several types of ground. The seed—God's word— like all seeds contains the potential for fruit, and that fruit contains the potential for a forest of fruit trees. The potential of a seed is limitless. When I hold a simple acorn in my hands, I hold not just the potential for an oak tree but for a whole forest of oak trees, each with its own acorns. The word of God has the same limitless power if planted in a heart that is ready to receive it. But not all hearts are ready. Some receive the word but do not take the time to understand it, and the word is snatched from their soil, even before conception can take place (v.4). For the preacher, a major barrier to conception is the busyness of life, which can easily crowd out a solid devotional life.

Other seed lands on rocky ground. Conception takes place and the seed begins to grow, but when the sun comes out, the new seedling dies because the word had no developed root to sustain it in the heat. With pressures such as ministry conflicts and struggles with church boards, there is never a shortage of "heat" in the preacher's life to test the ablest of hearts. The question is what will we allow the heat to do to our hearts? The heat will be present, but will we allow God to use it to melt our hearts like wax, or will we allow the heat to harden our hearts like clay? The issue is our heart's response when the heat is present, and that response is our choice.

Then there are the worries of everyday life and ministry, worries that Paul himself admitted can be quite a burden (2 Cor. 11:27-29). It is so easy to let anxiety do its deadly work in our hearts, even when we are warned that worry is not worth our time and energy (Matt. 6:25-34; Phil. 4:6,7). It's just as easy to allow our success to choke our hearts with pride. If left unchecked, over time pride, worry, and other corrosive heart attitudes can choke the word that was conceived in our hearts. The temptation to nurse long-term anger and bitterness is so easy to succumb to in any ministry setting, because we are in relationship with so many people. But we cannot afford to allow ourselves that indulgence. If we do, the word in our hearts will be choked. [55]

This is serious business. In the parable, the same powerful and transformative word was scattered on each type of soil, but only twenty-five percent of the seed endured to produce some kind of fruit. Even then, the quantity of the fruit varied—some thirty-, sixty-, or a hundredfold. The condition of the heart and its constant fertility are of the utmost importance in the life of the preacher. Can you see why the heart must be guarded the way a watchtower full of guards watches a maximum security prison? Spiritual barriers can shut down the conception of the word in our hearts if allowed to remain. The issues of life that spring from the heart are so fragile, and so many are counting on us. To return to our metaphor from Song of Solomon, we must catch the little foxes before they spoil the vineyard.

Dullness of Heart

Jesus' whole point in telling the parable of the sower can be found in Matt. 13:13-15, where Jesus quotes the Scriptures from Isa. 6:9,10:

[13] "Therefore I speak to them in parables; because while seeing they do not see, and while hearing they do not hear, nor do they understand. [14] "In their case the prophecy of Isaiah is being fulfilled, which says, 'YOU WILL KEEP ON HEARING, BUT WILL NOT UNDERSTAND; YOU WILL KEEP ON SEE-ING, BUT WILL NOT PERCEIVE; [15] FOR THE HEART OF THIS PEOPLE HAS BECOME DULL, WITH THEIR EARS THEY SCARCELY HEAR, AND THEY HAVE CLOSED THEIR EYES, OTHERWISE THEY WOULD

---

[55] In the Greek there are several words for anger that are recognizable because they have made their way into English. There is "ὀργίζω" (*orgizo*), from which the word "orgy" originates and refers to the abiding presence of anger. The word "χολάω" (*cholao*), from which the word "melancholy" originates, is also used. There is also "θυμός" (*thumos*), from which the English word "thermos" originates and which signifies a more sudden outburst of wrath. We cannot allow melancholy (an angry attitude of the heart) to remain over time or it acts as a spiritual contraceptive. We cannot afford abiding anger or to let anger remain "hot" over time because these kinds of intense anger likewise act as barriers. The Scriptures tell us plainly that we can be "angry and sin not" by placing boundaries around the anger and resolving it Eph. 4:26,27. Anger is God-given—it drives us emotionally to find a solution to something that could harm or destroy. The preacher must be disciplined to learn to feel the anger and then resolve it in a timely manner lest it dull or harden the heart and act as a kind of birth control that prevents the conception of the word.

SEE WITH THEIR EYES, HEAR WITH THEIR EARS, AND UNDER-
STAND WITH THEIR HEART AND RETURN, AND I WOULD HEAL
THEM.'

The Scriptures record God's ongoing frustration with people ". . . Who have
eyes but do not see, Who have ear, but do not hear" (Jer. 5:21). It's one thing to
have a set of eyes and a pair of ears, but it's another thing to use them. Parables
are wonderful because they carry truth in story form available to all, but it is the
heart condition of the hearer that determines what is heard. People with open
hearts hear the truth conveyed by the parable. For people with hardened hearts
the truth is concealed. Human beings are notoriously effective at hearing what
we want to hear. Our spiritual eyes and ears can become dull (Isa. 6:10). We
listen and see selectively on our own terms, often when it is convenient and expected. Spiritual blindness and dullness of hearing can occur when we drift
away from proper relationship with God.

Many times the drift involves issues of lordship. In the Western world,
since the Renaissance and the introduction of its humanistic thought processes,
we have been trained to think that life and the world revolve around us. We have
been sold on the fact that I am at the center of my universe, I make decisions for
my life, and I sit on my throne as the captain of my life. Such self-centered
thinking is reminiscent of the boasting of the rich man in Luke 12:16-21. Self-
centeredness wars against intimacy with God, because in self-absorption, there
is no room left for Him. Death is the great equalizer and ultimately exposes who
is in control. We do not own our bodies, we do not control how long we live,
and we ultimately realize how many things in life are out of our control.

When we usurp God's place and try to sit on the throne, we are acting like
Lucifer himself (Isa. 14:12-17). Taking God's place on the throne of our lives
produces a terrible dulling effect in our hearts that can quickly act as a barrier to
conception of the word. When dullness sets in, we can no longer see with 20/20
vision, because our vision is blocked by someone in our field of view—and that
someone is me. Spiritually, we can no longer hear, either. We become dull of
hearing, because our ears are stopped up with our own words and thoughts—
there is not enough room for God's words or thoughts.

Hardness of Heart

If we fail to catch the little foxes, and they continue to nibble away at our
intimacy with God, eventually a more serious state of dullness sets in—hardness
of heart. When our hearts grow hard, it seems as if God is nowhere to be found.
As when calluses build up on my hands and I lose feeling in those places, when
my heart grows hard, I feel more and more distant from God, until I cannot
sense Him at all. That does not mean He has left me—after all, our hand is still
intact under a callus. It's just that I cannot feel His presence. My heart grows

even more hardened, and hardness hinders me from seeing what God is doing in my life and from hearing what He is saying (Acts 28:27). It prevents God from communicating with me effectively, if at all (Ezek. 12:2). The condition of my heart does not diminish His love for me nor His desire to break through to me. Rather, He is patiently waiting for me to catch the little foxes and make the first move back toward softness of heart though repentance, turning from my consuming focus on self and renewing fellowship with Him (1 John 1:9,10; James 4:8-10).

I am talking here specifically about hardness of heart in the lives of Christians and of Christian preachers and teachers. Dullness of hearing and heart, as well as the eventual hardness of heart, sets in because of disappointments, unforgiveness, and taking offense at others—all of which are so easy to give in to when serving God's people. I become focused on my rights, my pain, my hard work for God, and I justify my right to remain angry and bear unforgiveness (Matt. 6:15; 18:35). But when such reasoning prevails, the ground of my heart becomes hard and conception is blocked. The little foxes have spoiled the vineyard.

A Soft Heart

Hardness is a warning sign that it is time to restore an open heart toward God. He cannot do that for us—it is our job to come to Him and to allow His Spirit to soften our hearts (James 4:8-10). Softening is a daily process, as when oil is applied to leather, to keep the heart pliable. I come to God with an open heart, confessing my need (Rev. 3:20). I lay down my agenda and open myself to God's agenda—He is much better at planning anyway. I go back to the Scriptures and begin to read them in faith, trusting that God's Spirit will illuminate a word, phrase, or passage that will explode in my heart and release softening life and power. I seek fresh bread—new manna for today—leaving yesterday's manna to rot, as it certainly will. I let the Scriptures speak to me once more as I approach them like a little child, waiting for "Daddy" to speak. Even if I feel nothing at first, I approach the Scriptures in faith, the same way I choose to love in a relationship with a friend or my spouse after a difficult time.

Making up after things have not gone well can be one of the best experiences in our human relationships. The intimacy that can come with making up is the sweetest, as love is renewed and commitment affirmed. Our relationships grow stronger and the fellowship sweeter through these healing seasons. The same pattern applies in our relationship with God. We come to our beloved in repentance and need, and we leave with new love blossoming and with softness of heart. Conception is once again possible as intimacy flows and barriers to conception are removed. My beloved is mine, and I am His.

Let Us Run Together

Hopefully this chapter has inspired a new yearning in your heart for the kind of relationship with God that makes conception of the word in your heart and transformational preaching possible. When we desire the "kisses of His mouth" and remain determined to deepen our intimacy with God, conception of the word becomes possible.[56] When we, like Solomon's bride, begin to cry out, "Let me hear your voice," renewing a passionate relationship with His written Word, the illumination of the Holy Spirit begins to flow, and the written Word of God takes upon itself flesh once again in the womb of our hearts. If we are diligent to watch over our hearts the way a tower of watchmen guard a prison, then we can avoid or counteract the dullness and hardness that so easily creep in and cut off the flow of transformational life.

If this kind of deep relationship work and approach to preaching seem overwhelming or impossible, then you've got it right. Fulfillment of one's calling to preach is impossible from a human standpoint—there are too many hazards, obstacles, and barriers in the way, and we are far too weak. But the challenge is also the joy of calling. The bride cries out, "Draw me after you and let us run together," and suddenly we are no longer alone. He is with us. It is precisely when we are weak and helpless that He is strong (2 Cor. 12:9,10). Our part is to be vulnerable—the "soft one" —ready for intimacy and conception. His job is to be the strong one, ready with seed.[57] This is where the word again mingles with human flesh and something incarnational takes place as the word is conceived in the womb of the preacher's heart. Now the task is to grow and mature the word so it can come to full term and be ready for delivery.

---

[56] Time fails us with all the additional metaphors for relationship with God and its parallels with human love. Worship also mirrors that kind of deep, romantic intimacy—one of the Greek words for worship is "προσκυνέω" (proskuneo), which literally translated means "to kiss toward"!

[57] I marvel at the word that Adam called his bride when he first met her. In Hebrew, Adam was man "אִישׁ" (ish), but Eve was "אִשָּׁה" (ishshah)—as some have translated it, "soft one." That term for Eve describes the role of the believer as God's bride and the preacher as he or she "runs with Him" to fulfill calling. The softness and vulnerability of my heart are all important to the conception of the word.

Chapter 4
Life Happens: Life Experience as a Catalyst for Growth

I got married at a young age to a beautiful Italian girl. Her brown eyes gleamed with radiance the morning we were married. I remember standing at the altar, looking toward the back of the church at this beautiful creature wrapped in a wedding gown so completely that it seems all I could see were those round eyes and smiling face as she walked toward me that morning more than thirty years ago. I was a preacher by that time. I was used to holding things together in public and had no concern about my ability to do so that day. But I wasn't prepared for what I saw. I was completely undone when I saw my bride, and I lost it like a fool. Within seconds, I was reduced to a puddle of tears and mush at the altar.

The vision of my bride melted me. Sometimes life is too much to take in all at once. That is why we have events like weddings, funerals, and baptisms—so we can look back at what we did and try to take in the enormity of it all for the rest of our lives. I said "I do" that day, but I had no idea what those words really meant. It takes living out a lifetime of commitment to begin to understand what those two small words are about.

The next nine years were a blur of houses, cars, children, diapers, hours spent in the office at work, and nights and weekends spent at the church in ministry. Life seems to pass so quickly, and we often take the things we treasure for granted. That was certainly true for me until life came to a screeching halt one day with some bad news about my wife's health. She hadn't been feeling well, and we thought it might be a case of the flu. I was away on a business trip when I got a call in California from my wife three thousand miles away. She was in the hospital. Her kidneys were failing. I needed to get on a plane.

To say I was shocked, astonished, in denial—all those things would not capture what I felt when I heard my wife tell me the news. She was only twenty-eight years old. She was the mother of our four small children under six years of age. She was the picture of health and living a healthy lifestyle at the time. How could this be? She was that lovely woman I saw at the altar only nine years earlier—would she live to see our tenth anniversary? She was also a pastor's wife. I thought bad things didn't happen to "good" people. Where was God? Had we done something wrong to incur His wrath or anger? Had I sinned and now God was punishing me? Would He supernaturally heal her or would she die? Was I going to spend the rest of my life raising four kids with no wife? When you get really bad news, your world turns upside down, and reality is suspended for a time. You seem to have so many questions and so few answers. Our world was shaken to its core.

We spent the next month getting more bad news. My wife's kidneys were at the point of no return. The doctors had no idea why they had failed, especially since she was young, athletic, and took such great care of her health. She would shortly need to be on regular dialysis just to stay alive and to try to reverse the toxic, lethal buildup of poisons in her blood. Surgery and transplants were possibilities to be discussed later if she made it through the next few months. We were in a struggle to save her life, and there was no shortage of doctors to remind us that her life would be shorter than we had imagined, even if everything went well from here.

I was devastated. I couldn't eat or sleep properly and lost more than twenty pounds. I was exhausted and couldn't think straight. I was constantly tormented by thoughts of losing my wife and haunted by what it would be like to live life without her, raising our children without their mother. Time at the church actually made things worse in those early days of crisis. We are people that believe in divine intervention and healing. Surely God would answer prayers of faith and heal her in some miraculous way. Surely the dialysis needles, surgeons, catheters, and machines would not be necessary, and a transplant would not be needed. God would take care of everything our way with some kind of miraculous healing if we prayed hard enough—or so we thought. Meanwhile, the crisis continued.

In the midst of my despair, one day about a month after we first got the bad news, I dropped to my knees while out in the in the garage and wept, crying out to God. It was there I felt as if I finally connected with God in a solid way about my wife and her health. Chronic illness brings with it a grieving period like a death, because something physical has died and been lost, never to return. But after the initial denial, anger, and despair, God broke though in that garage with hope in a way I would not have expected. Let me emphasize that I'm not suggesting I heard God speak with audible words, but to my heart. This was one of those times when He spoke loudly and clearly to me, and I heard the words in my heart: "You are going to die." That got my attention. I began to ponder those words, and I remember thinking that if I died, at least I would not feel the pain of my wife's illness anymore. I also thought to myself that I would gladly die if my wife could live.

It was then I distinctly remember the Holy Spirit bringing words from the Scriptures to mind, words that flooded my soul like healing salve. They were from Psalm 139. The psalm says we are each fearfully and wonderfully made and that all our days are written in His book (vv. 13,16). His individual thoughts toward each of us outnumber the grains of sand by the sea (vv. 17,18). As I remembered these words, I realized in a deeper way that my wife and I were in God's hands and that all was under His control. Our birth, life, and death were His—not mine—to govern. My wife was, first and foremost, God's child, and He had things taken care of. He knew the day of her birth and the day of her death. I would die and she would die, but neither of us would die apart from God, His love, or His care.

The words of Isa. 46:9,10 also came up in my heart: God knows our end from our beginning. Like a Master Architect, God designs our lives, weaving each twist and turn toward the end that He has in mind. He uses what we perceive to be good, and He uses what we perceive to be bad. Life experiences are the tools He uses to transform us into the people He has in His mind, and His dealings are always perfectly suited for that plan, calling, and purpose. In those moments weeping in the garage, I realized what the passages I had read so many times before were saying about all my worries. All the care and worry I could muster would not add one second to our brief lives (Matt. 6:27). If I could have done so, the care and worry I had shouldered in the previous weeks alone would have ensured our lives lasted well into our nineties.

In that brief moment of intimacy and connection with God, I learned more about how much God loves us and cares for us than in all the years I had put in studying those verses. This is what happens when God's written Word meets life experience: we encounter the depth of His love and are changed forever. His love for His bride is like, but much greater than, my love for my bride. I would have died for my wife if I could have made her well, but that was not necessary. Jesus already did. In that moment, my life experience gave me a perfect word picture for understanding the depth of God's concern and care: His thoughts toward my wife and me outnumber the grains of sand by the seashore. In that word picture, I could literally "see" that God had things under control. God reserves the right to use all the preacher's life experiences as a birthing ground for transformational sermons. My life experience, as painful as it was, would become a source of tremendous growth for my wife and me in the years ahead as God made the words of Psalm 139 and Isaiah 46 come to life—or, come into *our* lives.

Because of my wife's illness, faith is not an abstract theological concept to us but a trustful surrender that must sustain our souls each day. We are not sure what tomorrow will bring, but we know God is already there, waiting to meet us. He has already planned for it. To us, God's faithfulness is not simply a theological proposition. His faithfulness has a shape in our lives—we can point to it, for instance, when we consider the times He has pulled my wife back from death's door when her heart wasn't beating right or when her mineral imbalances threatened to take her life. Our life experiences have proved to us the futility of worry—life has been so out of our control that we have learned to live and enjoy one day at a time, trusting He will provide a tomorrow. We have encountered peace a person—He is a person who can hold you close late at night in emergency rooms when life is uncertain and death threatens. Shall I go on? Can you see how God uses life experience to ground the word in our hearts and cause it to grow? When God's word and the Holy Spirit's illumination meet life experience, transformative power is released and growth occurs. Our lives and ministry have been shaped by this transformative power. Life happens. Are you ready to harness the power of life experience as a catalyst for growing the word in your heart?

Grains of Sand

From the story I just related, you might gather I am convinced life experience is one of the primary ways God grows the word in the preacher's heart. Life experience makes some theologians very uncomfortable. Many theological concepts are safe as long as they remain in the realm of abstraction, because that realm is neat, orderly, logical, and precise. Life is a different matter altogether. It is messy, chaotic, and notoriously difficult to predict—that is, unless you are God. I honestly don't know whether to consider myself a Calvinist or an Arminian.[1] Perhaps I am a Calminian or an Arvinist. From both the Scriptures and life experience, it is evident that we serve a sovereign God and that His sovereign plan unfolds each day in our lives. It is also abundantly clear that each person has a free will, somehow integrated into God's sovereign plan in a way

---

[1] John Calvin, a sixteenth-century reformer, espoused a theology that emphasized the sovereignty of God in the affairs of humanity. There is a broad spectrum of beliefs about God's sovereignty. Some emphasize God's sovereignty and others humanity's free will. Beliefs that emphasize God's sovereignty usually fall under the theological heading of Calvinism. The most ardent Calvinists embrace a view of the sovereignty of God that is nearly complete and borders on fatalism. Jacobus Arminius, who lived in the seventeenth century, espoused a different theology that made more room for the free will of humankind; that view has since become known as Arminianism. As with Calvinism, a broad spectrum of beliefs could be classified as Arminian. What those views have in common is the importance of human free will in God's plan. I refuse to be classified as either Arminian or Calvinist. Both describe attributes that seem to be irreconcilable but are ultimately quite reconcilable in the mystery that surrounds the nature of an infinite God. His nature remains a mystery—it cannot be understood by reason alone. This is another example of where the mind and reason fail us, and where the heart must guide.

that makes us responsible for our own choices and actions. To deny either position requires some significant biblical gymnastics, but to embrace both requires a reach beyond reason.

It seems that God's sovereignty *and* humanity's free will are both factually true at the same time, though they seem to be in opposition to one another. While seemingly contradictory, they are somehow reconciled in the infinite heart and nature of God, who refuses to be put in one clever theological box or the other. I realize that this way of understanding life in God may not be very neat, but it does allow for a vital element of knowing God—mystery. I am growing more comfortable with mystery all the time, and being able to abide mystery is essential for anyone seeking to allow the word to grow in his or her heart. A young life growing in the womb, while open to the eyes of God, is hidden in mystery, and life and its experiences have dimensions to them that are far beyond our human ability to comprehend (Ps. 139:13-15).

Transformative sermons flow from life and its experiences. When the preacher takes the time to get in touch with what God is already at work doing, life experiences give flesh to truth so that we can see, hear, touch, and handle it. What we see as everyday events and seemingly random occurrences are actually parts of a divinely orchestrated opportunity to experience truth and its application in everyday life. Life experiences deepen our understanding of truth and grow the word in our hearts. Charles Spurgeon said that:

> God is every day preaching to us by similitudes. The things which we see about us are God's thoughts and God's words to us; and if we were but wise there is not a step that we take, which we should not find to be full of mighty instruction.[2]

The Scriptures describe the tremendous detail with which God knows us and has planned our lives. Since the time my wife and I first learned of her illness, the word pictures in Psalm 139 have framed my understanding of God's detailed involvement with us. The depth of His involvement in my life has awakened in me a desire to mine everyday experience by observing with a heart open to God's Spirit life as it unfolds around me. I love the words that open the psalm:

> O LORD, You have searched me and known *me*. [2] You know when I sit down and when I rise up; You understand my thought from afar. [3] You scrutinize my path and my lying down, And are intimately acquainted with all my ways. [4] Even before there is a word on my tongue, Behold, O LORD, You know it all. [5] You have enclosed me behind and before, And laid Your hand upon me. [6] *Such*

---

[2] Charles H. Spurgeon, *The New Park Street Pulpit* (London: Alabaster & Passmore, 1859), 4:330, quoted in Wiersbe, 35.

knowledge is too wonderful for me; It is *too* high, I cannot attain to it (Ps. 139:1-6).

God is intimately acquainted with each little detail of my life to a level that is too much for me to fathom. He understands me completely, which is something I cannot even say of myself. His knowledge of me is so complete that He knows the words I am about to speak before I form them in my mind or utter them with my mouth. He surrounds me with His presence and lays His hand on the details of my life day by day. He does so in such a subtle and unassuming way that it is easy to mistake His tender touch for accident or coincidence. His intimate contact is true in the lives of the saved and the unsaved. He cannot love one more than the other. His thoughts toward me are detailed from before my conception, as He weaves and forms me in my mother's womb, and every day I have breath. Everyday life experience is a gold mine for the preacher—it is an opportunity to grow and to nurture truth that God has conceived in our hearts.

The level of detail that encompasses God's thoughts toward every human being is unimaginable—who can count the number of sands by the edge of the sea? The psalmist goes on to sing these words:

> [13] For You formed my inward parts; You wove me in my mother's womb. [14] I will give thanks to You, for I am fearfully and wonderfully made; Wonderful are Your works, And my soul knows it very well. [15] My frame was not hidden from You, When I was made in secret, *And* skillfully wrought in the depths of the earth; [16] Your eyes have seen my unformed substance; And in Your book were all written The days that were ordained *for me*, When as yet there was not one of them. [17] How precious also are Your thoughts to me, O God! How vast is the sum of them! [18] If I should count them, they would outnumber the sand. When I awake, I am still with You (Ps. 139:13-18).

This particular passage fascinates me. It is full of the kind of mystery and wonder I would have designed into life if I were God for a day. Frail humanity is in awe of how far technology has come and how much computers can do; but it all pales in comparison to what God has created in the form of the human brain. And the brain is nothing when compared to the infinite capacity for detail that God Himself possesses.

With this in mind, is it too much for us to believe that God also knows each sermon we will ever preach before one word is uttered? Is it too much to believe that He knows each person in the audience who will hear our words and that He has a design in mind to touch each life? Can we go one step further and dare to believe that in God's marvelous plan, any sermon He would have us preach would first sovereignly relate to our own lives and personal growth in multiple ways, even as it is also meant for others? Considering Psalm 139 and the dance of sovereignty and free will, we need to rethink what a sermon is, how it relates to our lives and the lives of others, and what methodology is appropriate to use in the sermon's development.

I maintain that in light of Psalm 139, we must see our sermons as part of life itself. God's thoughts toward each of us outnumber the sands by the sea. Because of calling, God has the right to use our lives, according to His plan, to mold and shape our communication. The everyday people, experiences, and situations that come our way do not catch Him unaware. I am not saying that God causes all of them—the dance of sovereignty and free will is more complicated than that. What I am saying is that God causes all things to work for our good (Rom. 8:28). Each day brings new encounters and experiences that can add to the growth of the word in our hearts. Every day we experience joy, pain, sorrow, triumph, defeat, and a host of other things that can potentially become part of our communication.

The people we meet, the things we experience, and the ways they affect our lives become a living context for the communication of God's word in our preaching and teaching. The Scriptures and the truth they convey frame the word we deliver to the listeners, but that word works in our own lives as it "takes upon itself flesh" and we live it before it is ever preached. Life experience is where the word becomes flesh, and experience acts as a catalyst to grow the word in the womb of our heart. Preaching is not so much conning God out of a sermon as it is having eyes to see and ears to hear what He is already at work doing and saying. Sermons are sometimes born on the garage floor while you are groaning before God in pain. God's answers to those groans can transform our lives and grow in our hearts the words of transformational life that can be given away to others.

Master Architect

I am not an architect, but I am married to a woman trained in interior design.[3] My wife has dabbled in the arts of architectural design and the construction of buildings. She has learned a bit about how to read and draw on her computer blueprints for construction. She has learned about how architects place floor beams, design walls and roofs, coordinate specifications for parking lots, and place windows, as well as designate all the locations for plumbing, electrical outlets, and utilities in a building. The catch is that architects do all these things in their minds, without ever touching a hammer or saw. My wife has learned to assist the architect—the master designer—in his or her work. She has learned to see things complete and finished, just as they should be, before they are ever

---

[3] I often joke with my wife that I too am an interior designer. As a teacher, I am an equipper—the Greek word for equipping comes from the root "καταρτισμός" (*katartismos*), which means to "furnish." My job as a teacher is one of interior design—it's just that I furnish the inner person of those I serve.

started. In the process of designing, she and the architects she works with are acting like their Creator.

God is the Master Architect. Like an architect, He sees things finished in His mind before they ever begin. Consider Isa. 46:9,10:

> [9] "Remember the former things long past, For I am God, and there is no other; *I am* God, and there is no one like Me, [10] Declaring the end from the beginning, And from ancient times things which have not been done, Saying, 'My purpose will be established, And I will accomplish all My good pleasure';

There is God and then there is humanity. When our minds are renewed, we begin to see that life revolves around God and His plan. Life is about His purpose and His good pleasure. Our lives exist in that context and not the other way around. What if our sermon preparation also existed in that context? God makes the arresting statement that He knows the end from the beginning. In doing so, He makes claim to being the Master Architect of our lives and the source of our very existence. Before any one of us is born, He sees our end. He knows what He wants us to be on the last day of our lives. If this is true, then He even knows what He wants me to preach next week, next month, or many years from now. Our free will dances with His sovereignty to move us toward the end He has in mind. As life unfolds, it becomes the living context for our sermons and preaching ministry.

God's vision is perfect, and He knows perfectly what He wants us to become. Our free will can get in the way and hinder the fulfillment of His picture. He leads in the dance, but we don't always follow. And yet He is the Master Architect and has the blueprint for our lives, and that blueprint seems often to work with, around, or in spite of our free will. How amazing. As David writes in Psalm 139 of God's involvement with him, "Such knowledge is too wonderful for me" (Ps. 139:6). And that knowledge extends to our sermons. God is involved before they are conceived in our hearts. Could it be that our sermons, which are part of the Master Architect's plans for ourselves and others, have been unfolding as a part of life for days, weeks, months, or even years ahead of time, and we have only to look around to see our next sermons unfolding?

The Preacher and Life Experience

Life unfolds in unexpected ways. God uses the lives of people like Mary and Joseph, people who seem to be ordinary or who come from small, no-name towns, to shake up the entire world. In recent history, God used another unlikely life to shake the world. A little more than a century ago, on January 1, 1901, a woman by the name of Agnes Ozman was attending a small Bible school in a little town called Topeka, Kansas. She was studying under a former Methodist pastor and Holiness teacher by the name of Charles Fox Parham when she experienced what was later called the "baptism in the Holy Spirit," accompanied by the gift of speaking in tongues.[4] This event was the herald of a century in which the same kind of experience became a part of the lives of more than five hundred million people in a revival that continues until today.[5] Agnes Ozman's experience and that of the five hundred million after her have changed the face of twenty-first-century Christianity by moving us back toward a more experiential expression of Christian spirituality.

The dimensions of the revival that started in Topeka are staggering. As of 2001, that revival had spread on a global basis to more than 150 non-Pentecostal traditions within more than 9,000 ethno-linguistic traditions, representing more than 8,000 languages and covering ninety-five percent of the earth.[6] The movement, which can trace its roots to John Wesley and eighteenth-century Methodism and the idea of a "second blessing," can today be found in practically every nation and ethnic group in the world.[7] The movement—actually comprised of several movements—has been a controversial one, to say the least, but it has risen to be the predominant global force behind church growth and evangelism in the Protestant church today.

The combined flow of the Holiness, Pentecostal, Charismatic, and Third Wave Movements that have taken place over the past hundred years is now called the Renewal Movement.[8] One of the reasons the Renewal Movement has taken the world by storm is because it represents an experiential Christianity that embraces a personal relationship with God, emphasizing daily life experience with Him through the abiding presence of the Holy Spirit. In many ways, the Renewal Movement was an answer to an Enlightenment mentality that evolved after the Reformation. Enlightenment thought caused a gravitation toward a more rational kind of Christianity, one that included little time or space for the supernatural or for personal experience. Over time, the experiential part of Christianity was neglected by many in Protestant Christianity, leaving a hunger for a more personal encounter with God.

Church history traces movement back toward a more experiential kind of Christianity to the 1700s and 1800s among many smaller Christian sects. In the 1700s, the theology of John Wesley proved to be fertile ground for a more experiential kind of Christianity that allowed experience to play a role in one's discovery of truth. Wesley helped to initiate the evangelical revivals of the eigh-

---

[4] Vinson Synan, *The Century of the Holy Spirit* (Nashville: Thomas Nelson, 2001), 1.

[5] Ibid., ix.

[6] David Barrett, "The Status of Christianity and Religions in the Modern World," in *World Christian Encyclopedia* (Oxford: Oxford Press, 2001), 19.

[7] Donald W. Dayton, *Theological Roots of Pentecostalism* (Peabody: Hendrickson, 1987), 38-54.

[8] The term *Renewal Movement* is used to combine the trans-denominational Holiness, Pentecostal, Charismatic, and Third Wave Movements of the twentieth century that have led to an ever evolving renewal globally since its inception.

teenth century, and his theology is at the root of the Renewal Movement in the twentieth century.

Wesley's theology was centered on a vital and experiential inward religion that he called "true religion."[9] His theology was a reaction against the coldness of many Protestant groups that had become more rational than experiential in their orientation. Wesley incorporated an experiential form of religion into his theology because he was deeply concerned that people would "die in formality, outside religion," which had ". . . almost driven heart religion out from the world."[10] The inward religion that John Wesley advocated emphasized a personal, spiritual relationship with God and a walk with God that was what Wesley called "experimental." He encouraged people to think of their relationship with God as experimental with the belief that individuals should become familiar with the Scriptures and put them to the test in everyday life.[11] As one would imagine, this emphasis on experience greatly affected Wesley's preaching ministry, which encompasses over forty thousand sermons and two hundred fifty thousand miles on horseback.

Wesley's experiential theology had deep roots in both the Reformed and the Anglican traditions of his time.[12] Wesley's concept of "heart religion" or "true scriptural religion" was strongly influenced by his studies at Christ Church College at the University of Oxford and was a radical departure from mainstream Protestant theology, which at that time encouraged believers to experience God within the walls of the church and emphasized a corporate church relationship with God.[13] Wesley's ideas were met with distrust and ridicule by some, such as John Locke, who used the term "Enthusiasm" to level charges that Wesley and his followers were claiming their own private inspiration. In Wesley's time, as is true today, an appeal to a personal experience with God made some nervous.[14]

To Wesley, his appeal to life experience as a vital part of Christianity was not an appeal to something new but to a more apostolic kind of Christianity that could be found in the Scriptures. He thought of his work as an affirmation of what had always been a part of vital and transformational Christianity but was

---

[9] Donald A.D. Thornsen, *The Wesleyan Quadrilateral* (Indianapolis: Life & Light, 1990), 87. I strongly recommend Thornsen's book to anyone interested in an in-depth treatment of Wesley's Quadrilateral, which will be discussed in the next few pages. Thornsen is an expert in Wesleyan theology and the roots of the Quadrilateral, and he provides a very readable and informational glimpse of how the concept of the Quadrilateral evolved from Wesley's teaching.

[10] John Wesley, Preface 6, "Sermons on Several Occasions," *Works* (Bicentennial ed.), 1:106, quoted in Thornsen, 201-202.

[11] Ibid.

[12] Ibid., 15.

[13] Ibid., 51.

[14] Ibid., 46-47.

now sadly lacking in the church of his time.[15] The Reformers (of the Protestant Reformation) reacted to the abuses inflicted in the name of tradition as the highest authority in the church by restoring the place of Scripture as the highest authority. As we have seen, their cry *sola scriptura* was an expression of the belief that the Scriptures themselves were the only sufficient source for faith and its practice. But though the Reformers emphasized the Scriptures as the highest authority for determining truth, their intent was not to exclude other means for determining truth—only to allow the Scriptures to be the final authority in judging what is true.[16]

Because of the Reformed influences in Wesley's life, respect for the Scriptures as the highest authority for judging truth was embedded in Wesleyan theology. That respect was also blended with respect for tradition and reason as powerful tools for determining what is true—in part a response to the Anglican tradition, which also strongly influenced his life. The Anglicans realized that the Reformers had integrated human experience, reason, and tradition into their theology, alongside the Scriptures.[17] The Scriptures themselves were the primary authority for judging truth, but according to the Reformers, they worked with reason, experience, and tradition—all in tension and balance—to create a powerful paradigm for the discovery of truth. The integration of these four facets found in Wesleyan theology—the Scriptures, reason, experience, and tradition—is at the heart of growing the word in the preacher's heart after its conception.

Working the Quadrilateral

In the 1960s, Albert Outler used the term *Wesley's Quadrilateral* to describe Wesley's paradigm for determining truth.[18] It important to note that Wesley did not use this term himself, but it was adopted by the United Methodist Church to describe the four primary ways for determining truth as set forth in Wesley's writings. The four points of the Quadrilateral include:

- Scripture—the unique and settled truth as revealed through the process of inspiration and, therefore, the highest authority as a standard for determining what is true;
- Reason—the human mind's critical thought as directed toward research and inquiry into what is true but subject to Scripture as final judge of truth;

---

[15] Ibid., 19.
[16] Ibid., 35.
[17] Ibid.
[18] Ibid., 21.

- Experience—the personal encounter with truth and its illumination for individuals in their daily walk with God but subject to Scripture as final judge of truth;
- Tradition—the collective wisdom and behaviors of past generations attempting to live out and exemplify what they believed to be true but subject to Scripture as final judge of truth.

The Quadrilateral was meant to be a heuristic, or experimental, tool to find truth and to discover potential solutions for problems we encounter in life. Wesley believed that the Scriptures, as divine revelation, stood as the sole arbitrator of what is true. But he also believed tradition was a powerful tool by which to discover truth, because things are the way they are for a reason. His view of tradition promotes a spirit of tolerance and ecumenism if kept in proper balance with the other three sides of the Quadrilateral. Wesley also gave reason its proper place in saying, ". . . to renounce reason is to renounce religion, that religion and reason go hand in hand, and that all irrational religion is false religion."[19] Wesleyan theology made room for revelation, tradition, and reason at the table of truth's discovery. What separates Wesley's theology is that he also pulled up a chair and invited experience to once again participate in the conversation.

All parts of the Quadrilateral must be kept in proper balance and given their place in the process of discovering truth. If tradition is king, then reason can easily be abandoned and experience silenced, as was seen in church history before the Reformation. If reason is king, then the Quadrilateral also becomes distorted. Reason can be used to dismiss the authority of the Scriptures and the validity of experience, as has often occurred since the time after the Reformation with the introduction of an Enlightenment form of Christianity. If the role of experience is exaggerated, then it can lead to the demise of common sense and reason and to the abandonment of tradition, leading to some of the excesses seen currently in the Renewal Movement. Scripture must be the highest authority, but reason, experience, and tradition must be given their voice, or the power of the Quadrilateral in the discovery of truth is lost. Tradition, experience, and reason are not slaves to the Scriptures. Instead, the Scriptures must act as the "fountainhead" of the other three sources of authority, and those sources must work to confirm or enhance our understanding of the truth.[20]

As Donald A. D. Thornsen observes, knowledge derived from a personal encounter with God is objective in the sense that it establishes contact with a real, but hidden, reality. Although such an encounter involves the personal experience of someone seeking the truth, that experience is not entirely subjective. Other acts of knowing (reason, tradition, etc.) also involve some degree of sub-

---

[19] John Wesley, "To Dr. Rutherford," March 28, 1768, *Letters* (Telford, ed.), 5:364, quoted in Thornsen, 169.
[20] Ibid., 77.

jectivity, because human beings participate.[21] Even the pursuit of understanding truth in Scripture is subject to the limitations of human interpretation, which introduces a degree of human subjectivity to the process. Human subjectivity is simply not a good enough reason to dismiss experience from the Quadrilateral in our pursuit of truth. To do so is to lop off one leg of the table and lose a powerful means to grow and nurture truth in our hearts.

Experimental Living

Wesleyan theology and its Quadrilateral firmly establish the place of life experience as a means by which to grow and nurture a word conceived in the preacher's heart. Since God knows us each intimately and His thoughts toward us ". . . outnumber the sand of the sea," the preacher needs to see everyday life as an experimental journey for truth discovery (Ps. 139:18,19). The Master Architect is sovereignly at work, and each day's events and circumstances have experiential potential to illuminate truth for our understanding (Isa. 46:9,10). Please notice how radically this way of thinking changes our perspective on God and sermon preparation. Each day is pregnant with a sermon in the making as truth unfolds before our eyes. If I embrace the day with an experimental attitude, then that day holds the potential for learning and discovery. God is busy doing things in the preacher's life to illustrate truth and to give it flesh, all guided by the gentle touch of the Spirit. Life becomes a Spirit-led experiment to discover truth as it unfolds each day. Jesus said life would be just that.

At the Last Supper, Jesus told the disciples that the Holy Spirit would be daily at work in the life of the believer, gently leading and guiding us (John 17:17; 14:21,26). Jesus made the disciples aware of God's master plan to send the Holy Spirit to dwell with each of us so that He, the Spirit, could translate life, circumstances, and their context into meaning for us—all in order to give us God's perspective. If we have little difficulty believing the Holy Spirit "broods over the face of the deep" of the Scriptures, waiting to "hatch" truth in our hearts by illuminating God's Word for us, is it too much to believe that the same Holy Spirit is willing to brood over our lives each day, illuminating truth so that we can experience it personally? Our personal experience nourishes and feeds the word conceived within us, allowing it to grow.

Experimental living was advocated by Henry Blackaby and Claude King in their book "Experiencing God." The authors' whole theology is based on the kind of experiential Christianity embodied in Wesley's writings. Blackaby and King outline seven essential "realities" of experiencing God in our daily lives:[22]

---

[21] Ibid., 201-202.
[22] Henry T. Blackaby and Claude V. King, *Experiencing God* (Nashville: Lifeway, 1990), 50.

- God is always at work around you;
- God pursues a love relationship with you that is real and personal;
- God invites you to become involved with Him in His work;
- God speaks by the Holy Spirit through the Bible, prayer, circumstances, and the church to reveal Himself, His purposes, and His ways;
- God's invitation to work with Him always leads you a crisis of belief that requires faith and action;
- You must make major adjustments in your life to join God in what He is doing;
- You come to know God by experience as you obey Him and He accomplishes His work through you.

Blackaby and King's theology is experimental Christianity at its best. It takes into account the sovereignty of God and His lordship by conceiving of a God who takes the initiative in executing His purpose in our lives before we are even aware. Purpose is grounded in His love for us. This experimental approach to living is not an invitation issued by us to God, asking Him to bless our work, but rather an invitation extended to us by God to join Him in what He is already at work doing, thus requiring our submission and obedience. God is sovereign Lord of our lives, and we take our place in proper submission to the Master Architect.

Most importantly, experimental Christianity requires that a person take abstract Scripture and put it to the test as a guiding factor in life so that it is lived out experimentally. We take what the Holy Spirit has conceived in our hearts through the illumination process and weave it together with life experience as we apply truth to everyday decisions and problems. As the word is tested in us, it grows and matures. Blackaby and King describe that testing as a "crisis of faith" that occurs as we respond to God's invitation to join Him in what He is already at work doing—that choice or response is where transformation takes place and transformational sermons are born.

God's Theater

In the midst of the preacher's everyday life experiences lies another powerful, but often neglected, catalyst to growing the word in our hearts. Many times in ministry, I have been so caught up in the whirlwind of meetings, counseling, weddings, and funerals that I have forgotten to open my eyes and experience God's creation. God's creation is overflowing with truth and word pictures that trumpet His truth to us. John Calvin in his *Institutes* called nature a "dazzling theater," "a most glorious theater."[23] He called creation the "book of the un-learned" and believed that even a person who could not read a printed book could learn much about God by simply opening his or her eyes and heart to study God's mark left on creation.[24] If one examines Jesus' sermons, it's easy to see His eyes were wide open to God's dazzling theater all around Him. The majority of His sermons are entwined with references to creation as He experienced it each day; Jesus used creation as a picture gallery for His sermons in order to illustrate truth. In doing so, He utilized the power of creation and word pictures to help His hearers grow in the word and in understanding.

As I mentioned before, created things always have multiple dimensions of purpose—a multitude of interwoven purposes seem to be working all at once. Creation has many functions, but its wonder and beauty also reflect the One who created it; creation shows forth His glory. God left the mark of His person, character, and nature in His creation. His mark on creation should not surprise us—every artist leaves something of him or herself on his or her artistic creations. If I mention Rembrandt, Leonardo da Vinci, Vincent van Gogh, or Norman Rockwell, a certain artistic style may come to mind. God too has left His mark on the "painting" of this physical universe:

> [18] For the wrath of God is revealed from heaven against all ungodliness and un-righteousness of men who suppress the truth in unrighteousness, [19] because that which is known about God is evident within them; for God made it evident to them. [20] For since the creation of the world His *invisible attributes, His eternal power and divine nature,* have been clearly seen, being understood through what has been made, so that they are without excuse (Rom. 1:18-20; emphasis added).

When we look at God's creation we see the attributes that make God who He is. We see His eternal omnipotence given "flesh" in the power of the ocean and its waves or in a volcano erupting. We see His divine wisdom captured in the cycles of day and night, the placement of the stars, the precision of the human body, and the intricacies of the atomic and subatomic world. God's divine nature is illustrated as each sunrise and sunset display His faithfulness and order. Light and darkness embody an eternal struggle between good and evil. God's stamp is all around us in creation. Some cultures have recognized this and have developed animistic religious systems that actually worship creation, mistaking it for God Himself. Nature is not God, but it tells us about Him. Nature all around us shouts truth to us about God, His nature, His wisdom, and His love if

---

[23] John Calvin, *Institutes of the Christian Religion* (Philadelphia: Westminster, 1960), 1:61, 72, 341, quoted in Wiersbe, 33. Warren W. Wiersbe's book *Preaching and Teaching with Imagination: The Quest for Biblical Ministry* is one of the best works I have read concerning metaphor and word pictures in preaching and teaching.

[24] John Calvin, *Commentaries* (Grand Rapids: Baker, 1981), 1:80, quoted in Wiersbe, 33.

we have ears to hear and eyes to see. Nature has the God-given ability to add flesh to the word as God uses it to grow our understanding of what has been conceived in our hearts.

The Power of Word Pictures

Because of the pace of ministry, it is easy for preachers to become disconnected from creation and the world around them. There is always another email to write, a call to answer, or another text message to send. We travel miles each day in air-conditioned cars and work in climate-controlled buildings designed to keep us comfortable. All of our modern conveniences are wonderful, but they have an unintended effect on us: we become enclosed in our own version of virtual reality and can be shocked to realize there is a whole created world outside waiting to be discovered.

Disconnection from creation would have been impossible even as recently as a few decades ago; the majority of the people on the planet at one time were intimately joined to nature because their daily survival depended on it. They saw the food they ate growing in the dirt or walking on legs in the field. Before weather forecasting or pesticides existed, people were vulnerable to storms and insect plagues. The clothes they wore did not come from a shopping mall but were made by spinning cotton from a plant or by using wool or skin just taken from their owners. We consider these folks and reflect on how fortunate we are, and on how difficult life was for them in comparison to our own. Life may have been more difficult, but our forbearers were in touch with a powerful tool for understanding truth and growing God's word in the heart—the word pictures that God Himself paints in the world around us.

Nature and life experience are powerful teachers of truth because through them we can harness the power of metaphor. Metaphor making is defined as the act of comparing dissimilar things on the basis of some underlying principle that unites them in order to construct a new reality of understanding and meaning.[25] Metaphor is the business of building bridges of meaning between things we understand and things we don't understand in order to construct new meaning. Metaphor is a primary device that human beings were designed to use in thought, language, and the construction of meaning. It is the raw material of learning and the bridge to growth in understanding. Metaphor draws on the things we have experienced in life and maps them into relationship with things we do not understand, making the unfamiliar more accessible and understanda-

---

[25] Ellen Y. Siegelman, *Metaphor and Meaning in Psychotherapy* (New York: Guilford, 1990), ix. This definition is in part constructed based on the ideas conveyed in Dr. Siegelman's book. The book is a fascinating use for its use of metaphor as a tool to construct meaning in the process of psychoanalysis.

ble.[26] This book is built on an extended metaphor comparing the incarnation of Jesus Christ to the process of preaching God's word.

The reason word pictures and metaphors can enable truth to grow in our hearts has to do with basic human design. All metaphor can ultimately be traced back to its origins in nature and the world around us.[27] God has designed human beings with two brains. Speaking from the standpoint of human anatomy, what we call "the brain" is actually two brains. There is a left brain that organizes and is the seat of logic, sequence, and their associated functions, such as interpreting rules, reading, writing, and mathematics. Our Western culture cherishes left-brain functions and is biased toward left-brain thought. The right brain is the metaphoric brain that invents and creates. It is responsible for drawing, music, and visualizing. It is also the part that visualizes special relationships and builds metaphoric bridges to create meaning and understanding—processes essential to preaching.

Both sides of the brain are connected by a thick nerve trunk called the *corpus callosum*, which allows the left brain to communicate with the right brain.[28] God's wisdom is apparent in this design. There is first of all duplicity. If one surgically removes half the brain, the other part is plastic enough to recover most functionality and adapt. Then there is the ability to develop both sides of the brain. This allows the person to literally fly with two wings—one side skilled at the rational logical side of life and the other at the art of creativity and imagination. That is why a proper balance of reason (left brain), tradition, and experience (right brain), all guided by revelation (beyond our brain) are so essential to growing the truth in our heart.

Vision and visual imagery are at the center of the metaphoric mind. Children are born "single brained." [29] Children begin to make sense of the world though their senses. Every action is an adventure in experimental learning for a child as he or she literally tastes, smells, touches, hears, or sees the world into reality. The sense of sight is especially important in constructing truth about our world. David Sless observes that the eyes could literally be thought of as part of the brain.[30] Immanuel Kant conceived of the brain as the "thinking eye," because he saw vision and thought as one, and he argued they could not be separated logically or physiologically.[31] There are over one hundred million light cells in the retina of the eye, and they are attached to the brain by large nerve trunk lines called the optic nerves. The miracle is that each eye is independently connected to each side of the brain via a split in the optic nerve as it moves from

---

[26] Ibid., 3.

[27] Samples, v.

[28] Ibid., 19-22. Samples is an excellent source of information on metaphor regarding how it relates to the anatomy and physiology of the human brain.

[29] Ibid., 23.

[30] David Sless, *Learning and Visual Communication* (New York: Wiley, 1981), 16.

[31] Ibid.

the eye toward the brain. The importance of the eyes can be seen by the fact that in the embryo, the eyes form first, and then the brain actually grows out from them.[32] Humans were designed to construct truth about the world by being able to see things, whether actual objects or as images in our minds. Seeing is the way we grow understanding in our hearts. Is it any wonder then that metaphor is essential to preaching and a deep wellspring for growing truth that has been conceived in our hearts?

As children mature and the neurons in their brains begin to grow and connect, they begin to try to make sense of what they are experiencing through the senses. That act occurs largely through the development of language. Language is the means by which a child begins to chop reality into individual, bite-sized pieces and create metaphoric bridges of meaning so that life can be understood.[33] Bob Samples calls this process "acculturation"—the process whereby the whole is deconstructed into pieces with labels (words) so that the whole can be understood in terms of its parts. He calls this process "semantic surgery." Nouns (names like Daddy and Mommy) come first, followed by words of control or action (verbs like eat, give me, etc). Later, organizing and symbolizing are factored into the process as the child learns rules of grammar and writing. The left brain fragments reality, analyzes it, and associates it with the rules of grammar and semantics. The right brain then reconstructs it into the whole again with new meaning. In this way, words can be strung together to create "necklaces of meaning."[34]

One model for understanding this process of making meaning is called "dual coding theory."[35] Dual coding theory was advanced by Allan Paivio at the University of Western Ontario to explain how the brain learns to read and write. The theory holds that visual and verbal clues are processed by two different systems in the brain. First, there is the verbal system. Individual sounds become the basic representational units in the verbal system of the brain. These individual sounds are different in each culture, because each language has different alphabets with letters or symbols having different sounds. When each language's sounds are strung together in sequentially arranged packets, they form the basic representational units of the brain's verbal system. Each unit is called a "logogen."[36] Logogens are the auditory units of grouped sounds that make up words,

---

[32] Sless, 16-17 and Samples, 22.

[33] Samples, 24.

[34] Ibid., 25-31.

[35] For an excellent explanation of dual code theory as it relates to learning and the reading and writing process, see Mark Sadowski and Allan Paivio, *Imagery and Text: A Dual Coding Theory for Reading and Writing* (Mahwah, New Jersey: Erlbaum, 2001). Though written primarily for those interested in education, the book explains a lot about why metaphor is so essential for human understanding—metaphor is hardwired into the way we learn.

[36] Sadowski, 42-45.

sounds, and syllables that are heard by the ear and processed by the left side of the brain. They are then basic representational units of the verbal learning system. At that point, they are merely symbolic abstractions, as anyone can tell you who has heard a language spoken that he or she has never learned.

An essential part of the learning process involves the association of the abstract sounds of logogens with images stored in the brain, Each image is called an "imagen." Imagens are the basic representational units of the nonverbal learning system, the second system. Meaning for the logogen that is heard occurs when the right brain constructs a metaphoric bridge with an imagen, associating logogen and imagen to bring abstraction into experience. The association allows us to "see" what is meant by the abstract sounds we hear by associating them with something we are familiar with and allowing us to make sense via images we have stored though experience. Dual Code Theory is incomplete in its ability to explain such a complex process as learning, but it illustrates how essential the function of visual metaphor is to the learning process. It also illustrates how profoundly connected the growth of the word in our understanding is to metaphor, word pictures, and the language we use to express God's word when we preach.

David Buttrick, renowned in the world of preaching, observes that by the time a child is two or three years of age, he or she experiences a linguistic explosion, developing a vocabulary of more than one thousand words. By age four, the child is in command of multiple thousands of words, nuanced grammar, and a whole set of language strategies suited for specific cultural situations and events.[37] Buttrick notes that "by naming, we think the world live." As an example, he cites Helen Keller, who could not hear or see. She describes herself as having no world until she was taught words and could name her world and construct a reality for herself from them.[38] It seems that words allowed her to "see" things around her that she could not hear or see with her natural ears or eyes.

When done effectively, preaching, through the spoken word, allows the hearer to see the world differently and to construct a new reality. We are literally blind to a truth and its meaning until some metaphoric bridge of understanding can be built in our hearts to help us understand what that truth is like, and so are the people who hear us preach. As we determine to walk each day in intimacy with the God, the Holy Spirit can use the things we experience in life and in God's creation all around us to build those metaphoric bridges. Can you see how important word pictures and life experience become to the growth of the word in our hearts?

---

[37] Buttrick, 6-7.
[38] Ibid.

Imagery as a Growth Engine for the Word

As mentioned before, Warren Wiersbe observes that ". . . no person can rise higher than the quality of the beauty and quality of the pictures that hang in the gallery of their heart."[39] Our metaphoric concepts literally determine how we perceive truth. As we are learning, humans are created with a conceptual system that assembles our reality in a fundamentally metaphoric way. George Lakoff observes that we describe abstract concepts with metaphoric language that is so second nature to us we often fail to even notice it.[40] The abstract idea of an "argument" can be expressed in the metaphoric language of war; one can attack with an argument, demolish, strategize, or even "shoot people down" with it. The abstract idea of an argument can also be expressed with the metaphor of "dance"; we move, interact, and flow with it and its "rhythm." I pointed out at the beginning of the book that the abstraction of "time" can be understood in terms of money; we can waste, save, give, spend, invest, budget, run out of, borrow, or lose time. The association of abstract thought with known metaphor is essential to the process of understanding and meaning. We make these associations subconsciously every day. Shouldn't we harness this power deliberately in our preaching and in nurturing a word that has been conceived in our hearts?

Language, whether the written symbols we see on the page or the words we hear spoken, is meaningless until associated with an image in our hearts. Buttrick observes that "theological meaning must always be embodied in images drawn from life."[41] Wiersbe goes on to quote theologian Sallie McFague in saying, "Images feed concepts; concepts discipline images. Images without concepts are blind; concepts without images are sterile."[42] But it follows that concepts *with* images are fertile—we're back to our incarnation metaphor and the processes of conception and growth. Life experience as it is lived out each day becomes fuel for the growth of the word in our hearts. Each person, circumstance, and event we experience becomes another opportunity to see the word unfolding before our eyes as we yield to it in surrender and apply it in our lives. It is sad that Western culture has conditioned us to become so analytical that we see the world around us and reduce it to parts and pieces but never reassemble it with God-centered pictures that help us understand the whole and its meaning.

A tree is more than its leaves, bark, phloem, xylem, and chlorophyll. It can represent the kind of steadfastness that cannot be moved (Ps. 1:3). It can

---

[39] Wiersbe, 41.

[40] George Lakoff and Mark Johnson, *Metaphors We Live By* (Chicago: University of Chicago, 1980), 3-5.

[41] Buttrick, 132, quoted in Wiersbe, 41.

[42] Sally McFague, *Metaphorical Theology* (London, SCM, 1983), 26, quoted in Wiersbe, 41.

represent life-giving potential (Rev. 22:14) or even be a cursed instrument of death (Gal. 3:13).

Westerners are good at naming the parts and the pieces, but what about the metaphors and images built into creation that can unlock understanding of spiritual truth? Life as it is experienced each day and creation itself embody truth in metaphoric form. As William Blake insinuated in a letter written in 1803, we in the West often suffer from "Newton's sleep."[43] We have adopted a more rigid, reason-based approach to life that scientifically dissects reality to uncover its meaning, but we miss out on the holistic truth it was meant to convey. We fail to take in the big picture because we are used to killing things so we can pull them apart and dissect them to find the truth.[44] We often approach Scripture the same way. But life is not lived that way and the Scriptures were not written that way—dissection can kill the big picture. To be sure, there is value in reducing the whole to its parts through word studies and exegesis—this book has certainly done its share of that kind of study to mine the treasures in the words and grammar of the written Word. The problem occurs when this becomes our only approach, and cold reason smothers the voices of tradition, experience, and even the Scriptures themselves in our quest to grow and nurture God's word in our hearts. That, dear preacher, can be the death of a transformational sermon.

Growing the Word in Your Heart

I have never been the same since that day nearly twenty-three years ago when I found out about my wife's illness. It is not the illness that has changed my wife and me but what we have been able to learn about God while coming to grips with the illness. Life happens, but God is always carefully working to weave life experience into a wonderful backdrop for understanding the truth. An experimental approach to life experience and living with eyes wide open to the creation each day are essential to growing the word in the preacher's heart. As we open ourselves to the Holy Spirit's teaching through these means, He does the work. He is the only one who could think all the thoughts necessary to customize life and all its complexities into a uniquely designed curriculum to grow the truth in our hearts. He is the only architect who can see our whole lives in advance to be sure that all the right experiences unfold to grow the right words in our hearts at the right time in order to meet the needs of the people to whom we will preach.

You and I must learn to see God already at work around us. He speaks volumes through our circumstances and through what we encounter in the world, sovereignly growing the word in our hearts. We must realize God was already at

---

[43] William Blake, an eighteenth-century poet, used the term "Newton's sleep" in a letter he wrote in 1803, quoted in Wiersbe, 37.

[44] Wiersbe, 39.

work executing His plan before we woke up this morning. I think the Hebrews have it right—the day really begins at sundown, when we are about to go to sleep. In the Jewish mind, the day begins as we begin to rest. God is at work while we rest, actively preparing the new day for when we awaken. We have to learn to open our eyes and see what He is already doing. We need to hear what He is already saying when we get up in the morning. Our times of intimacy with Him and His Word in the morning simply get us "in tune" with His frequency so we can understand what He is doing.

Jesus made extensive use of life experience to shape the words He would preach. People gathered by the thousands to hear Him teach, and His approach ensured transformation and new life to all who heard. He was laying down an incarnational pattern for us to follow in the preaching and teaching of God's word. Therefore, like Jesus, in communicating I must deliberately relate truth to the world around me, based on the circumstances and experiences that God works in my life so that the word I communicate is alive for my audience. I must have my eyes open to see God's truth in creation each day, expecting that it will yield its word pictures and metaphors to grow the word in my heart. If I give attention to these things, my life and experiences will literally become "living sermon material" and an experimental laboratory for discovering God's truth, acting as a catalyst of the growth of the word in my heart.

Life experience fuels the growth of the word in the preacher's heart. Experimental living adds to the size and shape of its truth in our hearts. The word takes on new depth and meaning as life and experience help us build new metaphoric bridges of understanding. But that does not mean word is ready for delivery. It is one thing to grow and another to mature. Consider teenagers. Every time one of my four children came of age to drive it deepened my prayer life significantly. My kids were growing, but they were not yet mature—growth does not equal maturity. Similarly, the growth of the word in our hearts does not necessarily signal that it has matured in our lives. The word must be personally integrated and applied to the preacher's life in order for maturity—of both the word and ourselves—to occur. We have seen how to grow the word in this chapter. Now let's move onward to maturity.

Chapter 5
Heart-shaping: Refinement as a
Pathway to Maturity

Growing up is difficult. As children, we want to grow up and be adults—we long for the freedoms and benefits of adulthood. But as adults, we find there is a price to be paid for freedom, a price called responsibility, and so we find ourselves longing for the carefree days of childhood. Life is an ever-changing march forward, and there is no going back. The only choice we have is to cooperate with the maturing process or protest, kicking and screaming, along the way. Some adults are not willing to pay the price to live responsible lives, and they live like children in adult bodies. By contrast, those who do decide to "grow up" and accept responsibility find they are in for quite a ride.

The journey into adulthood requires deep and foundation-shaking change. Change is not comfortable or easy but involves a lot of labor, toil, and pain. We discover romantic fairytales are for soap operas and novels, but real love takes commitment and hard work. We come to the painful realization that life does not revolve around us but only works if we become selfless and place others, like our spouses and children, first. We learn the pain of delayed gratification and suffer through times of want and sorrow. Some become disillusioned and retreat back into childishness, while others embrace the work of change and become mature men and women. This process is repeated spiritually every day in the church. Each of us, including preachers, make daily decisions about whether we will regress toward spiritual childhood or continue on the journey forward toward spiritual adulthood.

Deep spiritual maturity is at the heart of transformational preaching and teaching. In order to support the weight of the calling to preach, a person must undergo an enormous personal transformation in his or her own heart. The weight of preaching ministry is enormous. The words we speak carry the power of life and death for the individuals who hear them—words have consequences (James 3:5-8). Anyone who has been in ministry for some time begins to see how desperate people are for spiritual growth, wisdom, and solutions to incredibly complex problems. The ability to be intimate enough with God to sense His specific words for a specific occasion can help desperate people hear from heaven. Marriages are saved, divorces are cancelled, career pathways are altered, and the deadly consequences of sin and poor choices are averted because of transformational sermons, but the opposite can also be true when sermons without transformational life are preached.

A sermon's transformational life is often dependent on the degree to which the word has done its work in the preacher's own heart. Any word that has been conceived in the preacher's heart must be allowed to release its transformational power in the preacher's life before that word can be effectively imparted to others. Unless the word is first allowed to refine and shape the preachers heart, the preacher's words may not align with the preacher's life and actions. A lack of alignment between word and deed in the preacher's life can be devastating to the hearers, and some may never recover from broken trust and wounded faith. The refining and maturing work of the word of God in the inner life of the preacher is critical to transformational preaching as well as to the preacher's spiritual life, health, and vitality.

Deep Transformation

The maturing of the word in the womb of the preacher's heart is at the core of what makes that word transformational. Intimacy with God results in the conception of a word that is alive in the preacher's heart. The Holy Spirit then grows the word by illuminating truth in the preacher's life experience and in creation. While growth of the word in the preacher's heart may be significant, growth does not mean maturity—again, growing up is one thing; maturing is another. And without maturity, delivery of the word is at best a risky proposition. The maturing of the word occurs as the Holy Spirit begins the very personal work of applying that word to the preacher's own life for personal transformation. Personal transformation is a deep and sometimes painful work, but that is the price of maturity.

Notice we are already more than halfway through the book, and we haven't yet addressed the actual structure or form of the sermon itself. That is intentional. I believe transformational preaching is seventy-five percent internal and twenty-five percent external. If we don't get the conception, growth, and maturing part of preaching right, then we are not going to like what we see when the sermon is finally born.

The maturing process for a transformational sermon can be likened to the maturing of a baby in the womb—it is not easy, smooth, or predictable most of the time. Sometimes the sermon's growth is a fluid process, as if that sermon drops into our spirits right from heaven. But at other times, the growing pains are intense and the personal cost enormous. Excitement about a calling to preach and the conception of the word can quickly turn into sleepless nights, false labor, and second thoughts. The maturing process that occurs during the last months of pregnancy is often the most difficult phase in bringing a child into the world, and so it is with the maturing of the word in the preacher's heart. Yet this is also the phase when the word comes to fullness and is finally ready for delivery. If a baby is born early during those last few months of pregnancy, the complications can be vast. Complications also develop for a sermon delivered too soon without adequate time for the word to mature in the preacher's heart. Transformational sermons are a result of the maturing of the word in the womb of the preacher's heart, allowing that word to come to full term before the baby is born.

The Need for Personal Transformation

The first chapter of this book outlined some arresting statistics related to the condition of ministerial health and wellbeing. Ministers and their families are experiencing an alarming rate of crash-and-burn outcomes in ministry. I have watched ministers crash and burn around me over the last several decades. Of my five most significant mentors in ministry, three have fallen to moral failure and two are no longer in ministry. No less than seven of my closest friends in ministry have suffered divorce and family break-up with devastating consequences. I do not believe that what I have seen is the exception, and I would guess that many of you reading this book are seeing similar things happen in the lives of those around you in ministry.

As I related in chapter 1, Dr. Richard J. Krejcir of the Francis Schaeffer Institute of Church Leadership Development (FASICD)—in two separate studies at separate pastors conferences in Orange County, California, in 2005 and 2006, involving a combined total of 1,050 pastors—found that:[1]

- 100% of the pastors surveyed stated that they had a close associate or friend from seminary who had left the ministry due to burnout, conflict in the church, or moral failure;
- 90% state that they were frequently worn out on a daily or weekly basis;

---

[1] Dr. Richard J. Krejcir, "Statistics on Pastors," The Francis Schaeffer Institute (FA-SICD),http://www.intothyword.org/apps/articles/default.asp?articleid=36562&columnid= 3958 (accessed July 2, 2009). The Francis Schaeffer Institute exists to provide biblical resources for the church. It specializes in providing research for insight and application for church leaders and pastors. Its research findings are often made public at http://www.intothyword.org/pages.asp?pageid=56972. Dr. Krejcir is co-founder of FA-SICD.

- 89% had considered leaving the ministry, and 57% said they would leave the ministry if they had a better place to go, including secular work;
- 77% said they felt they did not have a good marriage;
- 72% stated that they only study the Bible when they are preparing for sermons or lessons;
- 38% had been divorced or were in the process of getting a divorce;
- 30% admitted to having an ongoing affair or sexual encounter with a parishioner;
- 26% had regular devotions and felt adequately fed spiritually;
- 23% felt happy or content with who they are in Christ, at church, and at home.

These figures point to the desperate need for personal transformation in the lives of ministers and their families. The statistics relate behaviors and attitudes that are problematic, but the real problems lie much deeper—at the heart level.

A Pure Heart

Marriage and sexual problems; sexual indiscretions; spiritual, mental, and physical burnout; and dissatisfaction with life are all problems that must be addressed in the lives of ministers, but what are the root causes? How can individuals with a calling from heaven have such problems? How can people who have these kinds of problems purport to speak for God each week from the pulpit when their own lives are in disarray? How can God use a preacher's words to change people's lives when the preacher's life is so lacking in transformational power?

A very general answer to the questions above requires only one word—grace. The Word of God itself is powerful and has the potential to change people's lives regardless of the state of the preacher's life, though the word may be greatly hindered if the preacher's heart is not right. This is a very deceptive part of the calling to preach the word—God will still anoint and bless that word to some degree, even if things are not right in the preacher's heart. Beyond God's grace, a cure for the root causes of the problems listed above is personal transformation. The preacher's heart must be changed; then attitudes and behavior will follow. There is simply no substitute for a deep transformational work in the preacher's heart—anything else would be superficial. The word must release its transformational life in our hearts before we can give life away to others.

Regardless of God's grace, the Scriptures are clear—the one with the pure heart has the best chance of long-term ministry that is high impact and transformational. In the book of Psalms, we are told that a pure heart is essential for intimacy with God:

> [3] Who may ascend into the hill of the LORD? And who may stand in His holy place? [4] He who has clean hands and a pure heart, Who has not lifted up his soul to falsehood And has not sworn deceitfully. [5] He shall receive a blessing from the LORD And righteousness from the God of his salvation.

These words are echoed in the words of Jesus when He says, "Blessed are the pure in heart for they shall see God" (Matt. 5:8). The word used for "pure" in the text has a message for us—it is the root that gives us the English word catharsis.[2] The word is a violent word and pictures the process of the purification of metal in a furnace.

When I worked in industry before I went into full-time ministry, I worked for a specialty chemicals company that purified metal. I would see furnaces heated above 2,300 degrees Fahrenheit. Metal ingots were dropped into these furnaces. The furnaces were so hot that the very light they emitted was the heat itself—the light could set things on fire across the room when a furnace door was opened. I had to wear special goggles to protect my eyes from being burned. The hard metal ingot would melt like an ice cube before our eyes and disappear into an orange-white puddle of bubbling liquid—unless there was water trapped in the metal, in which case the ingot would explode. I will never forget seeing a white powdery substance floating to the surface of the liquid metal. That powder was the dross—impurities trapped in the metal were now floating up so we could see them. As I stood there observing the process of purification, my life experience was yielding another one of those precious teaching moments.

Purity in the life of the preacher is a violent thing. Most often, it takes place not in the study when we read the Word or commune with God in prayer but in the trying circumstances of life when the heat is turned to high. Purification is not a pretty thing. Our hearts are like that metal ingot—they are solid and have impurities trapped in them. God knows this. We are sinful and have a sin nature, of which we are well aware and which has not caught God off guard (Rom. 7:14–8:1). Jesus paid the price for our sin, and we are forgiven and without condemnation. Yet sin and its problems still remain trapped in us until God does His gradual, intricate work of purification over a lifetime. By using life circumstances, God turns up the heat in our lives to melt our hearts in order to release the dross. The heat is unpleasant and nearly unbearable at times, yet when the

---

[2] In Matt. 5:8, the Greek word "καθαρός" (*katharos*) is used for "pure." This word has with it the connotation of purification by fire and pictures what happens with metal when heated in the fire so the dross (impurities) come to the surface and the metal is rendered pure. The word also pictures a vine being pruned so that it is cleansed by that pruning in order to bear even more fruit. Both the heated metal and the pruned vine have undergone cathartic but necessary experiences for purification and growth.

heart has melted and the Holy Spirit has exposed the dross, the impurities can be swept away and our spirit come out refined.

Paul describes the refining process in Rom. 5:3-5:

> [3] And not only this, but we also exult in our tribulations, knowing that tribulation brings about perseverance; [4] and perseverance, proven character; and proven character, hope; [5] and hope does not disappoint, because the love of God has been poured out within our hearts through the Holy Spirit who was given to us.[3]

Paul uses specific words in this passage to describe how God purifies the heart. The word "tribulation" could be translated "pressures" in this passage. Each life has pressures, and preachers have their own unique, additional set of pressures. The Greek word for tribulation in the passage was used to describe the pressing of olives under slabs of heavy stone to extract olive oil and also type of execution whereby prisoners had heavy weights piled on their bodies until they could no longer breathe. This is a word picture for how trials sometimes feel as they pile up in our lives. But if allowed, God will use the pressure to mature us. If we determine with His help to bear up under pressure, it forms in us perseverance or, literally, "an overcoming spirit." Our heart is changed, and we develop the endurance and capacity to live and even thrive under pressure. We become like soldiers hardened by battle or plants moved from the greenhouse out into the elements to harden them and make them stronger.

God's refining process produces "proven character" in our hearts. The word used here in the original text is used to describe the refinement of metal. It pictures metal refined in the furnace, much as I described above. God uses the pressure and fire of a trial to melt our hearts, and dross comes to the surface. The refining process is repeated over and over until the desired degree of purity is attained. For metal, the pathway to greater purity is to heat and cool the metal many different times. When I worked with aluminum and gallium metals in industry, it took as many as six heating and cooling cycles to produce metal that

---

[3] This passage is pregnant with meaning in the Greek text. The word "tribulation," "θλῖψις" (*thlipsis*), means "a pressure"; it was used for the process of extracting olive oil from olives under the weight of heavy slabs of stone and for the execution of prisoners by piling weights on their bodies, creating pressure to stop the person's ability to breathe. This is how trials seem to us many times. Holding up under this pressure brings "perseverance"—"ὑπομονή" (*hupomone*), which literally means the "spirit that overcomes." Endurance brings an overcoming heart, which leads to "δοκιμή" (*dokime*), "proven character." Proven character literally translates to "refined" character, picturing the metal in the heat, which surfaces the dross so the metal can be purified. When this process is complete, new hope is gained, and God's love is poured out on a life that has been transformed—through fire.

was 99.9999% ("six-nines") purity. Each time the metal was heated and melted, more dross came to the surface.

You and I have trials we are facing right now in life. For most of us, ministry has added greatly to the intensity and frequency of these trials. I cannot tell you how much God has used my wife's physical trials to refine our personal lives, marriage, and ministry. Has this been pleasant? Far from it. Has it been effective? The purifying effects reverberate through our lives and ministry each day. Trials and their heat provide an ideal means for God to refine character—if we will agree to cooperate with the process and let the Holy Spirit do His work. Sometimes it takes the determination of those three Hebrew children who would not bow down to circumstances, though they faced death itself (Dan. 3:13-30). Because they were willing to face the literal fires of this trial, Shadrach, Meshach, and Abednego met the Son of God Himself. That meeting took place right in the midst of the fire.

For preachers, we often call out to meet with God, especially in times of message preparation. God determines where that meeting will take place, and as in the case of the Hebrew children, it may be in the middle of the fiery furnace. Isn't it just like God to hide the key to character development in the middle of a furnace, where we would least likely look and where few would dare to go? The furnace of life is where character gets refined. And fear of the furnace is often what keeps the preacher lagging behind in character development. We handle the Word, play with the Word, memorize the Word, and even speak the Word. The Word itself is powerful and has the ability to change lives. Yet without a deep work of the Holy Spirit in our own lives, we remain unchanged ourselves. When we refuse to cooperate with Him, we do not develop an overcoming spirit. We seek instead to avoid the fire and pressure of the trial and escape from its heat before it can melt our hearts and release the dross to the surface, and as a result, our character is not refined as it should be. No new hope to share with others is birthed, and we lose hope ourselves. We miss out on the genuine love and thanksgiving born in a heart that has been transformed as it comes though the fire and lives to tell about it on the other side.

The overcoming spirit, refined character, new hope, and greater experience of love does not happen by accident or as we read the Word—it happens as we live the Word, prove it in everyday life experience, and then allow it to do its work in our hearts to change us before a word is spoken from the pulpit. Words from a life that has been through the fire are different. Words from a life that has been refined are full of an experiential faith, hope, and love that can only be gained by first living the words we preach. If we live those words out in our lives, they are no longer abstract and theoretical but experimental, tested, and proved. God's Word becomes our word as it takes upon itself flesh. We cannot help but be changed by this process, and our words cannot help but be imbibed with transformational life.

Proven Character

God is after nothing less than a changed heart for His people, and how much more for the preacher? The statistics cited earlier regarding the condition of ministers and their health reveal much about the condition of our hearts. As I have mentioned before, every action is repeated twice—once in the mind and once in the lived world. That is why God seems to care so much about the inner life of each person—the condition of our hearts. God has always worked from the inside out, because until the inside is changed, the outside doesn't matter very much. If we do the right things for the wrong reasons, they end up being so much hay burned in the fire (1 Cor. 3:11-15). When we are saved, our spirit is the first thing transformed by the Holy Spirit (John 3:3-8); the mind is then changed over the course of a life time (Rom. 12:2). Right actions follow from a right heart. This inside-outside work of the Spirit creates alignment within a person—the heart is right and the actions that flow from the heart are right, so the person is one with his or her word. This is called integrity.

In case you missed this earlier, I want to state it again: God does not use people—He partners with them. He always has our best interests in mind when we are in ministry. Preachers are not an expendable commodity to be used up and then tossed on the garbage heap while God moves on to the next "victim." God always spends time developing the preacher's character to match his or her specific assignment. As Blackaby observes, "Nothing is more pathetic than having a small character in a big assignment."[4] Underdeveloped character that does not match the assignment is the root cause of many of the statistics shared earlier. Because God always has our best interests in mind, He always has a plan to develop our character in proportion to our assignment. The larger the assignment, the more character development is needed, and the more intense the refining process will be. Those with large ministry responsibilities inevitably pay a high price in their own personal development to get to the place of effective service.

More intense character development does not mean God is angry or trying to be especially hard on us—it is exactly the opposite. When He brings discipline into our lives in the form of a character-building experience, it is actually a sign of His love and confidence in us:

> [3] For consider Him who has endured such hostility by sinners against Himself, so that you will not grow weary and lose heart. [4] You have not yet resisted to the point of shedding blood in your striving against sin; [5] and you have forgotten the exhortation which is addressed to you as sons, "MY SON, DO NOT REGARD LIGHTLY THE DISCIPLINE OF THE LORD, NOR FAINT WHEN YOU ARE REPROVED BY HIM; [6] FOR THOSE WHOM THE LORD LOVES HE DISCIPLINES, AND HE SCOURGES EVERY SON

---

[4] Blackaby (1994), 146.

WHOM HE RECEIVES." [7] It is for discipline that you endure; God deals with you as with sons; for what son is there whom *his* father does not discipline? [8] But if you are without discipline, of which all have become partakers, then you are illegitimate children and not sons. [9] Furthermore, we had earthly fathers to discipline us, and we respected them; shall we not much rather be subject to the Father of spirits, and live? [10] For they disciplined us for a short time as seemed best to them, but He *disciplines us* for *our* good, so that we may share His holiness. [11] All discipline for the moment seems not to be joyful, but sorrowful; yet to those who have been trained by it, afterwards it yields the peaceful fruit of righteousness (Heb. 12:3-11).

Some of us have very negative memories attached to the word *discipline*. We see "discipline" in this text and envision physical discipline at the hand of an angry father or mother. Our parents' words echo in our souls: "This will hurt me more than it hurts you." As children, we had trouble believing that. But Heb. 12:3-11 does not refer to this kind of discipline. The Greek word used in this passage for discipline is the root word we translate "formation."[5] This word was used in Greek society to describe the process of forming someone to be a mature and responsible citizen so he or she could take a productive place in Greek society. The word has little to do with physical discipline and much to do with the training and cultivation of the correct virtues of the heart necessary for the fulfillment of destiny or calling. The writer of Hebrews borrowed that word to describe the development of a Christian's virtues at the hand of the Lord. When God uses life circumstances to test the word in our hearts and develop our character, it is a sign of His love. Virtue, when developed adequately, will allow us to assume a strong and responsible place in ministry. Proven character and refinement of my virtues are by-products of an incarnational preaching process—I am developed as the word develops in my heart and changes my life, resulting in a refined (pure) heart and a mature word that is lived out before it is ever spoken.

Heart-shaping

I love the term *heart-shaping* because it paints the picture of an ongoing work in the heart under the guidance of God's skillful hands as He molds and

---

[5] Here, the Greek word is "παιδεία" (*paideia*), which is the word for "formation." It was a word used by the Greeks to describe the process that a citizen went through in order to become an able member of Greek society. It involved education, socialization, and any number of pursuits to adequately form the individual for the responsibilities of Greek citizenship. The writer of Hebrews borrowed this word to describe the process of spiritual and mental formation that God brings into the lives of sons and daughters to form us adequately for our spiritual journey. This is a sign of His love for us—not His displeasure.

shapes our hearts the way a master artist does. I borrow the term from Reggie McNeal, who used it to describe the deep work God does in transforming a heart to be more like His.[6] The idea of heart-shaping is pregnant with the truth of God's providence and sovereignty in our affairs—the concept assumes He knows exactly what we need for life and ministry and that He knows just how to form us so that those needs are met. God is the only one with intimate knowledge of what we need at any point in our journey. The circumstances and situations He uses to shape us at any given moment in our life's history are perfectly chosen and right on time to do the precise shaping work we need.

Because it is something done over time, heart-shaping is a layered work. Perhaps the best illustration from nature is the way a pearl is formed inside an oyster. The pearl starts as an irritant, like a piece of sand, which is sucked into the oyster when it is filtering water for food. If that piece of sand becomes lodged in the tender tissues of the oyster, it begins to secret a substance called lacre to surround the irritant in order to protect itself. Over time, multiple layers of lacre are applied, and the result is a pearl. What was once an irritant is covered by layer after layer of beauty and becomes a gem—that is exactly what God does in the character-building process in our lives. Human beings culture pearls, and God cultures the inner life, if we will cooperate with that process.

The Image of God

We were made in God's image to bear His image. It's not about us, but it's all about Him. Paul reminds us in 2 Cor. 3:17,18:

> [17] Now the Lord is the Spirit, and where the Spirit of the Lord is, *there* is liberty. [18] But we all, with unveiled face, beholding as in a mirror the glory of the Lord, are being transformed into the same image from glory to glory, just as from the Lord, the Spirit.

Notice the link between the presence of the Spirit of the Lord and the transformation of the beholder's image. The Spirit's work is not external change but change in our very essence—at the level of character. All things relate back to Him, and everything is ultimately summed up in Him (Eph. 1:7-10). At the fall, our internal image was marred by sin and has never recovered. We have stopped seeing ourselves in God's image and have begun to see ourselves in another image—we're back to the pictures hanging on the walls of our heart. Our personal picture gallery is full of self-portraits that are abstract and distorted. They don't resemble God's image—because of our wounded hearts.

Character formation is the restoration of the image of God in our hearts. It involves the formation of character that is the very nature of God—character

---

[6] Reggie McNeal, *A Work of the Heart* (San Francisco: Jossey-Bass, 2000), xiii.

that looks like Him. As He does a deep formational work in our hearts, they become like His heart. His nature is imparted, and His image is restored—we start to look like God again, to those around us and to ourselves. As Graham Tomlin observes, the purpose of God was not simply to save humanity but to create a new kind of person—one who was renewed and could bear His image, live with Him forever, and live on a renewed and transformed earth.[7]

Ultimately, character development is God's invitation to participate in the divine nature—to experience God Himself, His very nature, and to be changed so that we more closely resemble Him while alive on the earth (2 Pet. 1:4-10).[8] The process is much like what we see in the creation narrative when the Holy Spirit broods over the face of chaos and darkness to birth something beautiful and good.[9] Can you see why good works are not enough to produce change? Good works and successful ministry do not have the power to transform—only an encounter with God in life's circumstances can do that.

There are several key assets God develops in our characters as He does His work bringing us closer to His image. These assets include:

- *New Beliefs*: The maturing of the word in our hearts must refine and change what we believe about truth. This means our beliefs about what is true should be in constant flux as God progressively reveals truth to us. A change in beliefs is exceptionally hard for preachers to accept, because we like to think that we have the truth and that the truth does not change. While the truth does not change, our comprehension and understanding of the truth must change in order for us to mature. Truth has length, width, and depth. We may understand parts of a truth and understand it in a two-dimensional way, but when the Spirit helps us to mine the depth of truth, our beliefs are subject to change;
- *New Values*: Values are the deeply held beliefs and convictions that are behind "why" we do what we do. They are uniquely embedded in our identity and frame who we are. They are the core motivators that determine how we act and respond in life. They are what we hold dearest. Our internal values system must be open to change as the word matures in us and is integrated into our lives. A values change is also exceptionally difficult due to the depth of transformation required in order for us to change our values. It often takes significant fire to refine this area of our lives;

---

[7] Graham Tomlin, *Spiritual Fitness* (New York, Continuum, 2006), 81.

[8] In 2 Pet. 1:4, the invitation is quite direct—we are invited to become "partners" or "κοινωνός" (*koinonos*) with God in His divine nature. The root for partner is also the root for our word "fellowship" in the Greek text. It defines one of God's purposes in offering fellowship to the believer—to transform our nature into His nature and to share in it with us.

[9] Ibid., 75.

- *New Attitudes*: Attitudes are the "spirit" that our souls project (Eph. 4:22-24). They are the spirit with which we relate to life and experience. The power of attitude to change life and circumstances is amazing. The maturing process of the word in our hearts must have the "right" to change our heart attitudes and refine or replace them with biblical ones;
- *New Actions*: New actions are the ultimate extension of transformation. When the word grows and matures to the point that it is evident in our actions, the word has taken upon itself flesh. The people around us can see the word, hear the word, and touch it as they touch us. We become that word and live it out as a living example, and it is ready to be spoken to others.

What we hold deepest in our hearts sets the course for our lives. Let's break down the areas in the list above so that we can understand more clearly what the internal work of the Holy Spirit looks like in these areas of our lives. Beliefs are what we hold to be true. Values are the truths that we hold dearest—they are the truths that motivate us and are the reasons behind our decisions, actions, and attitudes. A belief is always at the root of a value. If the core belief is faulty, so is the value.

There are biblical values and there are non-biblical values. Non-biblical values, such as selfishness, are based on faulty beliefs like "I have to look out for number one, because no one else will." In the case of selfishness, "number one" is me—I am on the throne and in control, and if I don't help myself, no one else will (belief). What about God? The faulty belief must take a trip to the cross and to God's Word. No one can help himself or herself—we are all equally helpless due to sin, and God must help us (Rom. 3:23; 6:23; Eph. 2:8-10). The truth demands we die to ourselves and become utterly dependent on God, His provision, and His help (Gal. 2:20,21; Ps. 46:1). I either depend on God or on myself, and no one can serve two masters. For those in ministry, God gives abundant opportunities for us to replace the value of selfishness with the value of servant leadership. Selfishness as a core value dies hard—in part because we may not realize it is a core value. But each day's experience provides us another opportunity to decide to nail selfishness to the cross and to embrace service to others by placing others first.

Change in values is a deep work of the Holy Spirit that comes as we allow Him to reorder our priorities and what we treasure. Where a man's treasure is, there his heart will be (Matt. 6:21). A reordering of one's values is a redistribution of one's treasure. I surrender non-biblical priorities and values. I learn what God values and begin to embrace those things. In the process, I am transformed and become in my inner person more like Him. I begin to live a life motivated by the things He values. My "why" has changed. I begin to serve others rather than myself as I learn the value of servant leadership. I begin to place others ahead of my own personal interests as I learn the value of sacrificial love. I begin to take the narrow road and the "road less traveled" as I learn that truth is costly. Love becomes my motivator. Service becomes my guide. Overcoming becomes my game plan. Discipline becomes my hammer and chisel. I become more like God Himself as He changes my core values into what He values. My values change and become a motivation to live out the truth for others to see. God gives the word flesh in my life for people to see and touch, so they can say, "This is what He looks like."

John Maxwell once observed that attitude is more important than the facts. Attitude can stare down a circumstance and make it bend to ultimate truth. Attitudes are the way we react to life—the "spirit" in which our soul approaches things. This can be seen in the command given by Paul in Eph. 4:22-24 to the church at Ephesus:

> . . . [22] that, in reference to your former manner of life, you lay aside the old self, which is being corrupted in accordance with the lusts of deceit, [23] and that you be renewed in the spirit of your mind, [24] and, put on the new self, which in *the likeness of* God has been created in righteousness and holiness of the truth.

Paul was addressing the "spirit of your mind," which is an old phrase used to describe one's attitude. The "old self" is to be laid aside and the new self is to be "put on" like clothing. The text does not say that God will put the new self on us, but rather that we are to put it on ourselves. God dresses us with white "robes of righteousness" when we are newly born into His kingdom. We continue the process by dressing ourselves with new attitudes—new outlooks and reactions to life changes—as we mature. Struggles become opportunities to overcome. Pressure becomes the furnace of character development. Each day becomes an opportunity to advance toward God's vision for our ultimate end. Insecurity fades as we draw closer to Him and learn to trust Him. Boldness results from faith that is rewarded. Death itself becomes a mere gateway to an eternal reward and inseparable fellowship with Him. Our attitudes change as the Word of God infiltrates our life and as the word that He has conceived does its work on those attitudes. The "old self" is removed and the "new self" emerges over time for all to see.

Attitude change is what should make a Christian different in the eyes of the world, though sadly this is not always the case. The world has its words and temporal images. They "fake it 'till they make it," only to have their lives and marriages fall apart because their house was built on sand. A person cannot build his or her life on a trumped-up image and expect it to weather the storm. A Christian who cooperates with God's process for attitude adjustment stands out in the crowd. Complaint ceases as focus is directed toward what God is doing in the midst of a challenge, injustice, or opposition. Courage is displayed in situations that allow one to become an overcomer rather than a whining "victim."

Love is displayed as we love people when they least deserve it or least expect it. These attitudes are characteristic of Jesus and His walk among humanity. They also progressively characterize the life dealt with by God though His Word and as the word is conceived, grows, and matures within us.

The ultimate substance of words that transform is the change they produce in someone's life. If there is no change or transformation that eventually works its way out into reality (actions), then there may be a problem with the "soil," or there is good reason to believe that the words lacked transformational substance. A personal encounter with God should ultimately work its way out into reality, because God is the author of change—it is His nature to change others because He Himself is perfect and unchangeable (Heb. 13:8). Change begins with words but ends with actions. That is why God is not as impressed with those who hear as He is with those who do what they hear (James 1:22-24).

Once the word that was implanted in the womb of our hearts has grown to sufficient size in us, it should begin to take over. Our lives should reflect the word, and the word should be thoroughly integrated into our beliefs, values, attitudes, and actions. Can you see why we must begin with the internal and let God have His way before the external is possible? When the incarnational process has changed us and becomes integrated into our beliefs, values, attitudes, and actions, we are then ready to deliver something that is alive and viable. Can you also see why trying to change people with mere words is impossible—why words must be "Spirit and life" in order to transform (John 6:63)? Take care of the internal first, and the external will nearly take care of itself. Cultivate the key virtues in your life, and reap transformation in your sermons as the word takes on flesh in a life aligned with the words you speak.

Key Virtues for Preachers

There are certain predictable patterns for the way the Holy Spirit will deal with preachers, because certain key character virtues are essential for ministry. Virtues are character traits found in the heart of God Himself. The Holy Spirit's plan for our character development always concentrates on building key virtues, because we cannot be fruitful in ministry without them. God is also at work developing these same virtues in other people's lives, but preachers incur a stricter judgment because we speak words on behalf of God due to divine calling and appointment (James 3:1). God is not being harder on preachers—our calling simply demands more purity in certain virtues for ministry success and fruitfulness. God is interested in the "six-nines" purity I mentioned earlier, so He is constantly heating things up, instigating further refinement to produce greater purity. He does this because He loves us, not to be hard on us.

Let's examine a few of the key virtues that are central to the development of a character that can support the weight of ministry. The list is far from exhaustive—consult passages like Gal. 5:22,23 on the fruit of the Spirit or 2 Pet. 1:5-10 to see which virtues can be "added to your faith."

Humility

Ministry is a never-ending journey toward humility. Jesus' example convinces us of this fact at every point in His ministry—with every narrative recorded in the Gospels, we see humility demonstrated by Jesus through his life experience. He incarnates humility, allowing us to see it, touch it, and understand what it is like.

Humility was an experimental part of Jesus' day-by-day experience and was abundantly tested each day. The Creator of the universe was rejected by His creation (John 1:10-12). He gave up all the trappings and privileges of deity to justify humanity but was condemned for doing so (Phil. 2:5-11). He received constant harassment and abuse from hypocritical leaders and still managed to answer them in a way that put their wellbeing first. He washed the feet of His own disciples and died naked on a cross in a manner fit for the lowest of criminals, the picture of utter humility. If our Master was constantly tested in the area of humility, can we expect anything less?

Your humility will be tested daily. People and life's circumstances provide no shortage of heat for refinement. Humility is the pipeline through which all of ministry to others must flow, and if not constantly being perfected, the pipe becomes easily clogged. Humility is strongly linked in the Scriptures with the "word implanted" (James 1:19-21):

> [19] *This* you know, my beloved brethren. But everyone must be quick to hear, slow to speak *and* slow to anger; [20] for the anger of man does not achieve the righteousness of God. [21] Therefore, putting aside all filthiness and *all* that remains of wickedness, in humility receive the word implanted, which is able to save your souls.

In James 1:21, a Greek word is used for "humility" that denotes meekness, which is strength under control. It was a key Greek virtue of the time—the ability to be strong and carry authority in a manner that was under control and therefore ensured victory in battle.[10] The English word "meek" today might be said to

---

[10] The Greek word used in James 1:21 has always interested me greatly. Its root is "πραΰτης" (*prautes*) and is translated "meekness" or "humility." It is the same root used in Matt. 5:5 when Jesus says, "Blessed are the meek, for they shall inherit the earth." Meekness was a key virtue for the Greeks, who were a warrior race. Aristotle speaks much of the virtue in his writings. He tended to define virtues by placing the virtue between two extremes to define the virtue by contrast. He placed meekness as a virtue between the extremes of excessive anger and excessive angerlessness. The word also had a history of use to describe domesticated animals among the Greeks. It described an animal

carry a connotation of weakness, because our culture has an element of machismo in it, valuing a display of strength for the sake of image. This is not the way battles are won. When one is assured of the power and authority he or she carries, there is no need for proof—that will come soon enough when strength is tested.

Those with true authority and spiritual strength learn to control their anger and forego the fleshly satisfaction that comes with an outburst. Instead, in humility, we yield to a better way—the word at work in our lives. We wait in patience for God's timing and wisdom to answer the things that come against us. The Greek word for "meekness" was also used to describe a domesticated animal with instincts that were under control, because the animal was submitted to authority. The animal might be capable of death and destruction, but its strength was in submission and channeled toward the master's purpose.

Preachers have God-given authority and power. Humility is the ability to place that authority and power in the hands of the Holy Spirit in everyday life. Doing this is very difficult when church boards, people in the congregation, or people in our community bring accusations and politics our way. We face the temptation to solve problems immediately, using our own strength, wisdom, and timing; but if we succumb, we fail to exercise the virtue of strength under control. We know the secrets of men's hearts and could destroy their reputations with one well-placed word of gossip, but that would not be strength under control. We can hide the facts or manipulate them to our own advantage to make a point or to get our own way with budgets and plans for the ministry, but again, we would not be exercising strength under control. There seems to be no end to the temptations that preachers face to cast aside prudence and self-control in order to display strength and authority so we can save face or protect our image. But Jesus sets a different example. Yielding to meekness and humility in the heat of these kinds of tests moves the refining process another step forward, and we are made more pure of heart.

The admonishment to be humble found in Philippians seems to get to the heart of how humility plays itself out in everyday life:

> [3] Do nothing from selfishness or empty conceit, but with humility of mind regard one another as more important than yourselves; [4] do not *merely* look out for your own personal interests, but also for the interests of others. [5] Have this attitude in yourselves which was also in Christ Jesus, [6] who, although He existed in the form of God, did not regard equality with God a thing to be

---

that had been successfully domesticated so that all of its natural instincts were in submission and under control—strength and power under control and submission. This is a wonderful word picture for the virtue in our lives, a virtue essential for ministers. For a more detailed description, see William Barclay, "The Gospel of Matthew," *The Daily Bible Study Series* (Philadelphia: Westminster, 1975), 96-98.

grasped, [7] but emptied Himself, taking the form of a bond-servant, *and* being made in the likeness of men (Phil. 2:3-7).

Here, a different word is used in the Greek text for humility—one that means "lowliness of mind."[11] This word, used in places like 1 Pet. 5:5 and Col. 3:12 , is a Christian construct using a Greek word root, because there was no word in the Greek language for this special kind of humility. The Greeks did not consider lowliness of mind to be a virtue but rather a display of weakness. The virtue of humility, as described by this constructed word, requires self-forgetfulness in order to serve the welfare of others and to seek their good, even above our own. In this passage, the Son of God Himself is our example—He who forgot His own welfare as He sat at the right hand of the Father in heaven and agreed to come to earth, leaving all the wonderful and deserved trappings of deity behind to rescue us. Lowliness of mind as described here by Jesus' example is literally the key to survival in ministry, and each day there will be multiple opportunities for this virtue to be tested in the preacher's life so that the word can become flesh.

Humility is the preacher's internal GPS—it keeps us on track and headed in the right direction. It is impossible, while placing others ahead of oneself, to divorce one's spouse, neglect one's children, or engage in sexual promiscuity. It is also impossible to survive the weekly grind of message preparation, counseling, weddings, and funerals without putting others first. Further, there are death traps in the ministry environment for which lowliness of mind is the only safeguard. Many of these traps involve the "pride of the praise of men," as Roger Barrier describes it. Below are some of the pride traps that daily test the preacher's heart:[12]

- A secret fondness of being noticed;
- A love of supremacy;
- An inclination to draw attention to myself, particularly in conversation;
- A desire to be first, prominent, and to have my name at the top of the list;
- An enjoyment of flattery;
- A forwardness in publicly displaying my talents and attainments;

---

[11] The Greek word is "ταπεινοφροσύνη" (*tapenophrosune*) , which is the most commonly translated word for "humility" in the New Testament. The root is a Greek word that means "abjectness, meanness, or baseness." Christians borrowed the root to construct a word that represents humility in the form of lowliness of mind as it relates to serving others. It is the opposite of pride and vainglory. It indicates a certain modesty but also the ability to forget oneself for the welfare of others. For more information, see Charles R. Eerdman, "The Epistle to the Philippians," *Commentaries on the New Testament Books* (Philadelphia: Westminster, 1977), 79-80.

[12] Roger Barrier, *The Sound of God's Voice* (Grand Rapids: Baker, 1998), 121-125.

- A hidden tendency to compliment myself instead of giving glory to God;
- A fear of launching out for God because of what people might say.

The attitudes and actions listed above are rooted in pride, which is the opposite of humility. Humility keeps us headed in the right direction. It is no wonder that pride has as its middle letter "I." Barrier's list reflects more subtle forms of pride and, in doing so, illustrates some of the things we as preachers face on a daily basis, revealing the extent of character development (or the lack thereof) in our hearts. I have been guilty of all these attitudes and behaviors in a single church board meeting. Grappling with the attitudes and actions listed above presents an opportunity for the Holy Spirit to conduct a long-term refining process in our lives and to mature the word in our hearts. As Tomlin observes:

> Michelangelo is reported to have said that he would choose a block of stone that felt as if it had the final statue hidden inside. His job was to reveal the beauty inside the rough stone, to chip away at it until, for example, the human form we see in his famous statue David was revealed. His chisel and hammer were merely the tools he used to bring out this perfect form. As James describes it, it is as if "trials of many kinds" are the tools God uses to form in us the qualities needed to display his glory to the world. . . . It is hard to escape the conclusion that God does his work in us apart from the experience of suffering and pain. . . . God uses the experience of suffering to build virtue in us.[13]

Our image before the world does not sustain the weight of ministry. Each day brings new opportunities for us to allow God to chisel away at our hearts. We choose to cooperate as we exercise humility. A preacher who fails to practice humility is saying no to the hammer and chisel in God's hands to his or her own detriment. There is no substitute for character development in the life of the preacher, and humility is most important.

A Forgiving Attitude

Forgiveness is not a virtue in itself, but it is an action based on several key virtues that have been refined and worked into the heart. Forgiveness is absolutely essential to ministry survival. Preachers must master the ability not only to forgive but also to walk in forgiveness as a lifestyle.

The ability to forgive tests the content of our character, its purity, and its state of development. To forgive is to act like God, and to refuse to forgive is one of the quickest ways to shut down intimacy with God. Unless there has been significant, Spirit-led character development in a preacher's life, he or she will

---

[13] Tomlin, 124-125.

find it impossible to forgive to the depth and degree required in ministry. Unforgiveness is one of the most prominent problems in preachers' lives, acting as a spiritual contraceptive for the conception, growth, and maturity of the word in the preacher's heart. Just as gluttony and greed are spiritual problems that have taken upon themselves flesh, so unforgiveness is simply the expression of inner problems in our character.

In order to forgive, we must practice the virtues of love, patience, kindness, and self-control. In many ways, forgiveness is the perfect test of these key virtues and an X-ray of the condition of our character. God's actions show us who He is on the inside—forgiveness arises from His very nature. Similarly, our actions reveal the degree of refinement within our nature. Forgiveness is the evidence of how God in His wisdom works all things together for good. Because of the fall of humanity, God has the opportunity to use our sin to show the world what forgiveness looks like and to give us a glimpse into the inner workings of His heart.

Our entire relationship with God is contingent on forgiveness. God can be found with a plan for forgiveness as early as the dialogue that occurred in the garden right after the fall (Gen. 3:15,16). God's plan to forgive was conceived in His heart before the world was created (Eph. 1:3-10). His heart of forgiveness compelled Him to place into effect a temporary way to forgive humanity's sin, covering that sin with the life in the blood of animals until more perfect blood was available.[14] He completely removed sin as a barrier through forgiveness based on the blood of His Son.[15] Forgiveness is an essential part of who God is. When we fail to forgive, it brings our parentage into question, because our Father is forgiveness and acts according to His nature.

I do not believe I ever had the opportunity to fully test the virtues associated with forgiveness until I stepped into my calling in ministry. Each of us has mul-

---

[14] Through the Old Testament, God instituted a way to cover humanity's sins until a more perfect way came in the form of His Son. The Old Testament word "כָּפַר" (kaphar) is the root for words that we translate that have to do with "atonement." Atonement is from an old English word that is a contraction of "at-one-ment." The word means "to cover over, pacify, or make propitiation." The sacrifice of animals was given because the wages of sin is death (Rom. 6:23) and that is the price of sin if justice is to be fulfilled. Lev. 17:11 says that the "life of the flesh is in the blood," and it is the life of animals that was shed through their blood that temporarily satisfied the price of death that sin demands. Because it was only the blood of an animal, the blood was only powerful enough to cover the sins rather than wash them away. The blood of Jesus Christ was more powerful because of the life that was in His blood, and it did not just cover but was the perfect life to pay the price for all death from all sin for all time (Heb. 10:4-19).

[15] In the New Testament, different language is used in relation to forgiveness. No longer is sin covered, but rather we are redeemed, "ἀπολύτρωσις" (apolutrosis—to obtain release by ransom), and justified "δικαιόω" (dikaioo—declared to be righteous), just as if we had never sinned.

tiple opportunities to forgive people in the course of everyday life, but the circumstances, nature, and discharge of ministry seem to exponentially increase the frequency and intensity of the need to forgive. Forgiveness is, first and foremost, a test of the quality of our love, because God is love. When God forgives, He simply acts out of His loving nature. When we forgive, the quality of His nature in us is being tested and refined. Perhaps forgiveness is so difficult because by its very nature it assumes that we have been genuinely wronged by someone and would have the right to take offense. Forgiveness is an act of mercy and love. I choose to forgo what is just and right for me and to release people from the debt they justifiably owe to me for wrong:

> [12] 'And forgive us our debts, as we also have forgiven our debtors. [13] 'And do not lead us into temptation, but deliver us from evil. *For Yours is the kingdom and the power and the glory forever. Amen.*' [14] "For if you forgive others for their transgressions, your heavenly Father will also forgive you. [15] "But if you do not forgive others, then your Father will not forgive your transgressions (Matt. 6:12-15). [16]

You will be wronged in the discharge of your ministry. You will be deeply hurt by wrongs done to you, because you love the people who have wronged you. The pain will burn in your soul and can affect your body with sleeplessness, lack of appetite, and physical exhaustion. Your mind will be vexed with the inability to concentrate and the temptation to dwell on the event and replay it over and over again. The people you count on the most and relate to most deeply will betray your trust and seek your harm. These are not the words of a paranoid person but the words of a seasoned preacher warning you of the realities of ministry. Jesus experienced these things long before you and me. He was betrayed by one of His closest friends and deserted by the rest. Jesus' anguish can be seen prophetically echoed in the Psalms as we see the pain of His betrayal by a close companion and friend with whom He shared sweet fellowship (Ps. 55:12-14). Betrayal and disappointment by others happened to Jesus on a daily basis, and it will happen (or is happening) to us on a daily basis.

The ability to walk in forgiveness requires a relentless, daily commitment to character development. In this commitment is where transformational sermons are born. Nowhere are the travails of the gestation process more apparent than when the Holy Spirit uses people's failures to turn up the heat and melt our

---

[16] Here in this text, the Greek root word "ἀφίημι" (*aphiemi*) is used for "forgive." It implies a release from a debt that is legally owed. The word is translated "release, leave alone, or send away." That is what God does when He forgives—He chooses to release us from a sin debt that we legally owe and send it away. This is so fundamental to the nature of God that it is unimaginable one would call him- or herself a Christian and not act in a like manner.

hearts in order to do His refining work. Put simply, I know of no greater opportunity for personal growth than the choice to walk in forgiveness—that choice is an ever present opportunity to mature the word in our hearts.

Perseverance

I have never experienced any endeavor that approaches ministry in either its demands or its rewards. I have also never experienced more opportunities to give up than I have in ministry. The difficult statistics cited earlier about ministers' health make my point by indicating the numbers of people who leave ministry each year. The casualty rates are enormous because the price to minister is so costly. The only way to remain in ministry and to finish well is to allow the Holy Spirit to gradually develop our ability to persevere.

The ability to persevere is a virtue because, as with all virtues, it defines who God is. We see who God is by what He does. God does not give up—He perseveres. When we learn to persevere, we are acting like Him. Ministry gives us no shortage of opportunities to act like Him by persevering. The key to building perseverance into one's character is in seizing each small opportunity that presents itself rather than waiting for big opportunities. When an athlete prepares for a long distance race, he or she does not run long distance on the first day of training. That runner starts with short distances to build endurance and strength. The long run is actually just a series of short runs strung together. The way to persevere through large trials is to build up your endurance with the small ones first.

Like forgiveness, the act of persevering is contingent upon the development of several other key virtues that are cited in Gal. 5:22-23 and 2 Pet. 1:5-10. Perseverance requires the application of diligence. It requires us to apply knowledge and wisdom as we work perseverance out in our lives. It also requires us to be faithful by not yielding to temptations to give up. Perseverance is an expression of godliness—an act of piety. As mentioned before in connection with James 1:2-8 and Rom. 5:3-5, trials give us the perfect opportunity to develop an overcoming spirit, which is the heart of the Greek word used in the text for perseverance. Talk is cheap when it comes to overcoming—we meet many would-be overcomers in ministry settings until there is something to overcome.

Training and sports word pictures are wonderful tools for describing perseverance. Paul exhorts Timothy, new to ministry responsibility in Ephesus, to "discipline" himself "for the purpose of godliness" (1 Tim. 4:7). The Greek root for "discipline" in this text is where we get the word "gymnasium" from in English.[17] The Greeks highly prized physical discipline, and Paul uses that value to show the greater importance of a value for spiritual discipline. The athlete who

---

[17] The Greek word for "discipline" here in the text is "γυμνασία" (*gumnasia*), from which come our words "gymnasium" and "gymnastics."

wins the prize is the one who trains hard and endures (1 Cor. 9:24-27). The athlete who continually buffets his or her body to condition it wins. It is impossible to win any race unless you finish, and it is impossible to finish without faithfulness and perseverance. The same is true for ministry. Athletes persevere for a perishable trophy or for a medal that will end up collecting dust in a drawer. Preachers persevere for the sake of eternal souls in desperate need of a word from God.

When you think of not persevering, think of the cost. If you are called, then God equips. He will not allow you to be tempted beyond your limits and will supply the way of escape if you keep in touch with Him and listen (1 Cor. 10:13). Remember Psalm 139 and the detail with which God knows your life. Remember Isaiah 46—God is the Master Architect. The circumstances in which you find yourself are accounted for in His plan for your development. Think about the sermons that are yet to be preached. Imagine the countless people awaiting answers from heaven. Think about the marriages that will be saved because you persevered and the impact your sermons will have on future generations. The cost of not persevering is immeasurable. Souls hang in the balance, preacher. Will you allow God to develop perseverance and the character necessary for you to overcome to preach another day?

Maturing the Word

The maturing of the word in our hearts is inseparable from the development of our character. The maturing process is where words are given flesh—the place where idea becomes transformational action. At conception, the word is still not viable in the real world outside the womb of the heart. The real development of the word only takes place after we have lived with it for a while and allowed it to change our very character and being. When the word has the opportunity to change our core beliefs, values, attitudes, and actions, we have something of substance to give away to others. It is at this point we truly have something to say. Before this point, all we have is words. But when we reach the point of inner transformation by the word, we have words that transform.

Pregnancy can seem to drag on and on. Expectant mothers pay the price for carrying children to full term. Yet when the baby is finally born, the memories of the pain and hardship seem strangely distant. That's the way it is with preaching. There is a price to be paid for carrying a word to full term, but there is nothing like giving birth to a transformational word. Conception has occurred. The baby has grown and matured. Now let's move on to delivery.

Chapter 6
Sermon-shaping: Birthing Sermons That Transform

As I reflect back on my life, the three most transformational events were my salvation, my marriage, and—if you count this series of four as one event—the births of my children. Each significant event involves an encounter with a person that changed my life in an irrevocable way. Watching my children's births was indescribable. Children are God's gift to us—if we are remembered for nothing else, they go on as our legacy into the future where we cannot go ourselves. We see them born; we nurture and raise them as best we can; and then we shoot them like arrows into the future, trusting God that their paths will be straight and true to His mark (Ps. 127:3-5). Sermons happen exactly the same way. We give birth to them, launch them, and trust God that they will hit the mark He intends.

The birth of my first child was one of the most amazing adventures of my lifetime. My wife and I had been married for about three years, and we sensed it was time to start our family. The day we found out she was pregnant with our firstborn is a day etched in my mind. Something alive was growing in her womb—a perfect blend of my wife and me and the fruit of our love. That there was a new life growing inside her was almost too much to comprehend, but all too soon it became very obvious. First, there was the morning sickness, which lasted about three months. Then there came the first flutters of life as she felt the baby quickening in her belly. Our excitement grew as we began to announce to our parents and friends that we were expecting our firstborn.

The next months were a blur of preparations as the baby grew. We got the nursery ready, had the baby shower, went to child-birthing classes, and watched my wife's stomach grow to an unimaginable size. Though she only gained about twenty pounds, it was amazing to see the baby grow so much you could see it moving and kicking around. Forget watching television—a wrestling match was occurring in her stomach each night! You could poke at her belly, and it seemed like the baby would poke right back. Soft music seemed to calm the baby down, and lively music made it dance. As we approached the nine-month mark, the baby grew to the point where my wife's womb could no longer contain it. First came the false labor, then the back pain, and finally, one day, those words that can stop a grown man in his tracks—"Honey, I think the baby is coming—let's get to the hospital!" There would be no argument from me. As we started off to the hospital that March day in 1981, I knew my life was about to change forever.

Actually, my life had already begun to change over the previous nine months as my wife carried the child. Finding out you are a father initiates a crash course in maturity. I had less time to think about me. I had to get my finances in order and make our home ready for a new resident. Then there was the concern for a baby I had not even seen yet—would the baby be healthy? Would everything be the way it should be at delivery? Would my precious wife be healthy through childbirth? We realized on our way to the hospital that all those questions would shortly be answered. The contractions grew stronger on the way. This baby was coming and nothing was going to stop it now. Once we got to the hospital, it was only few hours until they ushered my wife and I into the birthing suite.

First, the head—the baby had brown hair like Mom. Then those unmistakable eyes—big, round, and brown just like those eyes I saw peeking out from under that wedding veil a few years earlier on our wedding day. That body— kind of long, boney, and skinny—definitely like Dad. Then the moment we had been waiting for—it was a boy, Stephen, our firstborn son, which became obvious as he slipped out like a little fish. The nurses cut the cord, and a new life was launched into the world. My son's delivery and those moments almost three decades ago still bring tears to my eyes when I remember them. Some events change your life forever, and I knew this was one of them.

We have looked at the conception of the word in the womb of the preacher's heart. The conception of the word is a time of joy and wonder as the Holy Spirit conceives truth in the womb of our hearts by illuminating His word. Life experience and God's creation act as catalysts for the word's growth as the Holy Spirit develops the preacher's understanding of the word's meaning. The word matures in our hearts as we apply it to our own beliefs, values, attitudes, and actions, developing our character and preparing our life to support giving the word away to others. The womb of our heart expands and contracts with each belief, value, and attitude changed and with the new actions that follow. As we approach full term and are ready to deliver the word, there is that same sense of disquieting wonder one feels at the birth of a child. Will I come through this in one piece after I preach? Will the sermon survive delivery? Will it be a boy or a girl—what will the sermon's shape be? Will the delivery be quick and easy or painful and long? These questions will be answered at delivery. Ah, the wonder of giving birth to a child and the wonder of delivering a sermon—it is delightful agony.

Like the delivery of any child, the delivery of a sermon is both a science and an art. There is the scientific part—the part you can define, predict, and document and with a logical, linear flow the way knowledge is neatly ordered. There is also an art to sermon delivery that defies prediction and that no one can tell you how to do—the delivery is an expression of your uniqueness as a person. This book has so far addressed the internal aspects of the sermon, aspects we don't see treated as often in preaching literature. Now we will address the external dimensions of the sermon and its delivery, subjects for which there is abundant literature. I will approach the delivery of the word from the standpoint of its essence as science and art.

The Sermon as Science

Most women preparing for delivery are glad to be attended by someone with the experience and the credentials to guide them through the birthing process. Childbirth is a natural thing—a woman's body is designed to deliver a child—and in most cases, a woman's body will do the work automatically without a problem. But life is not always like that, and unexpected things occur. That's when it pays to have some knowledge and wisdom at hand. The same is true of sermons and preaching—we need help. Men and women who are called to ministry often have a God-given ability to communicate. For most of us, that raw ability is developed throughout our lives, and it is a natural expression of the way God created us. The mistake that many preachers make is in failing to build upon their natural abilities and giftedness with a solid deliberate understanding of preaching and how to communicate effectively—the science of preaching. Sadly, it has been my experience in teaching homiletics classes that the most naturally gifted communicators are least likely to believe they need to know the basics of sermon preparation and basic communication. They could benefit from a Speech 101 class but are often resistant to the formal study of the science behind the preaching.

The Sermon's Shape

One of the most common mistakes made in sermon preparation is failing to discern the proper sermon shape that is appropriate for the listeners. Shaping a sermon is science because a sermon's shape is definable and the presence or absence of a defined shape is tangible for those listening. Like any pregnancy, the development of a sermon can go well and its internal effect on the preacher can be a highly transformational experience, but the delivery is all important. When things go well with a child's delivery, the result is a new life that is kicking, screaming, and full of life. If the delivery goes poorly, then the child is found struggling for its very life, and so it is with the sermon. Each sermon must have deliberate shape in order to be effective for the specific audience it is meant to reach. The sermon's shape, and its mode of delivery, which we will get to later, entails a science that can be known and manipulated for greatest effect by the preacher. Let's begin by discussing how to properly shape a transformational sermon

There are six parts that define the shape of any transformational sermon. In describing them, I am going to access the power of metaphor by painting a word picture for each part in order to build a bridge between something abstract (form aspect) and our everyday experience. I will use the human body as a metaphor for describing what factors go into shaping a transformational sermon. The six distinct parts include:

- The Eye (Focus): Each sermon should have a defined focus that can be described in one sentence or less;
- The Skeleton (Structure): Each sermon should have an intentional structure that holds its parts together and gives the sermon support;
- The Heart (Emotion): Each sermon should express the emotion that the Holy Spirit feels about the content at its audience;
- The Joints (Transition): Each sermon should make use of deliberately chosen rhetorical devices during transitions between the themes in the sermon so the listeners are not lost;
- The Flesh (Illustration): Each sermon should include abundant illustrations from life, nature, and personal testimony as bridges between abstract truth and life experience;
- The Muscle (Application): Each sermon should have strong and obvious application to the lives of the hearers, driving them toward clearly articulated action.

Let's consider all the parts generally and then we will spend time on each one. First, eyesight is essential to any child—the human brain reserves up to eighty percent of its processing power for the purpose of bringing our world into focus. Proper sight and focus is no less important for a sermon. Like a child who cannot see, a sermon with little or no sight and focus faces challenges from the start. Bones give a child the ability to move and explore the world. This is also true for sermons; a sermon can't move properly toward God's transformational destination without strong healthy bones. We are made in God's image and share His capacity for emotions—is it strange to think that a God-given message must also be delivered with both correct words and precise, God-given emotion to accomplish His purpose? What about the joints, flesh, and muscle? These aspects of form are what make us human, and they are what make a sermon live and breathe as well. Let's examine the shape of the sermon with these attributes in mind.

The Eye

Blurry eyesight can make life miserable or even dangerous. Clear eyesight is essential for our ability to function unhindered in life. The eye is the gateway for the visual information our brains use to construct our perception of reality. The sermon too needs a clear eye in order to be effective in its mission. Every sermon must have clear, sharp focus to accomplish God's purpose. Which one of us wants to settle for anything less than clear and crisp sight? Unfortunately, that level of crispness and clarity is often lacking in sermons.

After weeks, months, or even years of living with a word, when the moment of delivery comes, the preacher must discern God's specific direction for the sermon. By specific, I contend that unless you can describe to someone in one sentence or less what you are attempting to communicate through the sermon, you are not yet ready to preach it. Focus is often achieved through wrestling with God, which can be quite painful—ask Jacob. Finding God's specific theme and purpose for a sermon is akin to the labor pains experienced by a woman giving birth. The preacher might spend countless hours in prayer, meditation, and study on the topic. He or she may have dozens or even hundreds of Scripture references, illustrations, word studies, and testimonies associated with the topic, accumulated over months or even years. But before the moment of delivery, it is essential that the preacher be able to see God's precise direction for the sermon clearly with as much focus as possible.

Jesus illustrated the importance of precise focus and the source of that focus when He said that He literally did nothing on His own initiative but spoke words at the Father's direction (John 8:28). Jesus was insistent that He only spoke what the Father specifically moved Him to say at any given moment for any specific setting and group of people (John 12:49). Discerning precise focus is a process that flows easily at times and at others seems nearly impossible, but this discernment is always one of the most important tasks of preaching. After accumulating mountains of resources during preparation, we must ask, what exactly does God want to say to the people through our sermon?

The Scriptures themselves must be the central focusing agent of the material, or the sermon begins to lose its transformational power. If our own ideas, rather than the Scriptures, become central, then the sermon becomes a lecture. If visual aids, technology, or testimonies become the central sources of focus, then the sermon becomes entertainment. Any extreme can distort the focus or clarity of the word as it is delivered, causing potential damage to God's purpose for the sermon.

If the central focusing agent of our sermon material is Scripture, then the focus of Scripture is the person of Jesus Christ. The Scriptures are very clear that Jesus Christ is the sole focus of history and time—quite simply, He is the reason for all, and everything only makes sense as it relates to Him (Eph. 1:10). Thus, any sermon must ultimately have as its focus the person of Jesus Christ. The Scriptures are important, as Jesus said when correcting the Jewish leaders, in that the Scriptures themselves exist to bear witness to Him (John 5:39). The Scriptures were written to point to Jesus. If we exalt the Scriptures without giving the person of Christ His proper place, then the eye of our sermon becomes blurred. That is why sermons designed to "proof text" a particular doctrine quickly lose their transformational power. When the Scriptures are the central focusing agent and allowed to direct us to the person of Christ, the sermon is aligned with God's purpose.

For example, expository sermons that focus on the meaning of the Scriptures themselves are most powerful when they lead to further illumination of the person of Christ rather than, as stated above, to the proof of a certain belief or doctrine. Topical sermons are most powerful if they focus on the place of that topic in the Scriptures and its relation to the person of Christ rather than slipping into a simple exposition on the topic. Narrative sermons that tell us a story must ultimately lead us to the Word and to Christ. When the Scriptures are used to illuminate the person of Jesus Christ, the sermon's eye is clear and wide open, giving the sermon proper focus and the opportunity to be transformational for the listeners.

Along with the Scriptures and the person of Christ, the cross of Christ must also be used to shape the sermon's focus. Our redemption and justification are central to God's plan. The Scriptures chronicle the Father's progressive revelation of the Son and His plan to buy back humanity from sin. When the Scriptures, the person of Christ, and God's redemptive plan are given proper place, God's specific purpose for a specific sermon comes into better focus.

Structured focus does not mean that there is no element of surprise in the sermon's delivery. Just like the delivery of a child, though there is planning and precision at work, the event is still full of surprises. There are times when the preacher will be called upon to draw from his or her reservoir of preaching experience for an extemporaneous moment. Extemporaneous preaching was at the heart of the Renewal Movement that we discussed in an earlier chapter. The roots of the Renewal Movement lie in revival meetings and famous preaching at places like Cain Ridge, Kentucky (1800), and Azusa Street (1906).[1] The preaching at these events was often extemporaneous, with little structure or preparation prior to the message. In fact, an extemporaneous preaching mode became associated with "the anointing" and God's transformational power, and this mode is

---

[1] For a detailed glimpse at the history of the Renewal Movement and its Holiness, Pentecostal, and Charismatic streams, see Vinson Synan, *The Century of the Holy Spirit* (Nashville: Thomas Nelson, 2001) and Harvey Cox, *Fire From Heaven* (Reading: Addison-Wesley, 1995).

certainly valid. But it is not the only preaching mode that brings transformation. In fact, it is not the mode of the preaching but the mode working with content and the Holy Spirit's direction that releases transformational power.

Considering the roots of the Renewal Movement a bit further, I will say here that it is easy for preachers in that tradition to associate extemporaneous preaching and a lack of preparation with the anointing (the Holy Spirit's transformational power) and deeper spirituality. This could not be further from the truth. Creation speaks of a highly ordered God. The human body and its design are such that if one system is out of order, then the whole system is thrown off-kilter. Sunrise, the tides, and the position of the stars are so precise we can set our clocks by them. It seems that the rule in God's world is order, and order is a part of His nature, expressed in creation when He brought order to formless chaos.

Unfortunately "formless" and "chaos" could describe some sermons based on the assumption that a lack of preparation and focus is more spiritual. When there is a lack of preparation, the preacher often spins his or her wheels to gain traction for a portion of the sermon until he or she finds what works. In the meantime, the audience gets covered in mud from the spinning wheels and cannot relate to what has been said. Focus is nonnegotiable. If God knows all things, then He knows what He wants to say through your mouth as you partner with Him in the incarnational process of preaching. The key is for you to allow God to open your eyes so He can help you craft a well-defined focus to shape the word for delivery.

The Skeleton

If we assume that God has something focused to say through our preaching, then it is also safe to assume that He has details in mind for the sermon's structure. Remember, His thoughts toward us outnumber the sands of the sea and He is moving us toward our destiny each day as the Master Architect (Psalm 139; Isa. 46:9,10). These two assumptions radically change the way we approach sermons—in thinking this way, we join God in what He is already doing and saying rather than construct something that we later ask Him to bless. When my words align with God's Word, there is transformation. A strong skeleton for the sermon is essential for this alignment.

We construct the skeleton of the sermon by discerning first, as we have learned, what God wants to say about the focus of the sermon. The skeleton is what supports the sermon, including the eye (focus). Much like the bone around the eyeball protects the eye from damage, a solid plan for the skeleton or structure of the sermon guards the sermon's focus. The adult human body has about three hundred fifty bones, and they are literally what keep us standing. Without their rigidity, we would be a pile of mush on the ground, forced to move like an amoeba from place to place. The skeleton of the sermon also lets the sermon move—without it, the sermon is mush.

The sermon is moving toward God's purpose. In *Homiletic*, David Buttrick discusses a sermon's "moves."[2] As Buttrick points out, all language has movement—it takes us from one place to another in our minds. Movement has to do with the nature of language itself—the logic behind the words moves the words in a direction toward a specific point or destination and brings the listener along. In this way, the spoken word moves a listener to a specifically intended meaning or conclusion—that is, if those words are constructed precisely and deliberately. If not so constructed, words often leave the listener confused. This is true in conversation just as it is in preaching.

Words generally move toward meaning in a linear direction—the rules of grammar and syntax are constructed that way. A sermon moves from one point to another, and this movement is accomplished through our spoken words. The sermon is actually a series of "moves" that make a point and allow the listeners to travel with the preacher in a specific direction toward a planned destination.[3] Ideally, that direction is God's direction, discerned through intimacy and wrestling with God.

I mention wrestling once again because the sermon's skeleton—the different subtopics or moves—is something that does not come clear easily. Wrestling with the specific points the sermon is designed to make can take an extraordinary amount of patience and time. Sometimes the specific points are not apparent until the sermon is about to be preached. When specific logic or direction for the sermon's skeleton does not flow, I plan according to my limited illumination, but as I preach, I remain open to the Holy Spirit for further instruction or guidance. Because of my openness to the Spirit's leading while preaching, I may find one sermon actually turns into a sermon series as I discern which moves are appropriate or even possible to deliver on a certain day. God knows what he wants to say (focus) and what He wants to say about what He wants to say (skeleton) on any given day for any specific sermon. The adventure begins when I try to understand His heart on this matter.

There are certain logistical considerations that determine the nature of a sermon's skeleton. One of the most important factors is speed. My most common error as a young preacher was to try to cram too much content into a sermon. My method was to talk quickly because that was the only way to cram all the content into my sermon. I did that until one of my "victims" kindly gave me some valuable feedback: "Great sermon, Pastor, but you wore me out!" The average auctioneer speaks at a rate 250 words per minute, and we perceive that to be fast. A speed of 200 words per minute is on the edge of many people's comprehension. Books on tape are generally recorded at 150 to 160 words per

---

[2] Buttrick, 23-24.
[3] Ibid.

minute. These statistics give preachers some idea of the limits of speed and human comprehension. The average sermon lasts thirty minutes. The preacher therefore has only 4,500 to 6,000 words through which to make his or her point. If we rush, we risk leaving some or most of our listeners behind. If listeners are left behind, then many times it is the preacher's fault, not the people's lack of attention or the absence of the Holy Spirit's anointing. In light of these statistics, preachers need to slow down, enunciate our words, and plan for impact.

Buttrick reminds us that we are forming ideas in the collective consciousness of the people who are listening to our sermons.[4] He advocates allowing for at least five minutes per move (subpoint or idea packet) and for no more than five or six moves in any twenty-minute period.[5] My experience tells me to double the amount of time allotted per move. I usually allow ten minutes for each subpoint and hang my sermon outline on these ten-minute idea packets—they become the skeleton. Ten minutes usually seems adequate for me to move in and out of a subpoint or idea packet. Here is generally what I do:

- Transition from the last point (the "joint" we will talk about next);
- Introduce the new subpoint or idea packet;
- Center the idea on Scripture by quoting or reading a passage;
- Give the idea "flesh" with an illustration, word picture, or personal experience;
- Apply (or move toward application) the point in the context of life experience;
- Transition out of the point and move toward the next.

The way I approach my preaching depends on the listeners, the sermon's focus, and many other factors, but I simply cannot do all the things in the list above for each move in less than about ten minutes. God bless you if you can!

Ten minutes for each move would allow for three specific points to be made in any thirty-minute period, hence the classic "three-point sermon." The average attention span of an adult in the West today ranges from five to seven minutes and is even less for young people. After five to seven minutes, the listener's mind begins to take a break from input and wander, because it grows weary. Movies are comprised of scenes and television shows inject commercials partly according to our attention span—viewers have been conditioned to receive information and learn in five-to-seven-minute time packets. Attention span varies greatly by culture and location. In my experience with preaching in India, I found audiences expecting a one- to two-hour sermon, which would have emptied my church back home. Attention span is conditioned and learned. The skeleton of my sermon is what keeps the sermon moving, but that sermon only has

---

[4] Ibid., 27.
[5] Ibid., 24.

so much time to make the trip. As is true of the focus of a sermon, a lack of structure is not a mark of spirituality or anointing. Barring a miracle, a sermon without structure cannot connect with an audience.

Before I leave this section, I must also make the point that the shape of the sermon is not about the preacher's preferences or tastes but about the audience and what best reaches them. I am serving others with the word, and I must learn to speak in their language rather than package the sermon some other way and risk their being unable to relate.

The Heart

Our human capacity for emotion is another vivid example of how humanity is made in the image of God. God has emotions—He gets angry, jealous, and grieved. God's emotions are expressed throughout the Scriptures, and they help to define His personality for us. We know the Holy Spirit is a person, not only because He can teach (John 14:26) and speak (John 16:13,14), but also because He can be grieved (Eph. 4:30).[6] God gave human beings the same capacity for emotions.

The body's design testifies to the power and importance of emotions. Most sensory input is routed directly to the brain's limbic system, which is the seat of our emotions. From there, raw sensory input is filtered and sent to the appropriate part of the brain to be processed. The processing of that information will determine the correct response. For example, the "fight-or-flight" response system may be engaged as we decide whether to avoid or confront danger, or the higher thought regions of the brain may kick in for logical, evaluative thought and processing.[7] Emotions are what make us human and give life its flavor—life would be so bland without them. Likewise, emotions are what give the sermon its flavor—a sermon without them is a sermon without a beating heart.

A sermon's emotional content is often a make-or-break issue for its success in connecting with hearers. A God-given word that has matured in the preacher's heart can be greatly damaged at delivery if that word either presents the wrong emotion or is conveyed by the preacher with the wrong emotion. The sermon's emotion should convey the heart of God and how He feels about a word that is being delivered. It is the job of every preacher to discern not only

---

[6] In Eph. 4:30, the word "λυπέω" (*lupeo*) is used for "grieve." It means "to make one feel sorry" and shows that the Spirit is a person.

[7] For a detailed description of the limbic system and other parts of the brain in layman's terms, see Robert M. Sapolsky, *Why Zebras Don't Get Ulcers* (New York: Henry Holt, 2004). The book is a valuable resource for understanding stress and its effects, an understanding that is so important for the minister and his or her family's well-being and personal health.

what God wants to say but also how He feels about what he wants to say, and then to convey that emotion properly.

If you think about it, emotion is the heart of human communication—we attach emotions to the words we speak, and those emotions determine meaning. The words we speak have their own meaning, but how we say them and the emotion attached to them flavor and shade their meaning in an essential way. Sometimes the emotions attached to words actually contain more information than the words themselves. The phrase "you are so pretty" can be said with so many different emotions. The phrase can express the emotion of want and desire. Those same words can also express sarcasm that cuts to the bone. All is determined by the way the person says those words to impart a particular emotion to spoken words. Some of the tools we can use to shape the emotions conveyed by our words include:

- Volume: the power-setting of the voice from soft to loud;
- Tone: the texture of the voice (i.e., full and bold or modest and shy);
- Speed: the rate at which we speak (i.e., slow and deliberate or rapid and excited);
- Quality: the "flavor" of our voice (i.e., low and raspy or shrill and exaggerated);
- Cadence: the rhythm and flow of our voice (i.e., starting, stopping, or using meter);
- Pause: the absence of our voice, used to make a point or to make the listener pause;
- Manner of Speech: the tone of our expression (i.e., humorous or tender).

I do not have enough space to enumerate all the nuances we build into our words. Emotion, when infused skillfully into a sermon, is one of the most unique aspects of incarnational preaching. Emotion is at the heart of transformation as well. There is a time to lecture and a time to preach. Some sermons are given with great sadness and weeping and others delivered boldly with the sting of God's rebuke. Think of a sermon on the topic of forgiveness. That sermon could be preached with weeping and pleading, following Jeremiah the prophet, or with fire and rebuke in the manner of the prophet Ezekiel. Jesus was a master at harnessing the emotion of God in His teaching and preaching. It is apparent that He knew not only what the Father wanted Him to say but with what emotion the Father wanted it said—His words conveyed the very heart of His Father to the listeners.

The need to discern God's emotional heart for any sermon tests the preacher's emotional intelligence—his or her emotional IQ. It takes some time and experience to discern what emotion is appropriate for a particular sermon and a particular group on a unique occasion. In rhetorical speech, the speaker's emotional posture is known as the *persona* of the speaker, hearkening back to Greek and Roman plays, in which the persona was the mask that the actor wore to express a particular emotion.[8] The correct emotion helps preachers embody the spirit of the text and the truth we are preaching, and emotion allows us to add the right spice to flavor the sermon for the specific occasion.

The human body itself is instrumental in conveying emotion, and the preacher must master the use of his or her body in conveying it. Cues to emotion are subtle and highly complicated, varying from culture to culture. The human body, particularly the face and its features, adapt strongly to convey emotion. As we use our bodies to communicate, we become one with the words we speak; we can actually feel those words on their way out of our mouths. The expressions of our hands, eyes, and faces are all read by our listeners. If our body language does not match our words, then we can confuse our listeners or appear rigid or without feeling. Further, the audience needs time to read and respond to our emotional cues. For this reason, it is important that a sermon not be rushed or overladen with detail. We must allow time for the emotion to come through, time for our words to create an effect, time for our own bodies to taste the words and express them on their way out. Just as intimacy cannot be rushed, so preaching cannot be rushed without great damage to the transformational power that emotions can covey.

Here I have another caution first for Renewal preachers and then for preachers from other traditions. In Renewal settings, emotions can run very high, and sermons often have deep, rich emotional content. This has much to do with the Renewal Movement's roots in revivalist preaching, which is often emphatic and laden with emotion. Emotionally rich environments are ideal for learning, because the brain stores not only the memory of the events but the senses associated with those events; and strong emotional associations make the events more vivid in our memory.

Thus, it is tempting in Renewal settings to begin to associate vivid emotion with the anointing and to substitute emotion for strong content. It is even more tempting to do the same to elicit a response from the audience. But emotionalism can easily eclipse the purpose God intended for a sermon. There is no substitute for a preacher who, along with emotional expression, delivers a sermon with a solid focus and structure. Focus, structure, and emotion, along with the other sermon attributes we will discuss, must all walk hand in hand in sermon delivery or the transformational impact suffers.

Similarly, in more traditional settings, there is no excuse for associating a *lack* of emotional expression with the anointing of God. Though emotional expression may be more reserved in certain environments, emotion is still a critical aspect of any sermon, and it often makes the difference between a sermon and a lecture. Again, the right words with the wrong emotions—or little to no emo-

---

[8] Lischer, 77. From *per-sonar*, to "sound through."

tion—can mar the message God wants to convey to His people. My goal as a preacher is to sense the heart of God during the delivery of any sermon so as to enhance the delivery of that word.

The Joints

People of all ages suffer from a disease called arthritis. There are currently more than 140 known types of arthritis, which is a degenerative condition of the joints of the body. Arthritis often creates intense pain and limits motion. Joints are important to motion. They are the junctures where bone meets bone, allowing the body to bend and twist. If we had bone but no joints, we would walk like sticks, or not walk at all, and have no capacity to bend or change direction. The anatomy of the shoulders, spine, and knees is replete with joints that are a wonder of God's creation in their complexity and wisdom of design. Joints make free motion possible for the human body and for a sermon.

Each sermon must have joints to help the listener transition from one point to another. We discern God's focus for the sermon and its skeleton, which helps us understand what He wants to say about that focus. We discern God's heart for the sermon—its emotional content and how that content will best be conveyed. Now, we must plan for graceful transitions from point to point to help the sermon bend and twist as it moves forward in a manner that best suits our audience and the Spirit's design. If we fail to build in transitions, then the sermon will be arthritic and its movement hindered. A sermon has to be able to move, bend, and twist appropriately in order to effectively convey the truth. Chances are you have encountered (or preached) a few arthritic sermons in your time. My goal as a preacher is to eliminate arthritic joints in order to allow the sermon to move freely and to serve the needs of the audience and the Spirit as I speak the word.

Because joints are so common in the human body, we take them for granted—until we injure one, it does not work properly, and it announces its injury loudly and clearly with pain. We build joints without even thinking into our human affairs—we take for granted transitions that are built into everyday life. Take, for example, our church services, which are filled with joints that we expect by conditioning. There might be a prayer offered to begin the service, followed perhaps by louder praise music to draw the people from daily life into worship. Then there might be a transition to slower paced music and to a different kind of worship as we approach the throne room in intimacy. Perhaps another prayer is offered, followed by greeting time, which in turn might be followed by announcements. The offering is taken but not without more praise and worship, which ushers us back into God's presence and prepares us to receive the word. The service ends with an altar call for response but not without more worship and a closing prayer. I have just described a very typical service for some reading this book, and that description is pregnant with examples of joints, which allow for graceful transitions and allow the congregation to prepare for what is next.

People most often like smooth and obvious transitions, and we expect joints to cue us that a transition is coming so we are not caught by surprise. We do not expect to be jolted back and forth from slow worship to boisterous praise in a service; we expect transitions to move us between the two. Likewise, announcements would not seem to fit into a service on the heels of a deep time of worship, but a time of greeting moves us more smoothly from a focus on heaven to focus on each other, and then makes room for announcements and the offering. All these joints represent transitions and clues that we are moving from one experience to another in a worship service. If we—if congregations—expect these transitions in a worship service, then should they expect any less in the sermon?

The preacher's job in the sermon is to make transitions from point to point obvious. A transition can be something as obvious as an overt statement like, ". . . and now for my next point." Still, many new preachers fail to give their listeners the courtesy of even those straightforward words. Another more interesting rhetorical device to signal transition is a story. In this book, I have used stories as I have transitioned from chapter to chapter. This book has a distinct focus (eye)—transformational preaching. The book has eight distinct subpoints for its skeleton, hence eight logical divisions called "chapters." Notice that many chapters use a story or an illustration to introduce you to the new subpoint. I could have begun each chapter by saying, "And now for my next point . . . ," but you would have grown bored with my arthritic joints.

A well-placed story that is shaped to make God's point can be a tremendous way to transition within the subpoints of a sermon while at the same time keeping your audience engaged. Jesus used stories all the time in His sermons, because He knew people love stories and can remember them long after the words of any sermon are forgotten. Stories are like that—they have the power to convey truth over time and across generations. The preacher who learns to shape and tell stories well can harness their raw power to convey emotion and focus for the listener. That preacher can also use stories to skillfully construct a joint between points. Both life experience and creation are pregnant with story potential just waiting to be discovered by the preacher and then woven into his or her sermon.

Humorous content, or even something as simple as a pregnant pause, also has the power to convey transition for the listener. We often miss the humor, some of it quite sarcastic, in the Scriptures, because of the translation from Hebrew or Greek to English. The people of God were busy praying for Peter's release from prison, and when he actually showed up at their door, Rhoda was so flustered she forgot to open the door for him (Acts 12:13-16)! Nicodemus just didn't get it when Jesus said he had to be born again and tried to imagine crawling back into his mother's womb (John 3:4). It took a donkey to straighten out a prophet one time (Num. 22:26-34). And Paul's lengthy preaching literally killed a guy (Acts 20:9). (Has that ever happened to you?) Paul was once so mad at the circumcision crowd he told them if they really wanted to get holy, then they should go for the whole thing (Gal. 5:12). If you are like me, life brings no shortage of humorous moments just waiting to be used as joints in a sermon to make a point while you make a transition. Joints are indispensible to the sermon's movement, another reason we cannot rush a sermon—we can easily sprain one of the joints if we do.

The Flesh

We've talked about using stories as joints in the sermon, but stories also add flesh to a sermon's bones. The preacher can use effective rhetoric to make a point, but when skillfully used, stories have the power to amplify that point and make it most memorable. The multibillion dollar entertainment industry is based on the appeal of story. Consider reality shows, which involve us in other people's lives. We are fascinated by life as it unfolds around us. Whether true or invented, stories help us make sense of life. The stories we hear, read, and view add texture and depth to our lives, touching us deeply.

Jesus knew how much people love stories and used this to His advantage when He preached. Sometimes He directly quoted from the Scriptures, but almost always He quoted from life experience or drew from creation, using stories. Jesus' communication is most noted for the parables, word pictures, and object lessons He created from the ordinary backdrop of everyday life. When he walked by a field of sheep, He talked about the Great Shepherd. When he walked through a vineyard, he spoke about the vine and its branches. He spoke about seeds, goats, pearls, dragnets, and a host of other common and ordinary things that the average person could relate to and understand. In doing so, He was accessing the power of story and of metaphor to build bridges of meaning between concrete, lived life and abstract spiritual truth.

As discussed earlier, testimonies, stories, word pictures, and metaphors are indispensible when it comes to preaching. Stories add flesh to our words, inviting our audience to experience life and truth through our words the way movies and television programs allow us to live through characters. Some people watch action movies so they can get the feel of driving a speeding car or beating up the bad guy. Others watch romance movies to experience that nostalgic feeling that comes when a man meets a woman and the couple hopefully lives happily ever after. Some watch movies for literary satisfaction but many for the visceral, gut-level experiences movies can generate. In fact, we often, or perhaps usually, rate our movie experience by the level of our visceral experience. The impact of a sermon is often gauged the same way.

There is a stream of thought in the field of homiletics that seems to diminish the importance of word pictures, stories, and other rhetorical devices in the sermon. A view along these lines can be found in the sermon suggestions outlined by Karl Barth.[9] Barth was zealous to protect the integrity of how God has revealed Himself in the Scriptures. In his zeal, Barth contends that the revelation in the written Word is enough and that the preacher should not attempt to add anything to that:

> Preaching cannot try to be a proof of the truth of God. It cannot set out to prove God by an intellectual demonstration, by setting and stressing certain propositions. There can be no other proof of God than that which God himself offers. Nor can it be the task of preaching to expound or present the truth of God aesthetically in form of a picture, an impression, or an aesthetic evocation of Jesus Christ. When Paul in Galatians 3:1 speaks of displaying Christ before the eyes, it is the apostle speaking. But we understand the command not to make any images. If God himself wills to speak the truth, preachers are forbidden to interfere with any science or art of their own. . . . [T]here is no place at all for the *scopus* of a sermon, whether theoretical (a formal theme or impressive proposition) or practical (the aim of directing listeners to a certain type of contact). . . . If preachers think they should present a theme of their own, it will anticipate what God himself wants to say. If they offer their congregation a clever conceptual picture, even though it is arrived at by serious and intensive exegesis, it will not be scripture itself that speaks, but something will merely be said about scripture.[10]

Barth's caution is excellent—preachers do need to let the Scriptures speak for themselves. My caution that one focus or center one's sermon on the Scriptures, the person of Christ, and God's redemptive plan is born of thinking similar to Barth's. However, Barth seems to go beyond caution in asking the preacher to add nothing else to God's Word. That position seems to violate the very pattern laid down in the teaching and preaching ministry of Jesus Christ. I am constantly pairing specific passages of Scripture with my life experience, word pictures from nature, and my surroundings in order through Scripture to make sense of them. We humans are designed to live, communicate, and think by building bridges to link abstraction with things we can see, hear, taste, smell, and touch. It would seem that using this same approach to life in crafting a sermon would make for a most effective means to communicate truth.

Why are stories so effective in preaching? Stories appeal to emotions and the senses, involving both the mind and the heart. The human body is alive with sensory capabilities. Our flesh has five known senses, and some consider intuition to be a sixth. The data gathered by the eyes, ears, tongue, nose, and touch are bombarding the brain with so much that the brain actually has to sort through

---

[9] Karl Barth, *Homiletics* (Louisville, Westminster-John Knox, 1991). This book, translated by Bromley and Daniels, provides an excellent look into the world of Barth's views on sermon preparation.

[10] Ibid., 47, 49.

and choose what to pay attention to. Can you imagine if we had to consciously think about the sensation of every breath or every heartbeat? Sensory power gives us contact with the world, and all of our sensory inputs are routed through a special processing center in the brain and shuffled off to the appropriate areas for conscious and unconscious processing.

As mentioned earlier, emotions are attached to this process by the limbic system of the brain—we do not just remember thoughts but also the powerful emotions we experienced with those thoughts and the very sensations we felt as we were thinking. The more vivid the sensation, the more vivid are the thought memories. Most of us over fifty years old remember the location, feelings, and thoughts we had when we heard about the Kennedy assassination in 1963. Younger folks may recall these same details regarding the explosion of the space shuttle in 1986 or the attack on the World Trade Center in 2001. These memories are so vivid because the brain is wired to amplify memories of things that are multisensory and highly emotional—the memories come alive and are more powerful because of the way we are wired.

My goal as a preacher is to create a multisensory experience for my listeners because that will give them the best shot at remembering what is said. I can create this experience using several important tools:[11]

- Word Pictures—I can evoke metaphor using life experience and nature;
- Testimonies—I can take listeners on an experiential journey by relating stories that illustrate the truth in action in real life;
- Props—I can use objects that convey truth, harnessing a powerful tool to impact listeners. No audience is too old for well-utilized props;
- Drama—I can incorporate dramatic representations of truth, utilizing actors;
- Multimedia—I can integrate a visual and sound presentation into my sermon;
- Multisensory tools—I can utilize incense or other scented instruments to create atmosphere. The Protestant church has largely lost the experience or impact of scents in a corporate setting.

---

[11] There is a wealth of excellent material out there for those interested in learning how to more effectively put "flesh" on the "bones of their incarnational sermons. This can be found in books like Mark Miller, *Experiential Storytelling* (Grand Rapids: Zondervan, 2003), which includes great ideas for the use of creative storytelling; Mark Galli and Craig Brian Larson, *Preaching that Connects* (Grand Rapids: Zondervan, 1994), which provides great advice from the journalistic technique; Ralph L. Lewis and Greg Lewis, *Learning to Preach Like Jesus* (Westchester: Crossway, 1989), which gives solid advice on the use of word pictures; Eugene L. Lowry, *How to Preach a Parable* (Nashville: Abingdon, 1989); J. Kent Edwards, *Deep Preaching,* Nashville: (B&H Academic, 2009), and my favorite, Warren W. Wiersbe, *Preaching and Teaching with Imagination: The Quest for Biblical Ministry* (Grand Rapids: Baker, 1994).

There are countless other tools we can use in our quest to create a multisensory memory with a sermon. Here I will introduce a new word to describe a multisensory preaching experience: *synesthetic*. I derive the word from the experience of people who have a condition called synesthesia. We know of anesthesia, which puts the senses to sleep (I certainly feel some of my sermons have had this effect in the past). Synesthesia is an awakening of sensory experiences that most of us do not experience. People who have synesthesia have brains that are wired differently. Medical experts believe that somehow unconscious processing in the metaphoric brain is actually a conscious experience for those with synesthesia. As a result, people with synesthesia can "see" sound, "taste" color, and "smell" sights. For some people with synesthesia, each number has a particular taste or color associated with it. These individuals have a blended sensory experience that is quite extraordinary, but their experiences make a point about our senses and the process of communication.

When we preach with transformational power, people can "taste and see" that the Lord is good (Ps. 34:8). That is precisely why Jesus spoke God's word using abundant word pictures from nature—sheep, goats, wheat, tares, pearls, fishing nets, and countless other metaphoric bridges from life and nature. In Bible days, the image of a shepherd invoked feelings of care, faithfulness, intimacy, and security. If we look at the miracles recorded in the Bible closely, because of their placement in time, they are often amplifications of Jesus' teaching ministry. What better way existed to convey that Jesus was the "bread of life" than to create enough bread from a few small loaves to feed thousands (John 6:35)? Preaching takes upon itself flesh when the word is clothed in humanity—our stories and our testimonies. Without the flesh, all we have is dry bones. With flesh, the sermon is alive and transformational.

The Muscle

The muscles of our body get work done. Muscles are controlled by our central nervous system and are subject to our will, enabling us to move with efficiency and to get work accomplished. The sermon too depends on muscle to get the job done. The muscle of the sermon is the force and impact that drive home truth to the listener. The muscle of the sermon includes the way we introduce the sermon, the way the sermon moves toward application for the listeners, and the way we conclude the sermon. Muscles in the human body depend on deliberate use to remain fit and toned. A lack of use will cause the muscles to wither and waste away. Failing to use the right kind and degree of muscle in a sermon also can cause it to wither and waste away.

Mark Galli and Craig Brian Larson make the point that the way we introduce a sermon ". . . gives the preacher a psychological warrant to take people into the sermon's custody."[12] Today's audience has been conditioned by the entertainment industry to learn by vivid, digital, multimedia-rich presentations. We have also been well trained in how to filter out things that do not grab our attention. We can quickly lose interest when a sermon lacks a strong, well-planned, muscular introduction; rich, directed content; and a strong conclusion.

I have a habit of spending a lot of time on the formal preparation of the introduction of a sermon. I do this for several important reasons. First, I have only a few moments to capture the attention of the listeners and convince them that what I have to say is important enough for them to give me their precious time and attention. Time is not a renewable resource, and people are rightly stingy with it. In his or her first few words, the preacher must earn the right to be heard. Secondly, people are already testing the message according to my first words. Am I preaching something for them or for an audience that lived a long time ago? Does the message seem relevant and applicable, or is it outdated? I will keep people with me or lose them based on trust and on my ability to communicate in the first few moments of the sermon where I will be going.

Another practical reason to give a lot of attention to the introduction is to prepare for the unexpected. If I'm not well prepared, I find that in the first few moments of my sermons, I am most likely to stumble. I am most vulnerable in my communication at the moment when I have the most adrenalin pumping and the least audience feedback on my words. A well-prepared introduction can be worth its weight in gold during such moments and carry the preacher until the sermon develops a momentum of its own. A well-prepared introduction can also carry me through countless interruptions—the soloist right before the message who should have stayed home that day or the baby trying to tell Mom and Dad it's time to eat. A well-prepared, muscular introduction covers a multitude of sins and has saved the day many times in my preaching experience.

The conclusion of any sermon is just as important as its introduction. The introduction earns us the right to be heard, and a muscular conclusion seals what has been heard. If God has a particular focus, structure, emotion, and muscular movement for the sermon, then surely He knows how He wants to wrap the sermon up. What call is the Holy Spirit issuing to the listeners through the sermon, and how can that call be summed up in its concluding remarks? The sermon must be crafted to drive home the sermon's focus. People's lives and their decisions are hanging in the balance. If the sermon was worth their time and attention, then the preacher needs to hammer home the point of their experience with a muscular conclusion. Application and a call to action are powerful ways to give your conclusion muscle. Muscular sermons confront the listener with clear choices and force the issue of truth. In doing so, muscular sermons leave a

---

[12] Galli and Larson, 35. This resource offers a fascinating glimpse into how basic principles of communication embodied in the discipline of journalism apply to preaching and teaching. See how this applies to sermons on pp. 35-46.

powerful imprint on the memory as words become actions and the word takes upon itself flesh in the listeners' lives.

The sermon-shaping process is a science that is deliberate. Through that process, we can create sermons that live and breathe, sermons that carry transformational power into the lives of people. Keep your eyes open and have what you want to say in focus before you speak a word from the pulpit. Make sure the sermon's bones are healthy and strong. Don't forget to add joints to those bones so the truth can twist and turn as God intends and people can follow along. Remember to keep the sermon's heart beating strong and right in line with God's own emotion for maximum impact. Put flesh on each sermon's bones with an abundance of story, metaphor, and testimony. Add to that muscle and you have the makings of a transformational sermon that will breathe new life into dry bones.

The Sermon's Mode of Delivery

We've just discussed in detail the shape of the sermon we prepare to deliver. We've looked at its component parts and learned to create a living message born out of the word of God that has been maturing in our own lives. What we have yet to talk about is the overall mode of the sermon's delivery. We've done our preparation. We have the pieces. We understand what God wants to say. But how does He want to say it? In what mode does the sermon need to be delivered so that the listeners will best receive it?

What do I mean by mode of delivery? If the sermon's shape is comprised of different parts, then perhaps the mode of delivery is best understood as the manner in which one chooses to communicate that sermon. We've looked at the parts used to shape a transformational sermon, now let's look at the modes that can be used to shape its delivery. Will the sermon be a homily, exhorting the listener concerning a specific text? Will it be a narrative, using the elements of story to communicate? Will the sermon be textual—that is, structured around a particular passage of Scripture? When we consider the delivery mode, we are considering the overall structure used to covey the sermon—or, to use another metaphor, its delivery wineskin.

In planning the delivery mode of a sermon, there are many different wineskins that can guide the sermon's presentation and help to guide its logical flow. These different wineskins are what Larsen calls the "topology and morphology" of the sermon and are just a few examples of the delivery modes that sermons can assume.[13] *Topology* is a term used to describe the shape of a surface. *Morphology* is the overall shape of something. By using these terms, Larsen imparts a "touch/feel" dimension to the sermon's delivery mode, because each delivery mode seems to give a certain "texture" to the sermon.

---

[13] Larsen, 60-63.

Delivery mode for sermons might be considered along the lines of "genre" in the world of written communication. Fictional writing has its own texture that is unique from nonfiction. A biography is written differently than an academic dissertation. Each genre has its own specific rules and texture. Musical communication too has different modes—the feel and texture of classical music differ radically from the feel and texture of country music or hip -hop. All these written or musical delivery modes can use words to convey a message but vary in "texture" because of the musical or written wineskins in which they are packaged. So it is with the sermon—each unique delivery mode or wineskin has its own rules that dictate something about the shape of a sermon.[14] Some of the most common *delivery modes* are:[15]

- Homily—structured to make observations and exhortations about a topic or text;
- Topical—structured to inform on a specific topic;
- Textual-Topical—structured around a text in order to develop a specific topic;
- Textual—structured on several verses and their meaning;
- Expository—structured around a biblical text (*lectio selecta*) or even a series of texts (*lectio continua*);
- Narrative—structured as or around a story used to convey truth;
- Extemporaneous—structured deliberately to be loose and free-flowing.

These delivery modes can also be shaped by two different *rhetorical forms*:

- Didactic—a teaching rhetorical form (*didache*) meant to ground the listener in the word;
- Kergymatic—a preaching rhetorical form (*kergyma*) that is more exhortative as to proclaim truth.

At the heart of these two rhetorical forms lie two different *rhetorical methods* of conveying truth:

- Deductive Method—states the truth for the listener and convinces the listener of its truth;
- Inductive Method—allows the listener to discover truth for him- or herself.

---

[14] For an excellent discussion of inductive versus deductive forms, see Ralph L. Lewis and Gregg Lewis, *Inductive Preaching* (Wheaton, Crossway, 1983), 79-137.
[15] For an excellent discussion of the different forms that a sermon can take, see Larsen, 30-32 and Lowry, 22-28.

I believe the delivery mode is meant to be a servant of the sermon's God-given focus and skeleton. The delivery mode carries the movement of God's word along in a manner that best suits the audience and the need. The audience and their conditioning should determine which delivery mode is best suited to shape the sermon. For some, the best mode will be extemporaneous preaching. For others, the best mode will be very linear and orderly teaching in *lectio continua* as a journey through the Scriptures. Within each mode, there is a pattern, texture, and flow. Some modes serve an audience more conditioned to words and others an audience more conditioned to story and image. The preacher's job is to discern the best delivery mode and build an appropriate structure to move the sermon on a journey toward illumination of the truth best suited for the specific audience.

Many high quality texts exist that specifically address this delivery aspect of sermon preparation and do so quite well, so I will be brief.[16] As I have said, the delivery mode should be suited to a preacher's audience. In fact, the mode of the delivery of a sermon represents one of the finest ways to calibrate a high-impact sermon for a specific audience of listeners. Preachers often gravitate to the delivery mode with which they feel most comfortable, but in doing so, they miss a great opportunity to shape the sermon in a way that could create higher transformational impact for their audiences. I do not believe preachers have the luxury of choosing a mode that simply suits us. The sermon is not ultimately about the preacher but about the audience. The ultimate point of the sermon is to preach for transformation in the hearers' lives by whatever means best suits their needs.

As I consider the different wineskin options for delivery mode presented, it occurs to me how structured the list above is. The summary is very linear and makes the assumption that a sermon's shape neatly fits into one of those categories, which do not resemble life. Most sermons cannot fit neatly into one of the delivery-shaping boxes, such as topical or expository, but rather end up flowing between the categories. I prefer to think of the sermon's delivery mode as something that slides on a continuum between different blends of mode. The real question one might ask is where the sermon lies on the delivery shaping *continuum*. Is it topical-expository or expository-topical? Or maybe expository-topical-extemporaneous? A sermon rarely fits into one neat category.

As I've listed above, the delivery mode of a sermon also has *rhetorical form* to it. Two of the rhetorical forms most common to delivery mode are teaching and preaching. The word in the original Greek text for teaching has the meaning

---

[16] By far my favorite book on the subject of sermon format and the shape possibilities for delivery is Ralph L. Lewis and Gregg Lewis, *Inductive Preaching* (Wheaton, Crossway, 1983). The book presents a comprehensive review of the flow of various kinds of sermon delivery shapes, including extensive information for experimenting with inductive form, which is new to many individuals.

of "grounding" the listener in God's Word.[17] The rules governing rhetorical form for teaching suit its purpose. Teaching is slower; it is more linear, methodical, and detailed. As a result of its slow, deliberate, linear flow, teaching is more suited for conveying detailed knowledge. By contrast, preaching comes from a word in the Scriptures that could be translated "proclaim or herald."[18] This rhetorical form once again follows function, because preaching is meant to exhort or encourage an audience and is therefore usually much more passionate and often less linear in its flow.

As with the other aspects of delivery mode, teaching and preaching are hard to put into a neat box, and sermons most often are a blend on a continuum between the two. Sermons quite often are "teachy-preaching" or "preachy-teaching." Sliding on this continuum should be the goal of any sermon, depending on what rhetorical form the listeners are most receptive to. Again, the object is to create a high-impact experience for the listener that gives the word being delivered the greatest possibility of being received. The "ear" of the listener has been conditioned by life, church, culture, and context to be most in tune with a certain delivery form. The preacher needs to be conversant in a number of different forms to reach his or her audience.

Considering that last two-point list above, deductive and inductive *rhetorical methods* lie at the heart of teaching and preaching.[19] Deductive method declares what is true and proves that truth with a set of linear arguments. Deduction is implicit in teaching because of its logical flow and linearity. Induction, though, is different. Inductive method points to life experience and then draws parallels between life and principles of truth.[20] Induction's power lies in its ability to let the hearers draw their own conclusions about what is true. Deductive method tells the listener what is true and then sets out to prove the point. Inductive method points to life by providing principles of truth alongside word pictures, allowing the listener to decide what is true. Inductive method's power is in the involvement of the listener—he or she is not passive but actively involved in the illumination process.[21]

---

[17] The Greek word "διδάσκω" (*didasko*) is used for "teach" (e.g., Mark 4:1). It conveys a grounding effect through its action. It is also the root of our word "didactic," which describes teaching methodology.

[18] The Greek word for "preach" is "κηρύσσω" (*kerusso*) (e.g., Matt. 4:17), which means to proclaim or exhort.

[19] It bears repeating that an excellent book on this subject is *Inductive Preaching* by Ralph and Greg Lewis (1983). This book is especially good for coaching people who are new to inductive preaching. It would be helpful for preachers who are used to deductive form and who do not know how to experiment with a more inductive delivery.

[20] Lewis and Lewis, (1983), 32.

[21] Ibid., 19.

Inductive method involves three distinct phases:

- Observing—looking for truth in life, nature, and experience;
- Interpreting—building a metaphoric bridge between truth and what we observe in order to produce meaning;
- Applying—taking the meaning of new truth and putting it into action in our lives in a tangible way.

Perhaps you have already made the connection—the incarnational preaching and teaching paradigm used in this book is strongly related to inductive method. The phases of this incarnational paradigm flow alongside the three distinct phases of induction:

- Observing—conception of the word in our hearts as we observe in life and the Scriptures while walking in intimate fellowship with God;
- Interpreting—growth of the word through the building of metaphoric bridges between the truth in God's Word and life experience and creation in order to produce meaning;
- Applying—maturing of the word in our hearts as the Holy Spirit helps us to apply new truth to change our beliefs, values, attitudes, and actions.

Delivery is the overflow of an incarnational inductive process that has transformed us and made us ready to be agents of transformation for others.

As with preaching and teaching delivery forms, there is a continuum between deductive and inductive methods, and sermons are often a mix of both. The context, culture, conditioning, and needs of the moment are important factors in considering how to slide on this continuum between induction and deduction for the sermon's delivery method. Incarnational preaching presents a natural opportunity for inductive method because of the centrality of life experience, metaphor, and imagery in conveying truth.

As I end this section, I issue a caution and an encouragement for the reader. Preaching is a science with a body of knowledge and practices that operate in prescribed manners with predictable results. It is important for any preacher to learn and master the science of preaching to the best of his or her ability. Mastering the science of preaching is vital to excellent delivery of the word. If the shape of the sermon is lacking in eye, skeleton, heart, joints, flesh, or muscle, then the transformational impact will suffer. If the sermon's delivery mode is lacking because the preacher does not understand the context and culture in which he or she is preaching as well as the people to whom he or she is preaching, then the sermon's impact is diminished.

Those are my cautions. Now for the encouragement: God bids us to come to Him as little children. When He called us to preach, He knew our human frailties and weaknesses. We are inadequate for the job, and preaching by its very nature requires divine partnership. If you had never heard of the incarnational preaching paradigm, the parts of a well-shaped sermon, or a sermon's different delivery modes, you could still fulfill your calling to preach. People who have never heard of these things often learn them intuitively, but with many starts and stops and the wounds that learning this way can bring. In fact, that would describe me before I learned the things I have just related to you. Ultimately, the science of preaching is best learned in the context of life as you live it out and experiment and find out what works and what doesn't. If all this information seems overwhelming for now, then let it rest and trust that God will teach it to you by the Holy Spirit's leading and at precisely the right time. Because it is inductive by nature, incarnational preaching is actually something to be discovered. That brings us to another inescapable conclusion—preaching is not only a science but also an art.

The Sermon as Art

Science is a logical, left-brain activity, and many gravitate to it because it brings a sense of order to our chaotic world. But try as you may, you can only go so far in understanding truth with science as a guide. Science is limited by the boundaries of logic and linearity. Life—with its complexity and nonlinearity— often defies logic. That is where art comes in. Art is an expression of the creative right side of the brain. Art relies more on intuition than logic. While the left brain analyzes, computes, and looks for logical patterns in order to discern truth, the right brain subconsciously combines all that left-brain data, discerning what is true through intuition or what many call a "gut feeling." A person with highly developed left-brain capacities but lower-level right-brain abilities can easily miss the truth, because truth cannot always be understood through analysis. Truth is very delicate. When dissected into pieces by the left brain, truth sometimes dies in our hands. We might come away understanding the pieces but forgetting how they relate to the whole. Truth is sometimes best understood intuitively. Sermons require both the preacher's logic and intuition, because preaching is both a science and an art.

My wife is an artist. God had a sense of humor pairing up a mad-scientist type like me with a person alive with art and a joy for experiencing life. My idea of fun is to sit with a book, read, and think. My wife's idea of fun is to look at flowers and landscapes and then try to capture with paint on canvas what she sees. I was attracted to her because she could see things that I could not. I could exegete passages from the Hebrew text about the dawn and sunset (Ps. 65:8), but she could experience the joy and wonder of the dawn and sunset with such life and excitement that it stirred my soul. My wife can get excited and dance— literally jump for joy like a child—when she sees the sun shining at a certain angle on a patch of wild lilies. I was with her recently as she arose at five in the morning to take pictures of a sunrise over the ocean (she came away with about 150 pictures). I am most likely to wonder about the Latin genus and species of those lilies or the precise time of the sunrise or sunset. Both kinds of thinking are necessary, but I must admit that my wife's way sure does seem like a lot more fun. She is an artist, and I have learned to be more like her over the last thirty-four years.

If we do not understand preaching as both science and art, we lose some powerful perspective on preaching's true nature. Some understanding of preaching as an art form is essential to sermon preparation, but this troubles many preachers because most of us have been conditioned by Western culture to think of it predominantly in terms of its science. The art of preaching is often unpredictable and serendipitous, which unnerves more left-brain types. The art of preaching is the aspect of the sermon that flows and bubbles with imagination and creativity. Imagination and creativity are such important parts of sermon delivery that we will spend the next chapter on them. In the meantime, let's look at some big-picture concepts for preaching as an art by listening to some advice given to my wife by a master artist.

My wife is currently studying art with a master impressionist artist named Charles Kello.[22] When we talk about what she is learning, I learn in greater detail the ways preaching truly is an art. Charles Kello was born in 1942 during World War II and apprenticed in his father's print shop beginning at age nine. In his biography posted on his website, he describes his father as ". . . an uncompromising craftsman. He simply didn't accept failure and he demanded perfection in every facet of art including lettering and design. We had many subjects and media to work with and you painted what you were handed and you did it right.'"[23] Because he learned under an exacting craftsman, Kello became an award-winning impressionist artist by age fourteen and hosted sellout exhibits in New York by age twenty-four. Let's allow the words of a master artist to guide us in our study of preaching as an art as we conclude this chapter on sermon-shaping and summarize what we have learned:[24]

To be a successful painter, always adapt your style to the subject you are working on. It is tempting for an artist to adopt one approach and get comforta-

---

[22] More information can be found at Charles Kello Galleries, CharlesKelloGallaries.com, http://charleskellogalleries.com/default.aspx (accessed July 1, 2009).

[23] Charles Kello Galleries, "Charles Kello III," http://charleskellogalleries.com/Bio.aspx (accessed July 1, 2009).

[24] The artistic statements in italics that follow are the comments made by Charles Kello as recorded by my wife while studying art under his instruction, and they are used with his permission. The non-italicized words that follow are my interpretation of those words and my adaptation of the principles to the art and craft of preaching. I should also emphasize that the master artist's comments are addressed to the specific genre of impressionism and may not hold true for every genre but are wonderfully applicable to preaching and teaching.

ble with it. A master artist advises us not to restrict our style to one approach but to let the subject we are painting shape our approach. How true this is for preaching. You may be comfortable with one kind of rhetorical form, such as teaching or preaching, but your subject and the listeners demand flexibility. A preacher cannot afford to get stuck in one kind of rhetorical form or delivery mode lest he or she miss the mark. Each different subject and context for preaching demands a different approach. You will always be strongest in a few different delivery modes and rhetorical forms or methods, but don't let fear limit you. Serve the people to whom you preach. Let the subject of your sermon and your preaching context determine the most effective approach.

Spotlight your subject—always have a hotspot for your viewers to look at. As I understand it, in painting, it is vital for the artist to create a focal point on the canvas that draws the viewer's attention. That point on the painting guides the viewer and acts as a starting point for a journey. Other visual shapes and patterns flow out from the focal point to give the painting body, texture, and shape. A skilled artist learns to create a focal point and to let the painting develop out of that point, and so does the skilled preacher in his or her sermon. Remember the eye for the sermon and maintain your focal point throughout the message. Let the skeleton flow out from your focal point to bring pattern, texture, and meaning to your message. Add flesh and muscle to give your sermon texture and shape, allowing it to breathe with transformational life. Weaving these things together is an art, but we have the Master Artist to guide us.

Nature gives us far too much to look at—exaggerate the most important parts. My wife's teacher makes his living looking at creation and the world around him and then rendering it on a canvas. He sees things the rest of us do not see. That is because over the course of several decades, he has trained his eye to see what others don't. My wife is investing her time and money to learn to see things in nature that she has not seen before and to learn how to bring them to life on canvas. For artists, each day is an adventure in discovery—a sunrise on water, mist and water droplets on flowers as the sun sets, a tree losing its leaves. Seeing so much in creation often overwhelms my wife to the point that she gets a headache—there is simply too much to look at, overwhelming anyone with eyes to see. My wife looks, she sees, and then she picks the thing that stands out, and she paints it. It is inspiring to watch someone see beauty that we may miss and then make it alive on canvas, using shapes and colors.

Preacher, your job each day is to allow God to help you see things in life experience and creation that others can't see. The Bible is completely overwhelming. It is the preacher's job to go to the Scriptures during times of intimacy and let the Holy Spirit highlight truth. You must allow God to train your eye to see His truth, both in the Scriptures and at work around you, so you can choose the parts He wants to capture in your sermon. As you live this way, your sermons will come alive with texture, color, and shape that would not be there otherwise. Life experience and nature all around you await your trained artistic eye. What has God been highlighting in your life or in creation around you? What do you see that others don't? Jesus was a master at seeing truth in everyday life and nature around Him—a true artist who saw around Him what others did not see. Use Jesus as your example of a master artist busily at work painting pictures with His words so others can see.

Take your work seriously and not yourself. I don't know how many times I second-guess myself from the time I close the last study book until the time I preach. I am so bad at second-guessing myself that I had to make some rules about sermon preparation in order to keep myself sane. My rules allow me to look at the final text of my sermon one time before I go to bed the night before I preach and one time the morning I am going to preach. If I continue to look, I begin to obsess over each word. Part of the reason I obsess is rooted in pride—I do not want to make a fool of myself. The other part of the reason I obsess is because I want God to be pleased with the result.

As with a painting, the shape of any sermon makes or breaks its delivery, but at some point you have to let it go or you will overwork your subject. Focus on what God wants to say through the sermon and capture it the best you can. Pray, seek God, and then learn to commit what you have done to God as you preach. If the result depends that much on you, then you are in trouble from the start. Don't take yourself that seriously. Make room for God and realize you have done everything possible. Now it is up to Him. Make room too for your humanity and give yourself a break. At the end of the day, don't believe your own press. The sermon wasn't as good as some people said or as bad as others would have you believe. Please God, do your best, and release the rest to Him. And be sure not to take yourself too seriously.

Be a storyteller and not a reporter. Let them finish the picture in their minds! These words could be directed right at anyone shaping a transformational sermon. Learn the power of story, and it will be your friend. Stories are inductive by nature and put the responsibility to decide what is true in the hands of the listeners—the listeners become partners with you in learning and discerning truth. Become skilled at telling stories, and become a story collector. Open your eyes and ears to your own story as it unfolds in life, and collect stories from other people's lives that illustrate truth. Resist telling people what the truth is all the time—let them finish the picture in their own minds. Preach like Jesus did, using life and nature as your truth text.

Paint with enough realism to satisfy the average guy and enough artistic expression to satisfy the connoisseur. Remember the different kinds of people you have in each audience. Some relate best to facts and others to word pictures. Some like to discover truth and others like to be told what is true. You will have engineers and carpenters, doctors and homemakers, business professionals and custodians listening to your sermon, so make sure there is enough meat to satisfy the most analytical hearer and enough story and word picture for even a child to understand. Make sure the shape of your delivery is varied so that it appeals to a broad spectrum of hearers. Be sure to use a variety of delivery modes. Surprise them with an expository series on Philippians and switch to a topical mode the next month. Use deductive method to be a reporter, and at other times, use inductive method to be storyteller. Paint word pictures from life experience. Tell stories. Build metaphoric bridge between abstract truth and life experience so others can see and experience the beauty of what God has allowed you to see.

Does this all seem a bit overwhelming to you? Living things are always a bit overwhelming, and by now you can see that a sermon is alive. Do your best to apply what we have learned about sermon-shaping, and give the rest to God. Know that sermon-shaping is a skill learned over time. It requires much patience—the average artist can paint and repaint a canvas dozens of times before he or she gets the painting right. One of the most daunting challenges in sermon-shaping is the amount of imagination and creativity required to shape a transformational sermon. Creativity and imagination are so integral to building a transformational sermon that they require their own space. Let's move onward and examine the transformational power creativity and imagination contribute in bringing your sermons to life.

Chapter 7
Imagine That! Creativity and Imagination in Sermon-shaping

Creativity and imagination are essential to the sermon-shaping process because they are the key sources of texture and depth in any sermon. In the fine arts, depth is called *perspective*. Before the Renaissance, most Western art was created with little depth—figures appeared flat and had an other-worldly feel to them, as is commonly seen in iconography. In the early 1400s, artists began to experiment with perspective, giving their paintings a more three-dimensional look, and a revolution in art took place.[1] Preaching resembles a painting in that the preacher can choose the amount of depth, texture, and perspective added to each sermon. In preaching, creativity and imagination add depth or perspective to a sermon, and when they are used effectively, they help to release a sermon's transformational power.

God wants to work through our imaginations. The words of an innocent prayer again echo in my mind: "Lord, all of You and none of me. . ." It's not that preachers who pray this way lack a pure heart—this prayer entreats the Lord to infuse the message with His power, direction, and anointing. But the content of the prayer is off base. It is impossible for a sermon to be all of God and in-

---

[1] The development of perspective in art literally fed the Renaissance and the art that came from that period. Masaccio (1401–1428) died as a young artist but was the father of much that evolved in the art of painting during the Renaissance period that followed. His use of perspective added depth to paintings and started a revolution. For more information, see Francis A. Schaeffer, *How Should We Then Live?* (Old Tappen: Revell, 1976), 62-65 and Carol Strickland, *The Annotated Mona Lisa: A Crash Course in Art History* (Kansas City: University Press, 1992), 32-33. In many ways, the development of perspective is a milestone in the development of our consciousness. Sermons also took on a new depth with the Reformation.

clude nothing of the preacher. God never intended it to work that way, and He is not interested in a dimensionless word that has no flesh on it. That is why He sent his Son rather than sending just words from the mouth of an angel or written words on a page. God does not want all of Himself and nothing of us in our sermons, because then those sermons would lack the perspective and depth our humanity is meant to bring.

Creativity and imagination are so important to preaching because of their link to effective communication. They are at the root of multisensory experience, powerful memories, and transformational human experiences. Creativity and imagination are closely linked to metaphor; they link abstract truth to everyday things we understand in the world around us. Creativity and imagination allow us to build bridges of meaning into the hearts of our listeners through the words we preach. As Thomas H. Troeger observes:

> Any preaching strategy worthy of the gospel will combine, then, two elements: an openness to the Spirit *and* the strenuous work of human thought and creation. To hold these together is no easy task, as the presentation of God's word makes clear.[2]

This book has devoted much time to advocating openness to the Spirit because His guidance is essential for incarnational sermon preparation. It is always the Lord's presence in a sermon's words that give them transformational life, and life originates in the heart of a preacher who has been first transformed by that word. Some time must now be spent on emphasizing what the preacher can do to facilitate that process. Ignorance about creativity and imagination can greatly hinder preaching, but wisdom in the use of these tools makes the preacher a master artist—they become the preacher's paintbrush and palate of color. The depth, perspective, and richness of color that a sermon has when delivered with excellent creativity and imagination is a true work of art.

Imagine That!

It saddens me that in some church circles, imagination and creativity are viewed with suspicion. The church has such a rich tradition of integrating art and creativity into its buildings, windows, and art work. In the early church, stained glass windows told the story of the gospel in visual form for people who could not read for themselves. And yet, as time progressed, in some church settings, creativity and imagination were perceived to be worldly or contrary to holiness. These views in part come out of a bigger historical context, as we will explore shortly, but we need to stop and consider our prejudices. God knows the church cannot get enough of His holiness and needs to be more like Him and

---

[2] Troeger, 8.

less like the world, but is abandoning creativity and imagination really the pathway that leads to greater holiness?

When we neglect creativity and imagination, we actually look a lot less like God. In their zeal to protect the integrity of God's Word, some like Barth have advocated that nothing creative or imaginative be added to a sermon. As we saw earlier, Barth's position was that it is ". . . not the task of preaching to expound or present the truth of God aesthetically in the form of a picture, an impression, or an aesthetic evocation of Jesus Christ."[3] Barth justifies this position based on the passage in Gal. 3:1, which forbids us to make any images, stating that:

> When Paul in Galatians 3:1 speaks of displaying Christ before the eyes, it is the apostle speaking. But we stand under the commandment not to make any images. If God himself wills to speak his truth, preachers are forbidden to interfere with any science or art of their own."[4]

According to Barth, such interference would include ". . . the constructing of mental images of God."[5] Though Barth clearly seems intent on protecting the Word, the deliberate elimination of creativity and imagination in the preacher's delivery of the word can drain a sermon of its transformational power. One need only look to Jesus and Paul and their communication of the word to see vast displays of creativity and imagination at work with transformational results.

In still other church circles, reason has been exalted to the point that it has smothered even the embers of the creative soul. Christianity is a relationship with a person not a set of propositions to which we add our intellectual assent. Albert Einstein himself said, "There are only two ways to live your life. One is as though nothing is a miracle. The other is as though everything is a miracle." He was one of the greatest intellectuals of the twentieth century but acknowledged that "The most beautiful thing we can experience is the mysterious."

Reason and creativity have walked together with imagination to produce some of the most powerful inventions humanity possesses. Indeed, invention is a function of the marriage of creativity and reason as the left and right brain dance together to give birth to something new. Many in secular settings have come to this realization and seek to nurture creativity and imagination. Unfortunately, in the church, some have allowed their creativity to lie dormant, concerned that God will not be given His proper place if creativity is allowed to awaken. And yet, God's image is perfectly expressed in creativity that is guided by truth. I have often wondered about the fullness of the meaning of the word for "eternal life" in the Scriptures. The Greek word is *zoev aioniov*, which might be translated "the life of the ages," and it seems to describe who God is in His creative power. Just knowing God recreates the human heart, because His nearness ra-

---

[3] Barth, 47-48.
[4] Ibid., 48.
[5] Ibid.

diates eternal life (John 17:3). Whatever God touches seems to ooze with holy creativity and life. Is it surprising that when He touches us, we can also flow with that same kind of creative life?

God is the Creator, and so He creates with unmatched creativity. As we view the Scriptures, it is clear from the very beginning that God not only creates but that in creating, He is expressing His very nature. When the Holy Spirit brooded over the face of the deep in creation, He could not help but respond creatively to God the Father's word. As mentioned before, God's nature is to bring order to chaos and beauty to that which is formless (Gen. 1:2).[6] In that text, the words "formless and void" are used to describe the state that existed before creation. The words in the original text convey a sense of utter formlessness, confusion, emptiness, and absence of physical reality before creation. With His spoken word and the movement of the Holy Spirit, God imparted form, order, reality, and fullness to what we now see around us. His act of creation sprung from the imagination of the Master Architect, who saw creation perfectly in His mind before it was ever created (Isa. 46:9,10). When the preacher speaks God's word under the leading and movement of the Holy Spirit, it too should be infused with creativity and imagination. When the preacher speaks this way, he or she is acting like God. If God is the Creator, then how can something that we assert is from God lack in creativity and imagination? Creativity and imagination are basic traits of God and are anchored in His very nature—He can't help but be that way. Christians, especially preachers, should therefore be among the most imaginative and creative people in the world.

God is ultimately the source of creative ability, but sadly, often the church is not known for being imaginative or creative. Christians and preachers often retreat to what they consider a safe place and avoid anything too creative or imaginative so they don't transgress some invisible boundary that separates them from what is profane and thus become "stained" by the world. Others just rely on safe strategies that have worked in the past so as not to venture into uncharted, untested, or unpredictable waters. The problem is that playing it safe is actually very risky because in doing so we sacrifice the power of creativity. Life is meant to be an experiment and an adventure rather than something that is always predictable and ordinary.[7] By abandoning the power of creativity, the

---

[6] Here in the Hebrew text, the words "תהו" (*tohu*) and "בהו" (*bohu*) are used to describe what God did in creation. The Hebrew word *tohu* describes formlessness, confusion, emptiness, or a state of unreality. The word *bohu* describes emptiness. God's creative work gave form, order, reality, and fullness where there was none before. His creative power still does so and defines what transformation is.

[7] Here I must give credit to my good friend Mark Batterson of National Community Church in Washington, D.C. His church is growing rapidly right in the heart of Washington, D.C., and reaches a largely postmodern audience of people under thirty years old at multiple locations. He has powerfully articulated his church's values, among which are "irrelevance is irreverence," "playing it safe is risky," and "all life is an experiment." His

church has marginalized itself and actually been made less holy, because it is acting less like God.

Imagination and the Holy Spirit are not opposed or in conflict with each other. Creativity and imagination, like human speech, are God-given gifts, neutral in themselves but dynamic when placed in the hands of God. It is possible to use the human tongue to curse God and to harm others, but yielded to God, the tongue can preach and save souls. Should we abandon the gift of speech to be sure that it is never misused in an unholy manner? Neither should the church abandon creativity and imagination but rather surrender them to a holy God to harness the vast power of these gifts.

Church authorities in the Middle Ages often viewed creativity and imagination with suspicion. The church of the Middle Ages was highly controlling and ruled with an iron rod. That control can be seen in art of the Middle Ages. Most of the art was church-based and commissioned, and the subjects of the art were primarily themes and subjects from the Scriptures. Certainly, masterpieces were created during this period and great art was incorporated into the worship experience, but artists were bound in some ways by the strictures of the church. The art world took a different turn during the Renaissance as human creativity found greater freedom of expression due to financing outside the church, and life itself became fair game for the artist to render in paintings and sculpture.

As we saw earlier in this book, another revolution took place in the 1400s—the invention of the printing press. When Gutenberg made mass production of print media possible and ordinary people then gained access to the printed Scriptures in their own languages, the Reformation burst forth. As we have seen before, the cry of the reformation was *sola scriptura*—the Word alone. By Wesleyan standards, focus on the Scriptures restored them to their proper place in the Quadrilateral, and the role of tradition was put back in into better balance with reason and experience. Because of the shift that written words caused in the way people perceived reality, some would argue that things went too far in the years following the Reformation. A new imbalance was created as reason and the abstract written Word replaced relationship and the spoken word in people's consciousness as the basis of reality. When reason became more prominent, it began to crowd out the place of imagination and creativity in church circles.

After the Reformation, the emphasis on the printed word and reason displaced image, symbol, and art in the church. Sermons followed the same pattern. Mark Miller observes that the focus in the church became the printed Word of the Scriptures and the preaching of the printed Word with little consideration of anything that was creative or imaginative.[8] Reformed theology took that a step further, because it holds that humankind is utterly reprobate and that nothing

---

church can be accessed online, as can its complete set of values, at http://theaterchurch.com/.
[8] Mark Miller, 53.

good can be found within us. It is only a small leap from there to consign human creativity and imagination to the same reprobate scrap heap. If we do so, we also may as well throw into the scrap heap the gifts of reason, speech, and other human capacities endowed upon us by our Creator. All these capacities are redeemable under the blood of Jesus Christ and can be blood-washed tools in the hands of any believer, including the preacher.

Reason and the written Word must be mingled with creativity and imagination to unlock God's transformative power in the sermon. Reason, creativity, and imagination are all indispensible tools for any preacher. Exegesis is a wonderful thing because it unlocks a historical-grammatical interpretation of God's inspired Word and gives us wonderful clues to its meaning. But exegesis must be kept in careful balance with imagination and creativity. In the preacher's life, there must be both the conception of the word in intimacy with God and the reasoned study of the Scriptures. Remember that exegesis "draws out" meaning from the Word, in effect, emptying a language, whereas imagination fills it.[9] Imagination, reason, creativity, and exegesis must all work together in sermon preparation if the sermon is to have transformational impact.

The Wellsprings of Creativity and Imagination

Mark Miller defines creativity as "the ability to think or act differently. You allow your mind to soar to places it has not been for a long time, if ever."[10] Imagination is engaged when we dip into the wellspring of creativity that God has placed within us. Creativity is not the exclusive property of the Christian, and all of us have seen what can happen when creative power meets evil imagination— the results can be quite disturbing. God in his grace has endowed all human beings with the capacity for creativity and imagination, and He wills that these gifts be used as tools for good. For the Christian, there is a special advantage. Where God's word and His Spirit intersect, there is potential for divinely inspired creativity that is not always available to the non-believer. When God's Spirit met God's word at creation, everything that exists was created. When His Spirit and word meet in the heart and soul of the believer, the same kind of creative and transformational potential is available. For the preacher, the interaction between the word, His Spirit, and our hearts releases the power to communicate in a creative and transformational way.

Creativity and imagination involve special patterns of thought. Mark Galli and Craig Brian Lawson describe creativity as a subconscious process that oc-

---

[9] Wiersbe, 222.
[10] Mark Miller, 58.

curs after someone has absorbed a considerable amount of data on a subject.[11] That is why broad reading acts as such a catalyst for creativity and fuels our imaginations. The creative and imaginative processes seemed mystical to ancient people as can be seen in the Greek concept of the "muse." The Greeks believed there was a spirit or a goddess who inspired the creation of literature and the arts. There were several possible "muses" behind creative operation, and each person had to find his or her own muse in order to be inspired for creative work.[12] Exposure to new ideas helps us tap into our muse—the Spirit—by stoking the fires of creativity and imagination.

As we read broadly and experience everyday life, our conscious mind acquires information from a variety of sources. The conscious mind learns and then moves on to other things, but the subconscious mind continues to process the information and look for meaning and application. The left brain acquires the knowledge through evaluative thinking processes and helps us to learn. It evaluates the truthfulness, logic, relevancy, and importance of the new knowledge in that learning process. We are most often aware of these evaluative thought processes when we are involved in learning at a conscious level.[13] But all the while, on a largely unconscious level, the right brain digests and applies the things we have learned in order to produce meaning. That is the creative part of our minds at work.

The work of our left brain and its evaluative thought seed the efforts of our right brain and its creative thought. With the information we have gathered, the right brain goes to work. The right brain functions as a source of a different kind of thinking called generative thinking. Evaluative thinking is often conscious, linear, and logical. Generative thinking is often subconscious, freewheeling, and nonlinear. Generative thought is seeded by the evaluative thought and learning process; then it takes on a life of its own.

One common kind of generative thinking we can all relate to occurs when we dream. For many years, scientists believed that the brain rested each night during sleep. This could not be further from the truth. While many of our conscious thought processes take a rest, the subconscious mind can be highly active while we sleep. The latest research on sleep suggests that there are scheduled periods of sleep each night when a person enters a very deep state of sleep known as rapid eye movement (REM) sleep. During REM sleep, the subconscious mind is very active. REM sleep is often associated with dreaming, believed to be a subconscious generative thought process. In dreams, random in-

[11] Galli and Lawson, 28. Their book is written from the perspective of journalists. They have much to offer preachers in the way of suggestions for creativity and writing in communication.
[12] Ibid., 23. *"hai mousai"* (the muse) of the Greeks was considered the source of one's inspiration. We see the concept handed down today as actors speak of finding their muse, and ordinary, everyday folks seek "a-muse-ment" as a diversion to restore their creativity.
[13] Ibid., 24.

formation gathered by an individual during waking is being associated with other recorded memories through subconscious generative thought processes. When dreaming, random information gathered by an individual during his or her waking hours is being associated with other recorded memories through subconscious generative thought processes. It is as though God designed a period of cessation for the rational mind so the generative mind could have its way. REM sleep periods are when these generative thought processes literally produce and fuse neural pathways in the brain that allow information stored in the brain to have order and meaning to us so we can later access it while we are awake.[14]

REM sleep and its generative thought processes allow us to see how the brain uses creative and imaginative thought processes to create meaning. It seems that generative and evaluative thought work against one another. Evaluative thought is at its peak when generative thought is dormant. The opposite is also true—when the evaluative part of our brain is quiet, generative thought can be unleashed and is dominant.[15] The key to generative thought seems to be activities that give the rational part of our brain a rest. Again, when we sleep, the conscious evaluative thought process is quieted and the subconscious generative processes can become more dominant, allowing our brain time to try to make sense of everything we have observed, learned, and experienced that day. That is why dreams often seem to make little rational sense—creativity often abandons the limitations and rules of evaluative thought and soars beyond them in a kind of thinking that we call "out-of-the-box" thought. This kind of out-of-the-box generative thinking is what can make dreams seem so surreal to us. In dreaming, we can break the normal rules that guide more evaluative kinds of left-brained thinking.

Thinking "inside the box" with its set of unwritten rules is what keeps us bound to familiar patterns. When Einstein changed the whole way we thought about the universe with his general and special theories of relativity, he actually created nothing new; he simply used creative thought to see in the existing theories of his time what others could not see. His creative thought was often akin to a dream state—his caregivers would often find him dressed to leave for work but sitting in the foyer for hours deep in thought, having never left the house. Is it any wonder then that people often awake with solutions to their problems after a night's sleep? They may have been battling with rational, left-brained thinking all day and have arrived at no solution. Sleep has afforded them an opportunity to shut down the logical mind long enough to let the creative mind have its way.

---

[14] William J. Cromie, "Research Links Sleep, Dreams, and Learning," *The Harvard University Gazette*, February 8, 1996,
http://www.news.harvard.edu/gazette/1996/02.08/ResearchLinksSl.html (accessed on July 1, 2009).
[15] Galli and Lawson, 24.

Many inventions have been discovered while individuals have been asleep, awaking to record their innovative thoughts. Many a preacher, myself included, sleeps with a notepad right next to his or her bed. My first pastor (the one who gave me my first chance to preach) would go to sleep many nights and wake up to pray and study an hour or two later. This was his practice for many years, and I am convinced it was the secret to his creativity in preaching. Some of my most creative sermons often come together in the middle of the night as I wake up or in the morning as I first rise after a good night's sleep. It's amazing to see what can happen when the rational mind takes a break and the creative mind is released.

The secret to unlocking creativity is to find what unlocks your generative thought processes. We are at a disadvantage in the Western world because of our bias for evaluative thinking and against generative thinking. Western advances in science and technology have proven the value of evaluative thought and its place in scientific method. Logical deductive thinking has allowed science to make remarkable advancements that have benefited humanity, but often evaluative thought is exalted and generative thought is ignored or even demeaned.

As mentioned earlier, Wiersbe observes that homiletics is a science and an art and that the highest truths are not always reached by analysis.[16] He also quotes Hugh Black who says that the deepest appeal is not made to logic but to imagination, not to the intellect but to the heart.[17] The Scriptures themselves are not written deductively like a book of rules to be followed and logically figured out; they seem to be written inductively, appealing to both evaluative and generative thought. Life is not lived deductively but inductively. Life is abrupt, illogical, and disordered most of the time.[18] If you think about it, communication itself is often much more inductive and generative than deductive and logical—it flows from the heart. That is why creative generative thought is so important to preaching. Wiersbe observes that creativity is a result of the preacher's imagination bringing both the science and the art of preaching together.[19]

Feeding Your Creativity and Imagination

When we tap into our subconscious creativity, our imagination is activated. Imagination is the driving force behind the power of metaphor—it makes what is abstract seem to be concrete and comprehensible. Imagination must be fed; otherwise, it starves and cannot function. If the wellsprings of creativity and imagination are that important to preachers and to their communication, then what can be done to assure these gifts function at peak efficiency? What can be

[16] Lloyd M. Perry and Hugh Black, quoted in Wiersbe, 222-223.
[17] Black, quoted in Wiersbe, 223.
[18] Ibid., 227.
[19] Wiersbe, 292.

done to move away roadblocks that hinder our creativity and constrain our imaginations?

To start, preachers need examine how we are living our lives. As preachers,
we grow up quickly and face a myriad of challenges in ministry. If preaching
and sermon preparation were all that were expected of us, then things would be
different; but our job demands much more. Counseling loads, building projects,
congregational meetings, board and leadership decisions, and conflict are also
part of every minister's life. The tension, stress, and demands of ministry actually work against our effectiveness in the discharge of ministry when the burden
becomes too great. Stress also begins to shut down the wellsprings of creativity
and imagination as it drives us into survival mode.

With rare exception, people who are trying to survive are not at their most
creative or imaginative. When we are trying to survive, our energies are focused
on the evaluative thoughts of how make it through another day. The reality of
what is happening around us can consume us—there is no space for imagination.
The way out of this trap is to take steps that optimize our creative and imaginative resources. Releasing ourselves from the things that hinder our creativity and
imagination often requires major change that could look self-serving or down-
right selfish. But this kind of change is actually for the good of those we serve.
Spending time away from the crowd or saying no to good things in order to embrace the best things doesn't always sit well with those who need us, but the
personal and professional costs of allowing our creativity and imagination to
dwindle or dry up are simply too high both for ourselves and for those to whom
we minister. As an encouragement to preachers, let us always remember that we
have the most creative force in the universe within us, the Holy Spirit Himself, if
we can find away to let Him express Himself.[20]

Moving back toward creativity when it seems to be distant or lost first requires a change in attitude. Jesus illustrated the kind of attitude essential for
creativity when some little children were brought by their mothers to see Him.
The disciples surrounding Jesus assumed that He would be "too busy" with adult
things like healing the sick or raising the dead to schedule some time with kids.
His disciples were wrong. Jesus corrected His adult disciples by telling them
that unless they became as little children, they would not even see the kingdom
of God (Mark 10:14).

It seems that the secrets of the kingdom, and the kingdom itself, are reserved for children. Children's hearts are most likely to be caught up in the
wonder of life not locked tight by busyness. Children are busy to be sure, but
they are busy asking questions and alive with wonder about what they sense
around them. Their curiosity is in overdrive and their questions can seem limitless. Children are trying to piece this thing we call "life" together and make

---

[20] Mark Miller, 60.

sense of it all. Their curiosity can drive adults crazy at times, but they are on a mission—to discover what is true about their world—and they won't be denied.

Mark Miller observes that healthy curiosity is the first step toward creativity.[21] The Greeks considered curiosity, called *curiosita*, a virtue foundational for all formation and learning. Children are like two-winged birds. Hormonal changes that occur at puberty often select for left-brained-dominant thinking for boys and more right-brained-dominant thinking for girls.[22] But children can think with both the evaluative and generative parts of their brain—their left and right brains work in tandem to decode life and its meaning. To think effectively and to be at their creative peak once again, preachers have to take the admonition of Jesus literally and become as curious children once again.

When the well seems to be running dry, the first step toward regaining creativity and harnessing imagination is to become like a child. That happens as we reimage God as "Daddy" in our hearts. Wiersbe was quoted earlier in this book as saying that ". . . no man can rise higher than the beauty and the quality of the pictures that hang in the gallery of their own heart."[23] In this case, these words ring true for the preacher and the way he or she sees God. When He becomes "Daddy," I can rest in Him as a child, and it becomes safe once again to adopt some healthy childlike qualities.[24] In childlikeness, we begin to imagine again. Daddy has the rest taken care of, and we can leave it to Him. "Daddy" is the cry of Jesus in the garden when He faced death and asked if there was any other way (Mark 14:36). "Daddy" is also the cry of the Christian who has received the "spirit of adoption" (Rom. 8:15) and of the Holy Spirit Himself within us when we are saved (Gal. 4:6). "Daddy" must be the cry of every preacher if he or she is to draw from the wellsprings of creativity and imagination. When we return to childlikeness in our attitude, faith, and thinking, we render our imaginations fertile ground.

A return to childlikeness is a return to inductive thought and lifestyle. When life is lived like an adventure and an experiment, each day becomes infused with new creativity and imagination. Adult thought patterns and attitudes can often choke the word and the creative process needed for transformational preaching. Both anxiety over ministry and the affairs of life quickly choke the seed of the word and render it infertile, because they slowly drain the heart of life; anxiety, worry, and busyness become like weeds that drain the vital nutrients and water from the soil of the heart. In principle, though sadly this is not the case in many places, little children have not yet learned to be anxious, because Mom and Dad

---

[21] Mark Miller, 60.

[22] Rose Palazzolo, "Study: Boys' and Girls' Brain Process Differently," *ABC News*, July 10, 2009, http://abcnews.go.com/Health/story?id=117338&page=1 (accessed July 31, 2009).

[23] Wiersbe, 62.

[24] The beloved Hebrew word for "Father" is "אָב" (*ab*) from which comes the endearing term *abba* or "Daddy."

will take care of things. It can take a while for children to learn to let anger simmer and become bitterness. Children are generally quick to release hurts and problems because children do not have a sense that they are in control anyway. Anger and bitterness can get in the way of today's fun, so children may feel those emotions and then move on. The heart of a child is so different than that of an adult with all our adult concerns. That's what makes children so free to be imaginative and creative.

Becoming childlike as a preacher allows us to embrace an inductive outlook on life. As Eugene Lowry observes, we become "first listeners" once again as we lay aside our own agendas and learn to observe and to listen like children.[25] We move from the role of "great explainer" as preachers to "great listener" as any child should be. When we come to the Scriptures, we lay down our agenda. We cease to embrace the Scriptures as a document to prove what we believe and instead embrace them as a source to help us to discover the truth. We let the Bible read us instead of always just reading it. Inductive thought begins to rein-vigorate the soul and to get the soul's creative juices flowing. Induction shakes the cobwebs off our imagination, and we begin to discover as children once again. Inductive thinking begins to feed our starved imaginations, and the wellspring of new creativity begins to flow. Once creativity and imagination begin to flow, they often take on a life of their own and develop a momentum that carries them along with less effort on our part.

Revitalizing Creative Flow

The activity of ministry often crowds out our ability to feel. It is said that children often "wear their feelings on their sleeves." That word picture is meant to convey how easily one can tell what emotions a child is feeling. One look at a child's face and the expression leaves no doubt as to what that child feels at that moment. If we are not careful as adults, we can shut down the emotional part of our lives to our own detriment. Emotions will not be denied and are the essence of what makes us human beings. If they are not expressed outwardly, they often turn inward and become one of the leading causes of chronic ailments like ulcers and heart disease.

Many times a period of intense emotion will trip our emotional circuit breakers so that we live with emotions that are too intense and normally would melt our mental circuitry. For a period of time, the circuit breaker is off, helping us live with pain and heartache, but if the intensity continues, it can lead to a quality of life that is subhuman. We are made to feel as humans, and feelings are the substance of our consciousness and the atmosphere that causes our thinking

---

[25] Lowry, 33.

to live and breathe.[26] Many preachers live in a chronic state of emotional deprivation that borders on burnout, because of the demands of ministry and its emotional drain. In such seasons, there is no solution but to rest.

In American society, we associate activity with productivity and inactivity with waste. A moment not spent in activity toward some end is a moment wasted. Our famous phrase is "Don't just stand there, do something." I think God may be looking right back at us and saying, "Don't just do something, stand there." In the America, we have a crisis of overactivity, because we think that being active ensures fulfillment and good. The Scriptures are clear that fulfillment and good are found in rest. After God created the heavens and the earth, He rested (Gen. 2:2). The Hebrew word here for "rest" is the word that we draw upon for "Sabbath."[27] God did not rest because He was tired—He is all powerful. He rested to establish a pattern for humans to follow. He also rested to enjoy what He had created. Both would seem like a waste of time according to prevailing American thought. Why didn't God get on to something else instead of pausing for rest? If He wasn't tired, then why didn't He keep on creating? The answer: what He created was too wonderful to miss enjoying. Preachers need to take a lesson from God if they want to flow in the creative and imaginative power that is locked up inside them.

Resting is actually an act of recreation (re-creation). It is infused with the power to recharge the batteries of our creative soul. Unless the preacher is willing to build in regular rest and cease from his own works as God did from His, creativity and imagination are soon drained and cease to flow (Heb. 4:10). When we fail to rest, we actually become less productive, because creativity and imagination are so much a part of efficiency. Rest allows us time to re-center and discover that our ministry is not dependent on us but on God. Resting allows us to acknowledge our humanity and His divinity—that we are different than God, not having limitless energy and capacity.

Our uneasiness with rest betrays a subtle but deadly pride lurking in the preacher's heart—the thought that we are somehow indispensible and that because we are so important, we cannot "waste" the time to rest. A more severe case of this diseased thought process can be identified as a martyr complex, which somehow justifies no rest because we are "working for Jesus" and God's work is "never done." The martyr attitude has its root in pride and violates the commandment requiring that everyone (preachers included) honor the Sabbath and keep it holy (Deut 5:12). When we set aside time to rest, we honor God and His Word, and we are renewed. It is my contention that each preacher must have at least one day off per week, several days off per quarter, and at least a week to

---

[26] John MacMurray, a philosopher, quoted in Galli and Larson, 17. This is not a quote from MacMurray, but my thoughts are adapted from MacMurray's quote in Galli and Larson.

[27] The word used in Gen. 2:2 is "שָׁבַת" (sabbath), which means "to cease, rest, or desist."

ten days off per year. Many of the most experienced ministers step back from significant work for a month during a slow period, such as August in the United States. Many talented and successful ministers take time off, and, indeed, time off may be one of the sources of their unusual fruitfulness and longevity in ministry. Disciplined rest makes the difference between a ministry that goes off and burns out like a firecracker and one that is a slow-burning flame, lasting for decades.

Rest is the source of creativity and imagination and, like sleep, the source of generative thought. When the preacher is disciplined to rest, he or she creates opportunity for the kinds of activities that feed generative thought. Prayer and meditation are most often associated with generative rather than evaluative thought. Studies of the brain show that the mental states brought on while someone is praying or meditating actually alter brain physiology in a way that facilitates creativity.[28]

Rest allows for time to break out of the routine and rhythm of everyday life, and the break itself can renew creativity. Rest also allows time for us to connect with creative people. The preacher must surround him- or herself with creative people because creativity is contagious (so is a lack of creativity). Rest allows time for broad-based reading outside the general field of theology, and such reading can be a powerful tool for seeding the imagination. News, current events, hobbies, and outside interests are essential to the creative process and provide a cross-disciplinary avenue for feeding the imagination. Some of the best word pictures can be found as we experience the world around us or discover the wonders of our environment. God is the Supreme Artist and He is always original; as we have been learning, nature is a wonderful source for imaginative sermons.[29]

What do you like to do to rest? What activities do you pursue for recreation? By exposure to sound words, creative people, and God's creation as we rest, we feed the imagination and renew our creativity. The quality of what we expose ourselves to is important, as is the variety. Wiersbe observes that the imagination is fed by words, concepts, and visual images, but primarily through words and concepts.[30] Feeding the imagination and the intellect produces a holistic sense of satisfaction in our souls. By doing both, we become balanced in

---

[28] See "Brain Activity During Meditation," http://www.crystalinks.com/medbrain.html (accessed July 1, 2009). The site is a compendium of articles written on meditation and its effects on the physiology and psychology of the brain. This is not a Christian source but rather a collection of articles from a variety of sources that comment on this subject.

[29] See Wiersbe, 26-28. As Wiersbe observes, left-brained people often miss it. Nicodemus didn't get it about being born again (John 3:1-12). The Samaritan woman could not connect with where to get living water (John 4:1-15). The Jews stumbled over the requirement of eating Jesus' body and drinking His blood (John 6:52-59).

[30] Ibid., 73.

our creativity, not allowing either the science or the art of preaching to become extreme.[31]

Exposure to words seems to be more powerful than exposure to visual images, because words allow us to build our own metaphoric bridges and to create our own concept of reality, whereas visual images seem to go right into the heart with little such processing. Music also seems to access a creative language that taps into the imagination. The messages that visual images convey, on the other hand, tend to bypass our thinking and influence us subjectively in ways that we do not consciously comprehend.[32] Our own images are more meaningful than the ones that are fed to us as crafted by the media experts. This is an important point for preachers—time spent reading and hearing words is a more excellent way to rest than is sitting in front of the television or a movie. Often television and movies transport us to a fantasy world with little thought required on our parts—we are passive passengers on the journey. Visual entertainment often creates a fantasy world of escape for us. But imagination is not an escape from reality; rather, it is meant to help us penetrate truth and reality from a generative-thought perspective.

A Creative Mindset

Creativity can seem elusive because generative thought is so different from evaluative thought—it is so different that many people can talk themselves out of creative thought and creative ability, convincing themselves they are not "gifted" in that way. Each of us is uniquely gifted, and as with all gifts, we can develop what we have. Each of us has been given a measure of creativity, just as each of us has been given a measure of faith. What creativity we possess can be developed. As with faith, the quantity of creativity that you possess is not important—it is the quality of your creativity that counts. Creativity also mirrors faith in that creativity can only be refined as it is used, and its use can sometimes be intimidating.

The parallel between faith and creativity is striking because, like faith, creativity is not a one-time event but a lifestyle. It is up to us to refine our faith as we put it into practice in our daily walk (Rom. 12:2). Faith is not meant to be used in certain circumstances and then put to rest, but we walk by faith each day and move from faith to faith as though life were a body of water and faith were a string of rocks acting as our stepping stones. Life is meant to be a leap from rock to rock as we exercise faith each day, with no pause intended. In the same way, Wiersbe observes, creativity is not a set of techniques to be followed but rather a lifestyle meant to be lived out each day—or an approach to life itself. [33] Ap-

---

[31] Ibid., 60.

[32] Ibid., 73.

[33] Ibid., 290.

proaching the Scriptures and life in this creative, childlike, and inductive manner develops the gift of creativity resident within the preacher, making the gift become flesh as it clothes the word as it is preached.

The emotions involved in creative thinking frustrate many preachers. Creativity does not seem to correlate with intelligence, at least not the way intelligence is currently measured.[34] Many intelligent preachers get frustrated in their attempts to be creative because generative thinking can be quite intimidating, especially when preachers are so schooled in evaluative thought. Graduate-level seminary work is laden with evaluative approaches to ministry that provide neat sets of rules allowing us to cleverly rip things into pieces that are small enough to understand. People who are dominated by rules end up becoming imitators, while people with the ability to think outside the box in a generative way become innovators.[35] Innovation requires that we move beyond evaluation and tap into our creativity and imagination. The church is not lacking for imitators, but it is in desperate need of innovators.

The way to develop your creativity is by practicing—the same way artists develop their creativity. Practice includes developing an excellent filing system for your ideas. Do not let ideas get away from you. When creativity is flowing, write the ideas down and then develop a filing system so you can access those ideas in the future. Idea generation and creative activity are holy things and should be treated that way, but ideas will be lost if not recorded and filed in some meaningful way. They will be lost because of the way the brain stores information—you have not forgotten the thought but rather forgotten how to remember the thought.

Our memories are stored by association, and they require triggers for us to remember where they are stored. Certain words or sounds can set off a cascade of memories associated with them. Otherwise, those memories may remain hidden. Every sermon you ever preach should be stored in a file with one word on it to describe a topic or theme that is meaningful to you. The file might be a physical folder in a file cabinet or a virtual file on a computer hard drive. Accumulate sermons, articles, pictures, and newspaper and magazine clippings under these topics and let these files grow with time. Use the contents of these files to trigger memories and to seed generative thought on sermon topics. My files now encompass nearly thirty-five years of preaching and generative thought about sermon topics, and the files are a treasured source for word pictures and practical application for sermon preparation. How stimulating it is to look back at what I have preached in the past on a particular subject and at how it was preached. Looking back at these sermons and the things I have since thrown into their files provides me with major generative thought seeds for future sermons.

---

[34] Larsen, 112.
[35] Wiersbe, 290.

I like the word "imagineering" to describe the creative thought processes we use when crafting our sermons.[36] Preaching is an excellent way to tap into the power of imagineering because of the power preaching has been given by our Creator. Written words can appear to be disconnected from reality, because they do not come alive until we hear them with our ears or in our minds. Spoken words have more power than the printed word, because sound creates a greater reality than the printed word and gives those printed words life when we preach. Sound unites groups of people like the printed word could never do—the sound of a common language establishes identity and even locates someone. The sound of a song sung in unison produces oneness and community as we all literally vibrate together with the same pitch.

Walter Ong observes that the spoken word appears to be the closest sensory equivalent of fully developed inner thought.[37] The other senses—taste, smell, touch, and sight—can mirror or represent inner thought, but sound captures it most completely. Sound gives us the experience of being inside someone's heart. Touch, sight, taste, and smell are external experiences, but sound actually occurs as it moves inside of me; and as I listen to another speak, I experience what originated inside someone else. The thoughts of another person—thoughts that originated inside that person's heart and soul—are now within me and in my heart and soul. Because of the way our Creator designed words to penetrate the heart, I can share that kind of intimacy with someone else. Sermon-shaping is the process of skillfully shaping sound to optimize its ability to penetrate the heart deeply and with maximum impact. Creativity and imagination are the tools that do the shaping. Each preacher works as a creative imagineer in the shaping process.

Though this may at first seem counterintuitive, I find it necessary to treat creativity as a discipline. If I wait to feel creative, no sermons are written. Creative flow most often starts as I struggle with the rusty topic and try to force it open by beginning an imagineering session with a sermon. After I push through for a while, creativity begins to flow, and then it often comes in gushes. When I feel stuck without an ounce of creative juice flowing, I immediately begin to seed my imagination. The Psalms have always been a daily source of images and word pictures that spark creativity for me. The Psalms in general are an image engine expressing God and His ways in a poetic and creative manner—a highly image rich environment that can get the creative juices following.

---

[36] The term *imagineering* was used by Walt Disney as early as 1952 to describe his studios and their production of creative media for entertainment. Wiersbe also uses that term to describe the creative process and imagination that is used in sermon development (285).

[37] Walter J. Ong, S. J., *The Presence of the Word* (Minneapolis: University of Minnesota, 1967), 138-139. This book is a rich resource for understanding the psychology of sound and words and their impact on the human soul.

I might also deliberately begin with generative kinds of thought exercises. I may start with a kind of thinking exercise called "freewheeling."[38] When freewheeling, I deliberately let my mind wander in any direction it wants to go and watch where it takes me. Freewheeling is particularly effective for me when I am out for a walk or run and my inclination for evaluative thought is more silent. Music is also a powerful tool for facilitating the fresh flow of creativity, as is worship. At other times, I will do a kind of thinking called "clustering," recalling a specific memory, theme, or focus and then allowing my mind to associate these thoughts with the truth I am grappling with in my sermon. This exercise is especially helpful for me because it allows the imagination to act as a kind of "womb" in which I recall a memory and experience the feelings and perceptions stored with that memory, combining it with a truth that God may be currently highlighting in my life.[39]

In developing a creative mindset for sermon-shaping, it is essential that the preacher move into a different kind of prayer that is meditative and heuristic in nature.[40] Preachers often have no shortage of things to pray about in their ministry. The needs are great for both the preacher and the congregation he or she serves, and God invites us to ask so that we can have these needs met. But intercessory prayer and petition can easily become a trap if they become one-sided events. Prayer at its very core is meant to be a kind of communion with God. If prayer becomes a time when the preacher talks at God, then it will eventually become drained of its transformative power. When prayer begins to move into the realm of abiding with God, it can become highly transformational and can be a wonderful source for seeding creativity and imagination in the preacher's life. When we ponder or reflect in God's presence, we practice the ancient art of meditation and tap into its power.

Meditation in a biblical sense differs greatly from meditative practices associated with many other religions. In the practice of Eastern religions such as Buddhism, the goal is to completely empty the mind. In the practice of Christian meditation, as the word "meditation" in the Old Testament implies, we actually fill the mind.[41] When we speak to ourselves and to God by asking questions, this expresses curiosity and taps into heuristic thinking, which is a generative process. Simply pondering a thought, truth, or word picture is a kind of generative thought process that invites fresh ideas or perspectives. In normal conversa-

---

[38] See Galli and Larson, 25, for an excellent discussion on different kinds of thinking.

[39] This is Wiersbe's observation as well (25).

[40] Heuristic thought or action is based on discovery, using experience as a basis for learning how to solve life's problems.

[41] The Hebrew words that we translate "meditate" are very descriptive. The root "שׂוּחַ" (suach) means to muse or ponder something, and the word "הָגָה" (hagah) means "to moan, mutter, growl, or speak." Both are very active processes that fill the mind as opposed to the Eastern practice of trying to empty the mind. When Ps. 4:4 tells us to "meditate on our beds," it uses the root "אָמַר" (amar), which is the word root for "speak."

tion between close friends, pondering and questioning naturally flow. They are what make conversations interesting and should be at the core of our conversations with God.

Ultimately, fear can be the greatest enemy of a creative mindset. Fear and anxiety can quickly turn off the flow of creativity and imagination. Preachers grapple with fear and anxiety, because each time we preach, we are only one word away from infamy. Our fear of rejection is one of the strongest. It takes courage to preach and even more courage to preach a creative and imaginative sermon. Mark Miller observes that the fear of rejection cascades into a fear of failure, which eventually becomes a fear of even trying.[42] The preacher can take courage that God has not given us a spirit of timidity but one of power, love, and soundness of mind (2 Tim. 1:7).[43] We can't let timidity or fear get in the way, because we aim for transformation with our words, and people's lives hang in the balance.

Creativity and imagination are vital to the transformational impact of the sermon, and God has given you more than enough resources to do what He has called you to do. It is simply time to develop and foster the creative mindset that He has given you in order to impact lives with your words. Mark Miller reminds us that in the person of the Holy Spirit, we have the most creative force in the universe inside us.[44] Mark Twain reminds us that "It is never too late to rekindle our creativity, and that it is still there inside you, in greater quantities than you realize."[45] Imagine that!

Helping People Listen

Creativity and imagination are powerful, sermon-shaping tools because they help people listen. There is a vast difference between hearing and listening. Hearing starts when sound waves from the human voice box or from an object in our environment release energy sufficient to produce vibrations in the air around us. These sound waves hit the human ear and are funneled efficiently into an amazing network of bones and structures that translate that vibrating wave energy into nerve impulses that are relayed to the brain. The brain then decodes the sounds—their tone, pitch, quality, and sequence—into sounds that mean something. That is, if the brain is paying attention. We are constantly, every second, bombarded by a myriad of sensory inputs, and sound is just one of them. There are constant noises around us, and our brain is fine-tuned to dismiss and ignore things deemed unimportant or having no meaning to us at a given moment. The

---

[42] Mark Miller, 66-68.

[43] Here the specific word in the Greek text, often translated "fear," is actually "δειλία" (deilia), which should be translated "cowardice" or "timidity."

[44] Mark Miller, 62.

[45] Mark Twain, quoted in Mark Miller, 63.

brain's sorting action is a subconscious process of which we are unaware. Someone can be speaking, but we may not "hear" them. We actually do hear them, but they are being filtered out. We are not listening to them. Only those with "ears to hear" are actually listening. To those who are not listening, our words and their impact are lost. To the extent that it is within his or her power, it is the responsibility of the preacher to help an audience listen.

Most people are lousy listeners. This is because listening is not a passive process—we must decide to listen and exert energy in order to do it. We decide to listen because we decide the things being said are important, relevant, and worthy of the effort. Being listened to is an earned right, as any preacher soon finds out. Creativity and imagination are the preacher's best friends when it comes to earning the right to be heard.

Some might argue that the anointing and power of the Holy Spirit are what earn the preacher the right and give him or her the ability to be heard. After all, Paul says in 1 Cor. 2:4 that he did not come with persuasive words but in demonstration of the Spirit and power. The power of the Holy Spirit is wonderful as He convicts, teaches, reproves, and trains through the spoken word. But even His power does not guarantee people will listen. If it did, there would have been constant success in Jesus' preaching ministry, but many (if not most) of His words were rejected by the multitudes. After Jesus' first hometown sermon, they tried to throw Him of a local cliff (Luke 4:29). People hear all the time but selectively choose what they will listen to from among the noise. Being creative and imaginative with our sermons gives us the edge in earning the right to be heard.

Preaching Like Jesus

Jesus knew how to be heard. What He preached was certainly important—He said that He only preached as the Father gave Him words—yet many chose not to listen. Jesus made truth interesting for anyone who chose to listen. He was the master of telling stories. Jesus certainly knew the Scriptures and could quote them word for word from memory, as we see many times in the Gospels, but Jesus told stories more often than He quoted Scripture. Stories and parables account for more than one-third of Jesus' recorded words. He used at least seventy-seven parables in His teaching, depending on how you count them. He selected stories that were always perfect for the occasion, bringing abstract truth to life in a way that was simple, relevant, and immediately applicable to people's needs. John Maxwell calls the practice of simplicity in bringing abstract truth to life "putting the cookies on the bottom shelf," where the goodies can be reached by everyone. Stories help people listen.

Mark Miller observes that most sermons tell people what to do, whereas stories force people to think.[46] The inductive nature of a story capitalizes on the need for the listener to ponder meaning, which seems to be a basic drive in all human beings. Sadly, however, many preachers don't trust their listeners enough to think for themselves. We are convinced that if we don't think for them, they will not arrive at the truth on their own. Jesus seemed to think that they would, and He told them stories. He knew that stories open a door for the Holy Spirit to help in the discovery of meaning when people are seeking answers. Stories by their very nature invite the hearers of any sermon to come along on the journey and to participate in an active manner as they ponder the truth that the story attempts to convey. In this way, the listener actually is a participant in the sermon experience—through the listening process, he or she gets to experience the truth in the sermon.[47] We preachers become "story weavers" as we communicate like Jesus did and as God knits our hearts with the hearts of our audience into a beautiful tapestry of truth and understanding.

Stories are powerful because they do several things for the listener.[48] First, the story creates a context—a space in which the truth can exist. Stories create a narrative environment in which an abstract concept can live and breathe. Parables are so effective because they create a place for the truth to live. Parables are extended similes—they tell us in detail what something is like, building a metaphoric bridge between abstract truth and something that the truth is like in the world around us.[49] Parables are not like allegories, which are designed to serve a different purpose. Allegories are extended metaphors that often use symbols to convey meaning. Parables flow much more freely—they contain a lot of background description to paint a context for the truth. Every detail does not have a meaning—if meaning is forced on each descriptive element, as might be the case in an allegory, then the truth the parable attempts to convey is easily lost or obscured. If we are to preach like Jesus, we must become masters at telling stories, painting the backdrop with elements from our listeners' world so they can easily relate to our words.

Once the preacher has created a detail-rich context for the story being told, it is important to populate that context with characters and props that are familiar to the listener in everyday life. Jesus populated stories with sheep, goats, seeds, good Samaritans, and bad weeds. He used these characters and props because people encountered them in everyday life and were intimately acquainted with them. You knew sheep in Bible days because if you didn't, you had nothing

---

[46] Mark Miller, 41.

[47] Tomlin, 1.

[48] Mark Miller, 95. Here Miller gives an excellent description of the power of experiential storytelling and how to meld it into sermon preparation.

[49] The word "parable" is from the Greek word "παραβολή" (*parabole*) meaning "to cast alongside"—it implies that abstract truth is placed alongside something known in order to explain what it is like.

to wear and nothing to eat. You knew about seeds because if they didn't get planted in the right soil, you starved and died. You disliked Samaritans because they were considered "half-breeds," and you probably thought more of the priests than you should have—in fact, they were really "whitewashed tombs" full of "dead men's bones." People today don't live with sheep and are probably eating chicken or cow while wearing their acrylic clothing. Each generation is in need of its own characters and props to populate its own unique stories. Creativity and imagination are a preacher's best friends. Each day is an inductive adventure for the preacher with a creative mindset, and we can use what we learn in life as we integrate stories in our sermons.

It is important to give our characters and props texture and life as we preach, and we can do that with the skillful use of voice and body language. Preachers need to make use of varied tone, pitch, and cadence when presenting a story. My words must be designed to elicit emotion, and my body must feel the appropriate emotion as my words are spoken so can I embody the emotion for the audience to see and experience.

Remember, communication is far more than just the words we speak. As listeners, we learn about 7% from the actual content of a person's words, 38% from the tone of that person's voice, and 55% from facial expression.[50] Most of what we learn comes from the *way* a person speaks. Learning from the speaker's body language and other nonverbal cues constitutes an amazing 93% of what we learn. Thus, my expression as a preacher becomes an essential tool I use to paint word pictures with more vivid colors for the listener. Listeners should not have to settle for a "silent film" or a "black-and-white" sermon. My words are chosen to help the listener see what I am saying, taste and smell what I am describing, and touch the truth that I am preaching. Statistics show that we remember 10% of anything we hear and 30% of what we see. But we remember 60% of what we do or experience.[51] Do you see why it's so important that your audience enter a listening experience? Stories drive truth down into our consciousness and make truth memorable. These are the very reasons that Jesus' sermons were incarnational—His listeners actually experienced the truth as they listened to Jesus and were transformed by that experience.

Buttrick observes that effective stories take on a life beyond their words.[52] A story starts off like a picture, and we see the background. Then the story be-

---

[50] Albert Mehrabian did work with nonverbal communication and published several often cited studies that quantify the extent to which nonverbal communication influences our communication. For more information on his ground breaking studies, see Albert Mehrabian and Morton Wiener, "Decoding of Inconsistent Communications," *Journal of Personality and Social Psychology* 6, no.1 (1967): 109-114 and Albert Mehrabian and Susan R. Ferris, "Inference of Attitudes from Non-verbal Communication in Two Channels," *Journal of Consulting Psychology* 31, no. 3 (1967): 248-252.

[51] Lewis and Lewis, (1983), 29.

[52] Buttrick, 20.

comes a mirror as we see ourselves in the story and live it out in our own hearts. Finally, the story becomes a window through which we can see life, reality, and truth for ourselves, and we are changed.[53] If we stop and think about it, life is actually a collection of stories, and that is the way we perceive life as we move through time. Each of us has our own unique story with its unique context, population, and experiences. We access our individual story and its pieces as we try to make sense of life. This is what I have observed during my pastoral care of the sick and dying—they are constantly looking back, rehearsing their story, and trying to sum it up and bring it to a conclusion with some kind of meaning. Our own story approximates our life as it has been lived and frames our own beliefs, values, and understanding of the truth as lived out in our lives. Stories also leverage the power of experience. The preacher who wants his or her words to have transformational impact must master the art of storytelling and preach like Jesus did, helping people to listen. As Tomlin observes, we are story collectors, and each day brings another opportunity to see how the day will fit into our story and, ultimately, into God's story.[54]

Culture—Our Collective Story

Preachers must master the art of storytelling, but stories don't occur in a vacuum. Just as each person has his or her own story, so each distinct group of people have their own collective story. That collective story is what we call "culture." The act of adapting our communication to fit within a certain culture is called *contextualization*. Culture traditionally makes preachers nervous because we can't quite figure out what to do with it. Should we oppose culture to the best of our ability in the name of holiness? Should we embrace culture entirely and become like the world to minimize the offensiveness of the gospel? Should we enter culture and become its heroes and try to redeem it? Or enter and try to tolerate it while we hold our noses? Perhaps we should create a separate "Christian culture" of our very own and invite those on the outside to join us and try to figure us out.[55]

Jimmy Long points out that Christians have another choice—one that fits with the theme of this book.[56] He describes an incarnational theology of culture that allows us to live out and demonstrate the truths of the Scriptures as we fully inhabit our cultural space.[57] We join people where they are and participate in

---

[53] See Wiersbe, 52, who is the source for this powerful word picture.

[54] Tomlin, 65.

[55] Excellent discussions on the way we as Christians should relate to culture can be found in Lesslie Newbigin, *Foolishness to the Greeks* (Grand Rapids: Eerdmans, 1986) and Richard H. Niebuhr, *Christ and Culture* (New York: Harper & Row, 1956).

[56] Jimmy Long, *Generating Hope: A Strategy for Reaching the Post-Modern Generation* (Downers Grove: Intervarsity, 1997).

[57] Ibid., 79.

their culture so they can relate to us as people, earning us the right to be heard. We do not compromise our Christian principles to do this, but we contextualize our lives and message the way any person on the mission field would do to win the hearts of his or her listeners. We learn about our listeners' art and speak their language. This is precisely how Jesus conducted Himself and why people were so comfortable with Him. He did not make a point of trying to be different, and He did not set out to spread His own culture; He left that to the work of the Holy Spirit as He transformed lives through His words. Jesus did not seem to be anti-cultural or countercultural in some overt manner, nor did he try to create a Christian culture of His own. Instead, He used culture as a tool to reach the lost by dressing His words up properly for the occasion.

Preachers must become as skilled in the exegesis of their culture and the world around them as they are of the Hebrew and Greek words of the Scriptures. Culture is something alive and dynamic—it is the collective "soul" of any group of people. In it are embedded the hopes, dreams, and history of people. Effective communication is creative and imaginative enough to build culturally appropriate bridges of communication between the preacher and the listeners. The preacher who does so places him- or herself among the people, as Jesus did. To not build such bridges is to risk the inability to connect with an audience. Awareness of culture is my responsibility, just as it is that of any good missionary. If I watch the people, live with them, and get to know them, soon I will be speaking their language and sharing their experiences. I learn to speak with their words so that, ultimately, they can become more like Him. I learn how to clothe the truth with culturally proper garments—I learn what clothes to dress the message in when I preach. As the preacher, I stop pretending that the message should be dressed in one kind of clothing as if one size should fit all. In the missions world, we got over that about a hundred years ago when we stopped expecting people to dress like us and to speak our language as a part of accepting the gospel. I fear we have not made that same transition in the communication of our sermons.

Preachers must learn to use culture as a tool to help their audience listen. Paul skillfully used culture as a tool when he spoke to the Greeks in their Aeropagus (Acts 17:15-34). Paul had just been run out of town in Thessalonica for his preaching and was on his way to Athens, the heart of the Greek world and culture at that time. As he walked through town he was greatly provoked by all the idols of the Greek gods that were set up in the streets (v. 16). He spent time with the church in town but was anxious to speak with the local people about the gospel. He chose to do so in the heart of the city on a hill known as the Aeropagus, where city court was held and philosophers gathered to discuss their ideas. He took the gospel to the people of Athens on their ground and in a way they could understand.

Though provoked by the idols he had seen in the streets, he saw one that was dedicated to the "unknown god." There were many such altars throughout the city because of a disaster that had occurred several centuries before that time. A terrible pestilence had fallen on the city, but a Cretan poet by the name of Epimenides had an idea. A flock of black-and-white sheep were brought to the "Hill of Mars," now called the Aeropagus, and they were released into the city. Wherever one of the sheep lay down, it was sacrificed on the nearest altar to the god of that altar in order to stop the pestilence. If the altar had no idol, it was sacrificed to the "unknown god."[58] Paul decided that this bit of cultural history would be the bridge into the people's hearts.

Paul was met by the Epicureans and the Stoics, who took him to the Aeropagus to join the philosophical discussions that were taking place (vv. 17,18). The Epicureans believed everything happened by chance and that death was the end of existence. They thought of the gods as distant and remote and believed pleasure was the chief reason for humankind's existence. The Stoics believed that everything was god and that he was a fiery spirit that inhabited material things. A person's life was thought to be a spark of that spirit, which returned to him after that person's death. Stoics thought of every event as the will of this god and believed life circumstances should be accepted without emotion ("stoically") or complaint.[59] Paul made deliberate use of the stoic and epicurean beliefs in his address to them at the Aeropagus.

Paul used the Athenian concept of the "unknown God" and the history of the Aeropagus as a starting point for conversation. He built on the people's culture to help them listen. He addressed their philosophies by telling them of a personal God who cared for them. He even quoted the Greek poet Aratus of Cilicia (the town where Paul was born) to make his point that the gospel was for all people, including his listeners. Paul did all he could to use every tool at his disposal to help the people listen to the gospel. He was not compromising by meeting them on their turf. It was not wrong to use their idols or quote their poets in presenting the gospel. He did not overtly quote from the Scriptures, because these listeners did not know the Scriptures. Rather, Paul chose to clothe the good news in the attire of the people's culture. Not all chose to listen, but some did, because he spoke their language.

How can we as preachers ignore Paul's example when we preach? We do so at both our own peril and the peril of our audience. As Buttrick observes, communication is primarily a function of translation.[60] We do not understand what is said word for word, but we assign concepts to those words, and we actually understand our faith in contrast with our culture. Likewise, preaching involves the translation of the gospel into our cultural formulation—its characteristics, beliefs, and the particular assumptions of a certain people as they exist in space

---

[58] William Barclay, "The Acts of the Apostles," *The Daily Study Bible Series* (Philadelphia: Westminster, 1976), 131-132.
[59] Ibid., 130.
[60] Buttrick, 56.

and time.[61] This kind of translation has always been done in preaching. John used the *logos* of the Greeks to describe the concept of the Word as Logos in his writings. The word *logos* was a very common word used by the Greeks at that time—they used it the way we would use the word *idea* or *concept* in our day. John adapted the word to describe Jesus to his audience as the Logos—the very thought, idea, or expression of God. In doing this, John leveraged the power of a known Greek cultural artifact to make a point about who God really is.

To be sure, there must always be a tension between contextualization of the gospel to make it understandable to a specific culture and assimilation of the gospel where the meaning of the gospel is changed to suit a specific culture. If we use culture as a tool to help people listen, then culture has done its job. If the gospel becomes another attribute of the culture and is swallowed and digested by it, then the gospel loses its power. Every culture is in constant change because, as the collective soul of its people, culture is a living thing. Cultures affect and name the world and environment with new words that constantly come and go.[62] If I use the word *groovy* to describe something nice, you locate me in 1960s America, because the word reveals my time, space, and culture. Do you see the power that one word can have? Cultural subgroups are constantly giving birth to new metaphors and stories and words to tell their stories. The key for the preacher is to fully inhabit his or her cultural space in time and seize any opportunity to use it as a backdrop to help people listen to truth. As we have seen, Jesus was a master at this, as George MacLeod affirms:

> I simply say that the *cross* must be raised again at the center of the *marketplace* as well as the steeple of the church. I am claiming that *Jesus* was not crucified in a *cathedral* between two candles, but on a *cross* between two thieves; on a town *garbage heap*, at a crossroads so cosmopolitan that they had to write His title in Hebrew, Latin, and Greek. At the same place where cynics talk *smut*, and thieves *curse*, and soldiers *gamble*, because that is *where He died*, and that is *what He died about*, and that is *where churchmen ought to be*, and what churchmen *ought to be about* (emphasis added).[63]

Postmodern Culture and the Gospel

As this book is being written, the Western world is in a time of cultural change so dynamic that our time could be compared to the Renaissance or the Reformation. Just as with the shifts in culture that occurred more than five hundred years ago, technology is once again driving this change. Will the church

---

[61] Ibid.
[62] Ibid., 65-66.
[63] Quote is attributed to George Fielden MacLeod, a twentieth-century clergyman and soldier in Scotland who founded the Iona Community there in 1938 and was known as an unconventional minister of the Church of Scotland.

react as it has in times past, retreating from change to take cover or ignoring change so as not to become stained by the world? If so, then the church is retreating from one of the greatest opportunities to reach people with the gospel that has ever existed. Huge cultural shifts can be scary things for people. Culture is the way we know, experience, and understand our world. Culture's written and unwritten rules help us to construct reality, and when culture's fabric changes, the result is a cultural earthquake that upsets our very basis for understanding life.[64] When the old rules of culture change, people become insecure and look for answers. Again I ask, will the church retreat to try to keep itself pure and safe, or will it earn its right to answer some of the world's questions by conversing with culture and speaking the new language? As J. Randall Nichols once observed, people do not have a burning desire to hear about the Jebusites.[65] The exception would be if the preacher could tell us, using a language and communication style we understand, how those Jebusites can help us live life better today.

M. Rex Miller contends there have been four major cultural shifts in Western culture over the last several thousand years and that all these changes have been driven by technological advances. Here is the break down of eras as Miller defines it:[66]

- Oral Culture (4000 BC–1500 AD): During this time period, the primary means of communication was oral, taking the form of face-to-face stories, liturgy, ritual, and symbols;
- Print Culture (1500–1950 AD): With the invention of the printing press, the primary means of communication became printed text, spurring a cultural revolution (the Renaissance) and a religious revolution (the Reformation), as the Scriptures were printed in people's common languages;
- Broadcast Culture (1950–1990 AD): With the invention and spread of television, a media revolution occurred that moved communication from words to images even as it also began to bridge distance to create a global culture and community;
- Digital Culture (1990–???? AD): The introduction of the Internet has created yet another cultural shift by allowing an explosion of global communication and collaboration, as well as a shift toward multimedia communication.

---

[64] Mark Miller, 15.

[65] J. Randall Nichols, quoted in Larsen, 95.

[66] M. Rex Miller, *The Millennial Matrix* (2004), quoted in Mark Miller, 83-85. M. Rex Miller's book is a fascinating summary of how technology has influenced culture over the last several thousand years, concentrating on the way broadcast media and the Internet are creating a cultural tidal wave in our current culture.

Each time communication technology has shifted radically, the culture has shifted radically because of it. Many times in the past, the church has reacted negatively to changes in technology rather than embracing them and using that cultural shift to the advantage of the gospel. The church killed those who tried to use print media technology to get the Scriptures to people in their own languages. It denounced television as a tool of the devil until preachers discovered that people like Billy Graham could use it to propagate the gospel. Will we do better with the Internet and the changes that are happening in a postmodern culture, or will we make the same mistakes we have been famous for in the past?

The answer is probably a little of both. As I write this chapter, there are hopeful signs that the church "gets it" as preachers mobilize to use the Internet to deliver streaming audio and video of worship services and sermons globally, penetrating every country with the gospel message. Many are also using social networking capabilities such as Facebook, MySpace, and Twitter to create virtual communities of faith and to share the gospel. Others are standing back from it all because the change is overwhelming. Some walk the same path seen in the history of the church as they denounce the new technology as evil, consigning themselves to a place in the cultural corner. Would that we would act like Jesus and Paul, embracing the culture and wringing from it every opportunity and method by which to present the gospel in this time and space and in a language that is being spoken at this moment. This starts with our understanding culture as it exists right at this present time.

If we are to help people hear and listen to our sermons, then preachers must understand the people we are preaching to at this moment in history. Today's multimedia and visual culture has changed the way people think and process information. By the time people graduate from high school, they have spent more time in front of the television than they have in the classroom. The average person may spend fifty minutes a week in a church, listening to a sermon for a half-hour, but that person spends more than two thousand hours in any given year watching television.[67] Lewis and Lewis observe that today's bombardment by visual communication from television and multimedia sources on the Internet has literally rewired our brains and the way we think—our right brain is literally clamoring for involvement in life and demands to be fed visual images.[68] The wise preacher will see this as an opportunity and seize the day.

Incarnational communication is all about images and putting flesh on the bones of our sermons. The preacher who knows how to paint vivid and colorful images with his or her words will be speaking directly to this generation and communicating precisely in the way their brains have been trained to listen. In God's providence, people are more susceptible to stories, metaphors, and word pictures than ever before. The question is will we meet them where they live at

---

[67] Lewis and Lewis, (1983), 10.
[68] Ibid.

this cultural intersection or retreat to our own safe place and hope that things will go back to the way they used to be.

Tomlin observes that what we do now is critical. How we use culture for the gospel should be on the mind of every preacher as we prepare our sermons.[69] Preachers need to exegete our current culture and learn what its deepest desires are and then determine how those desires can be satisfied in God. We need to keep in mind that the desires are not the problem; the problem is how people decide to satisfy those desires. Desires become sin when we decide to satisfy them outside of God. If the preacher can build a bridge that helps people understand how they can be satisfied in God, then that preacher has built a cultural bridge to answer the questions that are being asked, making the preached word relevant to the culture. My fear is that preachers will decide to continue to ask questions that don't matter to people today and focus on the answers to the questions no one is asking. I never thought it did much good to preach a sermon to a bunch of folks who have been dead for fifty years.

Today's culture is in love with story and personal experiences. In oral culture, the preacher was rabbi or mentor. In print culture, the preacher was teacher and spoke to students. Broadcast and now digital cultures have created yet another shift in which the preacher leads communities in dialogue like an impartational leader or coach. People have become wired to live and think inductively because of the love for story. A generation ago, the focus was on collecting toys and material possessions. This generation also has its share of toys but is more likely to give priority to collecting experiences. This generation is also starved relationally because of the fragmentation of our families and the isolation that a virtual word ultimately creates. At the same time, the world is literally at our doorstep because distance has been erased by the virtual world of the Internet. We have the ability to communicate with ease across the street or across the world.

These changes might be scary to some, but they present an extraordinary opportunity for people with creativity and imagination. Incarnational preaching can feed a hunger for relationship, because the incarnational preaching process has the potential to create authentic men and women who preach with words and live them for people to see. Incarnational preaching is all about the very thing that makes this generation tick—images and word pictures. God has seen to it that the world is full of brains that are uniquely wired to hear words that paint pictures. People of this culture are screaming to be involved with messages that are preached inductively, inviting them to join in discovering the truth. Today's listeners do not like being lectured at but want to participate in the discovery experience. Preaching today also presents an extraordinary opportunity for the

---

[69] Tomlin, 19.

introduction of multimedia into sermons.[70] To be sure, that multimedia must be the flavoring on the message rather than the main course, but the addition of spice to food is what often makes the meal and gets the family to eat.

As always, God has seen to it that His church has been placed at the crossroads of history in a very fertile place. If we embrace this opportunity with a sense of mission and release the creative and imaginative power He has placed within us, then many will be drawn to the saving power of the gospel through our words. Preachers must become as little children again and take joy in experiencing life and then bring that joy into the pulpit as we share not only the word but the word in the context of life itself. To do this, we will have to draw deeply from the wellsprings of creativity and imagination. We will need to put others first and lay aside the comfort of our preferred preaching styles in favor of the ones that work for our listeners where and when they live in space and time. We become equipped to do these things as our listeners' story becomes our story and as we love them enough to understand their language, culture, and words. We will connect when we meet with people where they live instead of inviting them to join us where we live. That's what Jesus and Paul did, and they seemed to do quite well. God grant us the courage to do the same.

---

[70] See Thomas H. Troeger, *Ten Strategies for Preaching to a Multimedia Culture* (1996) for an excellent book on how to preach in a contextualized manner to this generation.

Chapter 8
Words That Transform: The Sermon's Power to Change

A fitting way to end a book on incarnation preaching and teaching is to give you a peak at my own experience with sermon preparation over the last thirty-five years. I do this the way I approach every sermon—with humility and the fear of God. Incarnational preaching requires a willingness to risk being authentic and transparent enough with your own life to deeply touch the life of another. I may never get the opportunity to meet you personally, but at least I can invite you into my world to experience some of my favorite preaching moments. In doing so, I hope these experiences spark new thoughts about how incarnational preaching can work for you.

I also pray that this chapter gives you new hope in your preaching ministry. We could all use a bit of that. The grind of weekly preaching is relentless. My hometown crowd never tried to throw me off a cliff as happened with Jesus, but preaching can drain the soul. Perhaps you are in one of those down times with little energy to spare and an abundance of critics. I hope this chapter yields some helpful insights, stirring your creativity and imagination. I hope it seeds to your own incarnational preaching journey and drives home some of the basics of how incarnational preaching works in everyday life.

How to Touch the Untouchables

I trust you have experienced dry times in your preaching—I certainly have. Dry times can cause us to feel like God has taken a break or is involved in multitasking with some other big cosmic issues more important than our own. It is as if God has left us in line waiting until He isn't quite as busy. Dry times often hit when ministry is at its busiest and critics are screaming their loudest. We are only human, and our spirits can only bear so much until the energy is gone and it seems as if God is a thousand miles away. When God seems distant, the feeling produces profound weakness for the preacher—even then we must appear in the pulpit several times that week and have our best ready each time. In dry times, Sunday seems to come so quickly, intruding like an uninvited guest.

I was only seventeen when I sensed God's calling to ministry. I could not imagine a higher calling or something quite as satisfying as preaching for a living. Spending hours in the study and parsing words in Hebrew and Greek texts for a living seemed like a dream job, and I could not wait to get started. I approached every preaching opportunity like it might be my last, and I sought God diligently for His words on each occasion. As a young associate pastor with a full-time job in the chemicals industry, my ministry responsibilities included weddings, funerals, counseling, and teaching. Life could not have been better. By then I had a wife, four small children, a small, twenty-acre farm to live on, a great job, and the chance to teach and preach from time to time in the church. When I entered full-time ministry some years later, I embraced the opportunity with great joy and expectation.

Full-time ministry was different than anything I could have ever imagined. Its propensity to consume your life and make you its property is overwhelming. Ministry will take your wife, children, sanity, and your salvation if you let it. I quickly found out how important balance, discernment, wisdom, and Sabbath rest were to anyone in full-time ministry. I also found out the hard way how not to do many things—one of those things was preaching. We all learn to preach by preaching. That, unfortunately, is the inescapable truth. I cannot believe what my patient congregation had to put up with in the early days.

Before going into full-time ministry, I felt very comfortable teaching periodically in a small-group environment with people who wanted to learn. Regular preaching on a full-time basis in a larger environment on a Sunday morning with hundreds of listeners presented a whole new challenge for me. I quickly found out that this kind of preaching had totally different dynamics. Once I entered full-time ministry, it took me at least five more years to figure out what some of those dynamics were, and I learned many of them by trial and error—mostly by error.

After being in full-time ministry for about three or four years, my sermons did not seem to be connecting as well with the crowd on Sundays. I now know that this was probably because they were getting used to me and I to them. Familiarity can dull the listening ability of any group of people. It was time to shake things up, but I was a sedate pastor who was a teacher and not much of a preacher. I was not used to using voice inflection or using my body to speak. I was what some call a "milk bucket preacher." I moved so little and delivered my messages with so little motion that my field of movement behind the pulpit was limited to about the width of a milk bucket. I might as well have been standing in one for my lack of motion and expression.

That all changed on a mission trip to India in the mid-1990s. My whole world was rocked by what I saw there and what I was asked to do. My first sermon in a remote village near Pondicherry south of Chennai was interrupted four different times. The crowd numbered about five hundred. I was asked to preach in an open area in a village of untouchables. The untouchables are a caste of people in Indian society who occupy the lowest social place. They are extremely poor and live in squalor and hopelessness because of their place in the caste system.

Because Hindus believe in karma and dharma, untouchables are consigned to their caste for the rest of their lives and are often intentionally left by the wider society to suffer. *Karma* is the accumulated good or bad that one generates in each lifetime, and *dharma* is the position in life that one is reborn into because of the good or bad karma generated in the last lifetime. The untouchables are doomed to live out a miserable, lonely existence because of the supposed sins they committed in the last life—their karma was bad enough that they were reborn into this life with the dharma of an Untouchable. To rescue them from their dharma in this lifetime would only prolong their need to remain as untouchables in following lives, so they are left destitute and helpless to suffer, paying an unjust price for deeds supposedly committed before they were born this time around. My heart was broken for these people as I saw their hopelessness, shame, and despair. Their homes were made of scrap wood and metal, and animal dung was used for the walls. They had little or no access to education or the outside world; the village was their world, and I had entered it. The injustice was eating away at me, and I could not wait to minister to these people.

I soon discovered that they did not want to hear me teach—they wanted me to preach. I had no microphone and would have had to project my voice if I was to be heard. Many in the audience had traveled for hours by foot to hear the preacher and would settle for no less than several hours of preaching. What an interesting situation for a teacher who relied heavily on his notes and was used to teaching for about thirty or forty minutes with little volume or expression. What followed was an incarnational, God-ordained lesson on preaching that taught me the sermon was not about me or my preferences but the needs of the people who were listening. I suddenly saw how little my preferences really mattered and how important it was for me to know my audience and give them what they needed so they would have the best chance of receiving the word. My job was to help them listen to me because many of them might not have another opportunity to hear the gospel.

Most of the people present could not read or write, and I quickly found out that I would not be able communicate effectively with words alone. I was speaking through a translator anyway; my words were not their words. More importantly, I saw how unprepared I was to clothe the words I spoke with images, metaphors, and references that these listeners understood or had experienced in their own cultural setting. I also discovered that words did not touch their hearts as deeply as word pictures from life around them. The chickens and cows that ran in the streets and the grain they collected from their gardens were much better subjects on which to build my sermon than exegesis from my Hebrew and Greek lectionaries—they were eighty-five hundred miles away anyway.

My encounter with preaching in that Hindu village taught me a lot about the art of preaching itself. As I mentioned, I had always relied upon carefully prepared outlines with juicy details and specific points (underlined and marked in yellow, of course) in my preaching. That changed when a drunken man from the crowd charged forward and grabbed my notes before being grabbed rather firmly and dragged away by some people from the audience. My carefully prepared notes were all out of order and wrinkled beyond readability—for the next several hours, I learned to preach extemporaneously.

I was used to rather sedate environments where there was a lot of give and take between the preacher and the audience. The environment I found myself in for the next several hours was anything but sedate. I can still see the fist fight that broke out twenty minutes after the drunken man was dragged way. As the fight erupted about twenty-five feet from where I was preaching, a crowd gathered around the two men to see who would win. After that, I heard a strange and unfamiliar sound in the distance, getting closer and closer as I tried to continue to preach. A group of Hindu priests and religious leaders were approaching with drums, tambourines, and shouts, marching in procession with several idols they were venerating and progressively drowning out my sermon. A little later, somewhere near the end of the sermon, a fire broke out in the village, and many who were listening rushed to the scene to put out the fire with buckets of water and save what little they could before homes were destroyed.

I guess I could blame all the distraction on the devil and his hatred of the word of God. That sounds spiritual. But whatever the source of these crazy interruptions and challenges, I learned too much that day about preaching to give the devil all the credit and let him steal the show. God used these events in my life to teach me lessons about serving others with the word that I might not have learned otherwise. Actually, I saw what it *meant* to serve others with the word and how necessary it was for me to leave my own comfort zone in preaching to meet their needs. I really don't know how much my sermon touched the people in the village that day, but I will never forget how much I learned. God taught me a valuable skill that serves me well to this day when I preach. I learned how to touch the Untouchable. Isn't that what preaching is all about?

An Encounter with Holiness

After my return from India, my preaching ministry changed radically. Now I was more like a two-winged bird—in the two weeks away the teacher learned to preach. I learned to feel the sermon I was presenting and to let my body, expressions, and voice communicate beyond the words I spoke. I learned freedom from my dependence on written outlines and aids—if I had them, they were my backup. I learned I needed to relax and enjoy freedom in my overall delivery. Perhaps most importantly, I discovered the impact word pictures and metaphors can have in preaching. Most of the people I taught in remote villages in India had not even seen a Bible before. Word pictures from everyday life joined with spiritual truths were the only bridges to the gospel available to me as I preached. I learned the power of metaphor and the way word pictures could be used to communicate cross-culturally with great effect. These were exceptionally valuable lessons that helped me preach more effectively to my own congregation, an activity that, for many preachers, can also seem like a cross-cultural experience at times.

Even though India transformed me as a preacher, when I returned, I went through a dry period. I was emotionally drained from several funerals in my congregation. One who died was a dear friend who had clung to life for months and slowly slipped away, leaving a wife and children to grieve. Both my personal loss and watching this friend's family suffer were almost too much for me. I needed strength. Despite what we experience in ministry, Sunday still comes each week and the people don't accept excuses. I needed to hear from God and quickly. But nothing was flowing. One week was particularly tough. I tried not to let what felt like God's absence upset me on Wednesday because Sunday was still a few days away. Thursday was still safe because I thought I had discerned some sermon direction by then, centering on the topic of holiness. I had preached on that subject many times before, so surely something would grow readily around that topic now. Friday was cutting it a little too close for comfort because though I had a general topic, I had no structure or anything else for that matter. I had some focus but little skeleton, flesh, or muscle for my sermon, and Sunday by now was only hours away.

If you have preached much, you can probably identify with my dilemma. Most preachers know what it feels like to have a burden to preach but no details and no idea how to move forward. When a preacher gets to this point, begging and pleading usually begin. We try to make deals with God and even promise not to commit our favorite sins anymore. In my case, the pleading turned to anger and then descended into despair. I rehearsed a hypothetical Sunday morning scene in my mind: I would walk up to the pulpit, confess that I had nothing to say that week, and then walk back down from the pulpit in disgrace and shame. So here it is Friday, I'm replaying this scenario in my head, and that morning my wife makes an awful discovery. I mean awful.

At this time in our lives, we lived on a farm out in the woods, and we did not have city water or sewage on the property. Instead, we had spring water from the hill behind the house and a septic tank carefully buried in the front yard to catch all the muck from our toilets and sinks. No one told me you were supposed to get the septic tank cleaned out every five years or so to keep it from clogging up. Well, by this time, it had been ten years since we moved in, and that septic tank had never been cleaned. You can probably imagine what I'm about to say: the septic tank picked this particular weekend to clog. The preacher had no sermon, and the septic tank was filled to the brim, which is not a good thing when you have a wife and four small kids at home. So I called the septic tank guy Friday, and he said he would be out first thing Saturday morning— right when I had scheduled my last-ditch attempt at prayer and study to pull out some kind of message for Sunday.

I don't mind telling you how angry I was that my last hope for sermon preparation was gone, especially considering that the final prep time was stolen by a septic tank packed with a decade's worth of muck. (I'm just being real here.) Anyway, the man did come out on Saturday, but for starters, he was late and did not get there until late afternoon, which meant we had to wait around all day without being able to use the bathroom in the house. When he arrived, he asked me how long it had been since the tank had been cleaned. I told him. He grinned and said I might want to stand back. Then he lifted the lid and used his truck to suck ten years of muck out of the tank. I gagged when the smell hit me. Within half a minute, I heard screams coming from the house some distance away as the kids caught the odor through closed windows!

After about fifteen minutes, the job was complete, the muck was sucked into the truck, and the septic tank was empty. But my problems were far from over. The kind gentleman informed me that the tank's standpipe, which allowed water to drain out, had broken and was at the bottom of the tank. The tank would not work unless that pipe was fixed. I asked him how one fixed a standpipe, and he explained that you had to climb down into the tank and glue the fittings back in place. I asked him how much he would charge to do that for me. He smiled and said that it would be several hundred dollars, which I did not have at that time. So I thanked him and said I would handle it myself, realizing that any stray moments I would have had to pull out my sermon on holiness would now be spent in a septic tank as I fought to make my bathrooms functional again. The man just smiled and said, "Have fun."

Now the preacher was really mad at God. How could He let this happen to me? Why should a man of the cloth have to get into a septic tank on Saturday night before he was to preach a sermon that wasn't even written yet? Where was God in all this anyway, and was He secretly amused with the situation? As much as I would've loved to sit pondering these mighty spiritual questions, the septic tank was calling, as were my wife and kids who really wanted to use our bathroom and sinks again.

At least I could take some solace in a clever little plan I had devised for fixing the standpipe. At about that time, the first *Mission Impossible* movie was out in the theaters. If you saw it, you may remember the scene in which Tom Cruise is lowered upside down from a ceiling into a secured vault to retrieve something. You guessed it—I rigged up a device whereby I could lower myself headfirst through the opening and into the septic tank. I used a pulley with a rope attached to my feet. Once I lowered my upper body partway into the tank, I could work upside down while hanging by my feet with my hands free to fix the standpipe. This plan may sound crazy, but I really didn't want to climb into the septic tank.

I will never forget the sight, sound, smell, feel, and even taste of hanging upside down in that tank. The walls were still coated with years of muck, and the bottom seemed alive with little white critters that squirmed and squiggled. I did not smell the smell as much as taste the smell while trying to breathe. Everything I came in contact with and touched was slimy and coated with ten-year-old defilement. The walls gleamed and dripped with crud. Despair and disgust would not adequately describe my feelings at that moment. And yet—would you believe it?—right then I had a life-changing encounter with God. As I mentioned earlier in the book, I am not one for visions or audible voices when it comes to God. I know what his "still, small voice" sounds like in my heart when He speaks. But this time the still, small voice seemed a bit louder and more distinct. Some people might attribute my "encounter" to sewer gasses or hanging upside down too long, but I heard God say a few simple words to my heart: "It's hard to live in unclean vessels." Hanging there in the septic tank, my whole concept of holiness and of God's redemptive love were changed forever.

Can you imagine what love and patience it takes for God to live on the inside of us each and every day? He is so holy and so different from us that it seems unimaginable He would send His Holy Spirit to come and dwell inside unclean vessels. He is so pure, clean, and unstained by sin. We are so full of muck—accumulated over a lifetime and often overflowing. Yet He is willing to come and clean out all the years of crud and dwell within us. Salvation cleans us up a good bit and makes us holy, but then there is our everyday walk with God, and often it does not go so well. We accumulate quite a bit of crud on the walls of our heart over the years. I was mad about having to spend a few moments in a septic tank, but our holy, loving God was willing to send His Son to die so He could come and live in unclean vessels for a lifetime.

The septic tank experience changed my whole perspective on God's love for me. I was broken that day. The experience in the septic tank helped me to see the price God pays to live inside me and what it must be like for Him when we take Him along with us as we sin. The experience literally built a metaphoric eight-lane expressway into my heart so I could understand something as abstract as holiness and helped me to begin to grasp the depth of God's mercy. To this day, when I share this story, I do so with tears in my eyes because of the transformation the experience worked in my life, giving me a more personal and direct understanding of holiness and God's love than ever before. It is hard for me to sin willingly without remembering what it is like to do time in a septic tank. Our God is a holy God, and we are unclean vessels. Yet He has chosen to live within us—His redemptive love compels Him. Coming out of the septic tank, I didn't have to wonder what to preach about the next day, and that sermon on holiness was one of the most powerful messages I have ever preached. When life's circumstances encounter God's Word and a preaching opportunity, even septic tanks can help accomplish His transformational purposes.

Words that Live

Sometimes the words in a passage of Scripture seem to jump off the page and take on a life of their own. The writers of the Old and New Testaments probably had no idea they were being used by God to write what would later become our Scripture. They were busy with life and ministry, writing letters to churches with very ordinary instructions, encouragement, language, and form. The Scriptures are rich in beautiful stories, metaphors, and word pictures—the language and communications of everyday folk. If a preacher keeps his or her eyes open, many times these words will jump off the page as we read. I cannot think of a better example of this kind of rich passage than Rom. 12:9-21. If I ever am ever asked to preach at a moment's notice and need extemporaneous words, you will find me beginning with this passage.

Once I was overseas on a preaching assignment and sitting with a group of students and teachers in a meeting that commemorated the founding of a new ministry. I was one of the only people in the room who was visiting from another country and must have looked like the perfect speaker for the occasion. I was listening to the leaders talk about the new ministry, its expected impact on the surrounding area, and about how God had sovereignly provided the physical structure and the ministry's financial needs. At this point, the woman speaking looked over at me and caught my attention. She smiled and said to the group, "And now, we will hear some words of exhortation from our beloved brother from the United States, Pastor Flynn."

I had one of those moments when I couldn't swallow and looked around to see what pastor she was talking about. As I've explained, I am one of those preachers who likes to plan a sermon in detail and have detailed notes; even if I don't use them much, they are still my security blanket. Not in this case, though. When everyone else politely smiled and turned to look at me, I knew I was the pastor the group leader meant. I too thought how interesting it would be to hear Pastor Flynn speak, because I had no idea at that point what he would say. You will have many such moments in preaching ministry. Remember, Paul warned preachers to be ready "in season and out of season," so we have had about a two-thousand-year notice (2 Tim. 4:2).

I instinctively opened to Rom. 12:9-21, because the passage is pregnant with word pictures, which can be life ropes for preachers in trouble. When you don't know a group or are ministering in a cross-cultural setting, you can always count on the richness of imagery and metaphor to help bridge the cultural divide. I started with verse nine because of the richness of the words in that text. There are several words that jump right off the page for me if I will lay aside my own personal agenda. When I got to this verse, instead of reading the Word, I tried to let the Word read me, letting God demonstrate His agenda through it. If we approach the Scriptures inductively, setting ourselves to learn and discover, sometimes words leap right of the pages of the book and straight into our listeners' hearts.

The first word to leap of the page was "hypocrisy."[1] The word jumps out to me because of the way it was used in Paul's time. The Greeks loved drama and acting, and Greek culture and religion were the common topics of their plays. Actors would pray to their gods sometimes and ask them to inhabit them during a play so they could literally become someone else for those moments onstage. The Greek word for "hypocrisy" used in this passage was associated with acting. Paul was exhorting the Romans to stop playacting as if they were someone else for the sake of outer appearances but rather to cultivate love from a sincere heart. Words about hypocrisy were very important to the people to whom I was speaking and struck right at the heart of their future ministry direction. Their local culture highly valued appearance and saving face. People were culturally conditioned to save face at all costs, even if that meant compromising the truth. Because of the need to save face, it was culturally acceptable to shun people of lower stature to protect one's honor. Shunning was all too common, even among Christians. The people at this ministry knew it was their duty to love even those of lower stature in society, but it was clearly difficult for them.

Duty is just one step away from indifference—if we love others because we are supposed to, we often do so in an emotionless and empty manner. Loving out of duty is sometimes better than not loving at all, but after a while, you begin to feel like an actor putting on a show. Love must be sincere and from the heart to have its full impact, and this message hit home with my audience that day. My audience was going to be involved in a lot of ministry with underprivileged people who were very needy and, from their culture's point of view, undesirable. God wanted the church to move into a different kind of love—a love that goes beyond simple duty and acting and flows from the heart.

The exhortation about hypocrisy was a bit bold coming from a visitor, but the words in the verses that followed continued to leap off the page in front of me as I preached. The next two words that stood out in the flowing verses are a preacher's dream because they are so filled with passion and potential. With the words "abhor" and "cling" there is no middle ground. These are very intense, passionate words. The word abhor in the Greek is a particularly violent word.[2]

---

[1] The word in the Greek text here is "ὑποκριτής" (*hupokrites*), which was a term used in drama and playacting. When an individual was playacting, the actor would speak, and someone would "answer back" in dialogue with the actor. The answer was not genuine or sincere, but just an actor playing his or her part in answering back. The idea of hypocrisy in the Greek mind is associated with being an actor. Paul was saying not to be an actor but to be the real thing. Love should not be an act but should be real and from the heart.

[2] The word for "abhor," which is "ἀποστυγέω" (*apostugeo*), builds upon the Greek word for hatred and takes it to another level. The word implies that we shudder in the horror of

Christians in New Testament times knew the root word for abhor was built upon their word for hatred, but abhor took hatred to another level. To abhor something means to shudder and shake with a hatred for that thing. It implies a deep, visceral reaction of disgust toward something.

Because it is such a visceral word, abhor is just waiting for word pictures to amplify its meaning. For the Jew, an abhorrence is eating pork. For the Muslim, an abhorrence is the thought of a dog living in one's house. If we get creative and use our imaginations, we can go further in picturing examples of things we abhor. What about two-week-old garbage that has cooked in the heat and humidity of the day and is crawling with so many maggots that you can hear them squirm in the decomposing heap? The people to whom I was preaching lived near the equator and had very little access to sanitation. They could surely understand that word picture. Maybe the thought of a dead animal left in the sun to bake for a few days would conjure up that feeling of abhorrence. Or a slaughterhouse and all of its contents. I chose the last one because I thought the example would resonate and I had personal experience with slaughterhouses. To illustrate abhorrence, I used a word picture from the days when I used to work in industry.

My work in industry took me to a rendering factory that was in need of my company's technology in order to streamline its production of animal food and cosmetics. The stench of the thirty-thousand-gallon vat of road kill and animal guts being ground up for "crude protein" found in animal food and cosmetics was bad, but the one-hundred-thousand-gallon vat of cow blood was a whole different story. The place was so hot and humid that the smell and sights went right through you. You could taste the smells and feel the sights. Talk about a multisensory experience! After spending four days there, I had to throw out my clothes, shoes, and underwear because the stench would not wash out. For six months, I felt like I was still smelling the wretchedness of that place; it left such a scar on me mentally. I learned the meaning of abhor that day and still remember that lesson when I read Romans 12.

Do we really "abhor" what is evil, or do we feel something less? I daresay that most of us do not really abhor it but actually play with evil sometimes—and maybe even are content to be entertained by it in a good book or movie. Adam and Eve got into trouble by getting to know evil. All they knew was good before they experimented with knowing evil; God had built into them the capacity for knowing good but not evil. We were never meant to know evil and were not designed with the capacity to survive the experience of knowing evil and remain intact. Adam and Eve were enticed by the thought of getting to know evil. They were warned by God not to go there because they were not designed with the capacity, and knowing evil would produce death in them. But they touched evil

---

our hatred. It is an emotionally packed reaction to an emotionally packed word. It describes how we should feel about evil.

anyway, got to know it, and it killed them. Knowing evil does the same for us—unless we abhor it.

God's call that we abhor evil is a warning to fragile men and women to treat evil as if it were disgusting. Illustrating disgust for the listener is crucial to driving home the point of the verse. The abhorrence of evil would be a very important tool in the hands of the people overseas to whom I was preaching. They operated in an area full of evil, one where prostitution and debauchery of every kind could be easily found within several blocks' distance. On any given day, the people could easily be exposed to sights—right there on the streets—that you and I would never see in our lifetimes. The people needed to understand what it meant to abhor something and understand that the "something" God was warning them about that day was the evil that was all around them.

Just as the word abhor provokes a visceral response, so does the word cling. The word cling can produce a windfall of imagery for any preacher if he or she is willing to be an artist.[3] In the Greek text, the word used for cling is the word for glue. Paul's exhortation in this passage urges us to be glued to what is good so that we are inseparable from it. What kinds of circumstances prompt us to cling? I have witnessed the panic in someone's eyes when the person thinks he or she is drowning. Panic begins to set in and take over the person's mind. Life is suspended and thinking yields to desperation—everything becomes about survival in that moment and the person will do just about anything to stop from drowning. A drowning man is actually quite dangerous and must be approached with caution. In his panic, he will literally grab on to you while you attempt to save him, dragging you down and potentially causing you both to drown. A drowning man tries to cling to you or to anything he can reach, because life depends on it. A drowning man knows what clinging is and will not soon release anything from his grip that might save him from a watery death.

I have never jumped out of an airplane, because I do not like heights. When I watch people doing it for fun or sport, it makes me wonder why anyone would choose to jump out of a perfectly good plane. But there are people who enjoy that sort of thing, and when I watch them do it, I get a sick feeling in my stomach. I imagine the rush of wind as the door is opened. I imagine looking down to the distant ground ten thousand feet below. I can see my fingers gripping the side of the plane as I get near the door to jump. At this point, my imagining stops, because you would have to pry my white fingers off the sides of the door for me to go any further. I would cling to the door and not let go until my fingers were bloody.

I have also seen another kind of clinging—a man and a woman holding each other about to be parted by travel and distance. It is especially intense when one is going off on deployment to a war zone. The couple kisses, hugs, and cries

---

[3] Here in the Greek text, the word "κολλάω" (kollao) is used and translated "cling." The word has the idea of gluing things together in a manner so they cannot be separated.

together, and then there is the moment when they say their last goodbye. They cling to each other like it might be the last time. I have seen that same kind of clinging as loved ones embrace a father, mother, or child who is dying. Do we cling to good with the same passion and intensity, resisting letting go with everything in us? Or do we release the good more easily?

When times get rough, I release good far too easily. The writer of Hebrews asks us in our struggles with sin if we have yet resisted to the point of blood (Heb. 12:4). I think for most of us, the answer is no. Have we made every effort to cling to good, even when it is difficult, unpopular, or painful? To what degree have we clung to good? Like a rock climber at the top of the climb or that person about to jump out of a plane? Like a loved one about to depart for war and saying goodbye to a spouse? This is the passion Paul conveys in his exhortation to cling to good—that we cling to good just as passionately as we abhor evil. What an important exhortation for my audience that day. In that culture, people had an overwhelming desire to be liked and respected and not to offend. Yet their ministry was taking them straight toward what would offend a decadent culture, and they would need to learn to cling to good rather than to the approval of people.

The final thing that caught my eye in that Romans passage (Rom. 12:9-21) was the way Paul asks us to be devoted to one serving one another. I could sense as I read the words that devotion to one another would be the cement that would hold this ministry together in the rough times of testing that surely lay ahead. The passage said clearly that we are to be "fervent" in service toward our Lord. Here the Greek word literally means "boiling."[4] How easy it would be for these people to settle into being "lukewarm" when they got established and were experiencing some measure of success (Rev. 3:15,16). Jesus demonstrated exactly how we are to serve God. He served with all His strength, soul, and passion to the very last breath He breathed. His service was all-encompassing and complete—hot and boiling in nature. The people I preached to would have a measure of success in their efforts to serve their community. In time that success might tempt them to relax a bit, take service for granted, and tone down the passion. That would be deadly for them because service cannot be allowed to mellow and grow passive. It must boil in its intensity if it is to have the impact God desires, like the strong tea that they drank each morning with no cream or sugar. Did they like their tea boiling hot or room temperature? They could not afford to fall into the trap of complacency, even for a short period of time (Rev. 3:16).

I learned a lot that day while preaching and was more surprised than any of the listeners by what the preacher had to say. A few little words found in a few verses written two thousand years ago changed my life, as I hoped was the case

---

[4] In the Greek text, the word "fervent is "ζέω" (zeo), meaning to boil or to be hot. God demands the same kind of passionate service toward Him that He gave to us in the form of His Son. Jesus gave His all, and so we must do also.

for those with whom I shared. I do not know what became of that ministry and have not seen or spoken to them since. Preachers are often placed in situations in which we have one chance to speak words that will transform and one chance only. Sometimes it comes down to a few words that leap off the page with transformational power. These words in Romans were infused with power not only because they were rich in imagery that could impact listeners in another cultural context but also because of the work the words had done in my life before I shared them with this group. I had lived in those verses and had been changed by them myself. If we live a life open to transformational words that change our own lives, then we have a reservoir to draw on for times when we are called upon to preach—in season or not.

Chickens and Eagles

Everyone goes through times when life seems to melt away our physical strength. When it gets really tough, strength seems to likewise drain from our spirit and our soul. We are constructed as three-part beings with a spirit (heart), soul (mind), and body (flesh)—three persons in one, just like the God in whose image we are created (1 Thess. 5:23). Each of these three parts of our being is infused with a finite amount of energy that allows us to function. My experience tells me the spirit, soul, and body are somehow connected and swap energy back and forth—they are like tanks that are interconnected with no values in the plumbing. When the body is physically drained, it seems to borrow energy from the soul and spirit. When we are mentally drained, we seem to draw down energy from the body and spirit. We can even become physically and mentally drained because of spiritual problems. All parts of our being seem to borrow energy from one another, until our energy reserves run so low that there is nothing left to swap out.

Low levels of energy in all three parts of our being define a condition called burnout. When we are burned out, our spirit may feel deserted by God, as if He is nowhere to be found. The soul has trouble thinking, and an awful numbness sets in that seems thick and tangible. The physical body is drained and even the smallest of activities seems nearly impossible, exhausting us. As ministers, we must watch over ourselves because the demands of being in ministry can quickly drain our being and leave us in a very dry land, hindering or crippling our ability to minister effectively. I am convinced that energy depletion to the point of burnout is a leading cause of the exodus we see from ministry each year, as represented in the statistics for ministerial dropout shared earlier in this book.

At a certain point, I found myself in a perfect storm of life events that were systematically draining my spirit, soul, and body. Ministry was relentless at the time with major events occurring in rapid succession. There were the usual problems with the board, the weekly sermons, and the tight finances and problems with staff members who were leaving. Life at home continued at its usual pace with my four kinds now ranging in age from ten to fifteen years old. The counseling load seemed especially high at the time, and there were major decisions to be made related to our Christian school and expanding toward a high school. The preaching load seemed overwhelming, and I seemed to be growing stale. I had very little creativity left. I was existing rather than living. I think the thing that tipped my ability to cope was the loss of several wonderful people in the church, followed by a major health setback for my wife.

We had been setting my wife up for her first kidney transplant after five years of dialysis when tests uncovered thyroid cancer. With everything happening at once in the church, my wife's health developments, and no significant time off for more than a year, I was a great candidate for burnout. I had never learned to take care of myself with proper sleep, diet, rest, and time away from ministry, and I had a martyr's mentality. I had forgotten that Jesus had already died for the church and would prefer that I stayed alive. My experience taught me what burnout means—it is a very dark experience that you will do all within your power to shun once you have been there. Still, in my case at this time, the ministry needed to go on, and the preacher needed to preach.

I found myself feeling spiritually deaf and far from God. I treasure God's closeness, so my inability to sense His presence or hear His voice was very disturbing. My devotional time seemed useless and empty, mocking me. Sermon preparation was like pulling teeth. God was faithful, but once again, I found myself approaching a Sunday morning with no sermon topic or even any idea what to preach. I remember playing "Bible roulette" (not a very biblical way to discern God's direction!) by opening the Bible indiscriminately and seeing where my finger pointed. By God's mercy, it was not the verse in the Gospels that reads ". . . and Judas went out and hung himself"! I happened to open to the book of Isaiah in chapter 40 and read these words:

> [28] Do you not know? Have you not heard? The Everlasting God, the LORD, the Creator of the ends of the earth Does not become weary or tired. His understanding is inscrutable. [29] He gives strength to the weary, And to *him who* lacks might He increases power. [30] Though youths grow weary and tired, And vigorous young men stumble badly, [31] Yet those who wait for the LORD Will gain new strength; They will mount up *with* wings like eagles, They will run and not get tired, They will walk and not become weary (Isa. 40:28-31).

I vaguely remember thinking to myself, "I guess this is a great verse for eagles." But I was not an eagle and had no wings. I also remembered that I had forgotten to go out to the chicken house on our little farm that morning and get the eggs. I figured getting the eggs would be a lot more productive than continuing to stare at the Bible, so I went out to the chicken coop to collect them. If I couldn't get a sermon, at least I'd get some fresh eggs and have a great omelet.

I had six chickens at that time because something had eaten the other ones. The chickens were Rhode Island Reds, and they each would lay at least one egg a day, some with double yokes. The trick was getting those tasty brown eggs from underneath the chickens. I have mentioned the Genesis passage in which the Holy Spirit is "hovering" over the face of the deep at creation. The Hebrew for hovering is better translated "brooding" over the face of the deep, painting quite a word picture—that of a mother hen sitting on her eggs trying to hatch them. A broody chicken is hard to separate from her eggs because she instinctively protects them and her future chicks. If you mess with a broody chicken, either she will sit there on the eggs like a statue refusing to be moved or take off and fly right at you. The trick is to trim one of the wings before a chicken gets broody. That means when she takes off at you, she will fly like a helicopter that has lost one of its blades, turning upside down and spinning toward the floor out of control. It is a funny sight to see. We have spent many evenings watching chickens trying to fly and laughing as they spiraled toward the ground. That is exactly what happened as I opened the door to the hen house the day I left the Bible and Isaiah for an omelet. Those chickens flew toward me, knowing I was coming for their precious eggs. The flutter and flapping of six pairs of wings with feathers flying was quite a sight. So was the chickens' short-lived attempt at flight as they spiraled toward the floor. They made their point, and I got my lunch anyway.

After I had a very tasty omelet, it was back to work in the study. My Bible was still open to Isaiah 40 when I got back. As I glanced at the passage, the words of verse 31 stood out to me—they will mount up with wings as of an eagle. I remember a still, small voice in my heart, whispering to me at that moment, "Do you want to continue to flap like a chicken or begin to soar like an eagle?" For the first time in a while, I had connected with the Lord, and the answer was obvious. God had my full attention. I was acting like the chickens I had just seen. I was treating problems and the life circumstances I encountered like they were mine. I was sitting on them trying to "hatch" a solution. I was flapping around helplessly like one of my chickens, brooding over my problem. The answer was not to flap around like a broody chicken but to learn to soar like an eagle.

Eagles are amazing creatures. They can weigh as much as fifteen pounds and have wing spans as wide as eight feet. With those wings, they can fly as far as one hundred miles in one day, looking for food. Eagles can fly as high as ten thousand feet (nearly two miles high) at speeds of sixty-five miles per hour. From that altitude, they can survey the air and land space below them, focusing on objects more than a mile below them as potential prey (using the "eagle eye" we so often hear about). When diving to catch prey, their descent speed can top two hundred miles per hour, and they kill their prey by simply hitting it with the talons on their feet—the speed is deadly. The key to this amazing behavior is not eagles' ability to fly but to soar. Eagles have mastered the art of finding updrafts in the atmosphere that provide natural lift and then simply spreading their wings to gain altitude and cover distance. It would literally be impossible for an eagle to "fly" one hundred miles in one day or to reach those high altitudes on their own energy and strength. For the eagle, it is a matter of life and death to learn to catch the updraft and soar. So it is for weary pastors and their congregations.

That moment with the words of Isaiah in my study, having just come out of the hen house, changed me and my approach to life, ministry, and sermon preparation forever. I realized that I did not have the strength to fly the distance in any of these realms and that God's intention was for me to soar instead. God had given me all I needed to soar in any realm of ministry but not to fly in my own strength for very long in any of them. I do not have the strength to go the distance, but like the eagle, I needed to seek God's updrafts every step of the way. I realized that would mean surrender to Him each day. You cannot predict or control the wind; you must wait for it. God designed life, ministry, and even sermon preparation itself to require us to soar with wings spread wide and to wait for the updraft of His Holy Spirit to carry us where the "wind" wants to blow.

My problem was I was flapping around like one of my own chickens. I flapped from day to day in life, trying to make things happen for God. In ministry, I was doing my best to do what had to be done to advance the church and care for His people. With sermons, I was literally exhausting myself looking for that best topic or trying to craft the perfect sermon with the highest impact. I realized that I was exhausted from all the flapping around—too much flying and too little soaring. From that day forward, I determined to "wait" for the updraft, begin to soar, and enjoy the view from ten thousand feet.

Waiting is hard for most people. I find it especially difficult. I am most prone to go do something and then figure things out while I am in motion. The idea of sitting around waiting nauseates me because I am most comfortable when I am engaged and in action. As I looked into the passage further, I saw that the Hebrew text was pregnant with meaning. The word "wait" does not imply sitting by wasting time until something happens—it is a very active word that would literally translate "to look for and eagerly to wait with great expectation."[5] That kind of waiting is my part. God's part is to create the updraft. When I do my part, God's updraft multiplies my strength many times over as I soar to new heights and cover great distances that I could not fly on my own. I am utterly dependent on His updrafts when I soar like an eagle; they take me where I need to go.

The congregation was surprised when I showed up the next morning with one of my chickens. I introduced the passage from Isaiah and told them about chickens and eagles. At a prearranged time, my assistant brought the chicken out with its freshly trimmed wing, and I threw it up in the air about ten feet. Many in

---

[5] Here in Isa. 40:31 the Hebrew word "קָוָה" (qavah) is used and is translated "wait." It is not a passive word but implies an active waiting in which the individual is waiting with eagerness and faith. Rather than passive waiting, this is an engaged and expectant waiting that assumes that something will happen.

the church had not even seen a chicken before, much less a chicken with one of its wings clipped and turning in circles, flapping its wings as it came rather gracelessly back to earth. The flapping, loose feathers, and wild clucking sounds presented the perfect picture of my life to that point as I tried to fly on my own strength. I told you—I will use anything, alive or dead, as a word picture if it will illustrate my point in preaching.

My point was made and now it was time for us as a congregation to begin to soar. I couldn't bring an eagle from the farm that day to show them the contrast. If only I'd had access to the kinds of multimedia available today and could have shown them an eagle gracefully soaring on the updrafts as a contrast to what they had just seen with my chicken. Instead, my words painted the picture of an eagle soaring majestically in flight, and to this day, I am convinced that many of us who were in the congregation that day approach life differently because of that sermon. I am always impressed when someone can remember my sermon a week later. To this day, over fifteen years later, I still have people remind me of the "Chicken Sermon," when I talked about chickens and eagles and we decided to soar like eagles rather than cluck like broody chickens. Truth is life-changing, especially when clothed with flesh. An encounter with that kind of truth can last a lifetime and change the course of a ministry and a church—it certainly did that for us.

Parting Words (That Transform)

I could go on from here. God has been good over the last thirty-four years, providing countless ideas for thousands of teaching and preaching opportunities. I'll finish now because I think you've got the idea. Perhaps God has conceived something new in your heart about preaching ministry that has begun to grow. You can take it from here. Let life and its daily circumstances grow the word in your heart to give truth depth and meaning. Be sure to visit God's theater (creation) regularly—admission is always free.

Always remember that a sermon is not an isolated event cut off from life but an experience intimately woven into life's tapestry. God is the Master Architect, and His thoughts toward you outnumber the sands of the sea. The seeds for your next sermon were already planted yesterday, and God intends today to be an adventure in discovery. Your job is to run with Him and to be vulnerable—to have ears to hear and eyes to see. Your life and the world around you are pregnant with God's truth and love. He is busily at work clothing his word with your flesh to produce words that transform—in your life first and then in the lives of those who hear your words in due season.

Let creativity be your close companion and imagination walk beside you each day. Dip deeply into their well and drink. Pay the price of personal transformation by allowing the word to do its work in you. Many are counting on you to pay the price. Some of those who will be counting on you have not even been born yet. You provide the flesh and God will provide the words. Can these bones live? The answer is a resounding yes! Talk to the bones, Ezekiel. Speak to them with words that transform.

Bibliography

Barna, George. *The Second Coming of the Church*. Nashville: Word, 1998.

Barrett, David. "The Status of Christianity and Religions in the Modern World." In *World Christian Encyclopedia*. Oxford: Oxford Press, 2001.

Barclay, William. "The Acts of the Apostles." *The Daily Study Bible Series*. Philadelphia: Westminster, 1976.

———. "The Gospel of Matthew." *The Daily Bible Study Series*. Philadelphia: Westminster, 1975.

Barrier, Roger. *The Sound of God's Voice*. Grand Rapids: Baker, 1998.

Barth, Karl. *Homiletics*. Louisville: John Knox, 1994.

Black, Hugh. *Listening to God*. New York: Revell, 1906.

Blackaby, Henry T. and Claude V. King. *Experiencing God*. Nashville: Lifeway, 1990.

Blackaby, Henry. *Experiencing God*. Nashville: Broadman & Holman, 1994.

Boman, Thorlief. *Hebrew Thought Compared with Greek*. London: SCM, 1960.

Buttrick, David. *Homiletic*. Philadelphia: Fortress, 1987.

Calvin, John. *Commentaries*. Grand Rapids: Baker, 1981.

———. *Institutes of the Christian Religion*. Philadelphia: Westminster, 1960.

Clarke, Adam. *Clarkes Commentary*. Nashville, Abingdon, n.d.

Crystal Links. "Mediation & Sleep." http://www.crystalinks.com/medbrain.html (accessed July 1, 2009).

Cox, Harvey. *Fire From Heaven*. Reading: Addison-Wesley, 1995.

Cromie, William J. "Research Links Sleep, Dreams, and Learning." *The Harvard University Gazette*, February 8, 1996. http://www.news.harvard.edu/gazette/ 1996/02.08 /ResearchLinksSl.html (accessedJuly 1, 2009).

Dayton, Donald W. *Theological Roots of Pentecostalism*. Peabody: Hendrickson, 1987.

Edersheim, Alfred. *The Life and Times of Jesus the Messiah*. Peabody: Hendrickson, 2004.

Edwards, J. Kent. *Deep Preaching*. Nashville: B&H Academic, 2009.

Eerdman, Charles R. "The Epistle to the Philippians." *Commentaries on the New Testament Books*. Philadelphia: Westminster, 1977.

Galli, Mark and Craig Brian Larson. *Preaching that Connects*. Grand Rapids: Zondervan, 1994.

Goetz, David. "Is the Pastor's Family Safe at Home?" *Leadership: A Practical Journal for Church Leaders* 13:4 (Fall 1992): 39.

Grudem, Wayne. *Systematic Theology*. Grand Rapids: Zondervan, 2000.

Harris, R. Laird, Gleason L. Archer, and Bruce K. Waltke. *The Theological Workbook of the Old Testament*. Chicago: Moody, 1980.

Heisler, Greg. *Spirit-Led Preaching*. Nashville: B&H Academic, 2007.

Henry, Carl F. H. *God, Revelation and Authority*. Waco: Word, 1976.

Hill, Andrew E. and John H. Walton. *A Survey of the Old Testament*. Grand Rapids: Zondervan, 2000.

Jackson, Anne. "Info-porn: Don't Spread the Bad Stats." FlowerDust.net. http://www.flowerdust.net/2007/12/26/christians-like-info-porn-don't-believe-the-stats/ (accessed July 02, 2009).

———. *Mad Church Disease*. Grand Rapids: Zondervan, 2009.

Charles Kello Galleries. "Charles Kello III." http://charleskellogalleries.com/Bio.aspx (accessed July 1, 2009).

————. "CharlesKelloGallaries.com." http://charleskellogalleries.com/default.aspx (accessed July 1, 2009).

Krejcir, Richard J. "Statistics on Pastors." The Francis Schaeffer Institute (FASICD). http://www.intothyword.org/apps/articles/default.asp?articleid=36562&columnid=39 58 (accessed July 2, 2009).

Lakoff, George and Mark Johnson. *Metaphors We Live By.* Chicago: University of Chicago, 1980.

Larsen, David. *The Anatomy of Preaching.* Grand Rapids: Kregal, 1989.

Lewis, Ralph L. and Greg Lewis. *Inductive Preaching.* Wheaton: Crossway, 1983.

————. *Learning to Preach Like Jesus.* Westchester: Crossway, 1989.

Lischer, Richard. *The End of Words.* Grand Rapids: Eerdmans, 2005.

Long, Jimmy. *Generating Hope: A Strategy for Reaching the Post-Modern Generation.* Downers Grove: Intervarsity, 1997.

Lowry, Eugene L. *How to Preach a Parable.* Nashville: Abingdon, 1989.

Mehrabian, Albert and Morton Wiener. "Decoding of Inconsistent Communications." *Journal of Personality and Social Psychology* 6, no.1 (1967): 109-114.

Mehrabian, Albert and Susan R. Ferris. "Inference of Attitudes from Non-verbal Communication in Two Channels." *Journal of Consulting Psychology* 31, no. 3 (1967): 248-252.

McFague, Sally. *Metaphorical Theology.* London: SCM, 1983.

McNeal, Reggie. *A Work of the Heart.* San Francisco: Jossey-Bass, 2000.

Miller, M. Rex. *The Millennium Matrix.* San Francisco: Jossey-Bass, 2004.

Miller, Mark. *Experiential Storytelling.* Grand Rapids: Zondervan, 2003.

Newbigin, Lesslie. *Foolishness to the Greeks.* Grand Rapids: Eerdmans, 1986.

Niebuhr, Richard H. *Christ and Culture.* New York: Harper & Row, 1956.

Olson, David T. *The American Church in Crisis.* Grand Rapids: Zondervan, 2008.

Ong, Walter J. *The Presence of the Word.* Minneapolis: University of Minnesota, 1967.

Palazzolo, Rose."Study: Boys' and Girls' Brain Process Differently." *ABC News,* July 10, 2009. http://abcnews.go.com/Health/story?id=117338&page=1 (accessed July 31, 2009).

Ramm, Bernard L. *The Pattern of Religious Authority.* Grand Rapids: Eerdmans, 1957.

Sadowski, Mark and Allan Paivio. *Imagery and Text: A Dual Code Theory for Reading and Writing.* Mahwah, New Jersey: Erlbaum, 2001.

Samples, Bob. *The Metaphoric Mind.* Menlo Park: Addison-Wesley, 1976.

Sapolsky, Robert M. *Why Zebras Don't Get Ulcers.* New York: Henry Holt, 2004.

Schaeffer, Francis A. *How Should We Then Live?* Old Tappen: Revell, 1976.

Scroggie, W. Graham. *A Guide to the Gospels.* Old Tappen: Revell, n.d.

Siegelman, Ellen Y. *Metaphor and Meaning in Psychotherapy.* New York: Guilford, 1990.

Sless, David. *Learning and Visual Communication.* New York: Wiley, 1981.

Spurgeon, Charles H. *The New Park Street Pulpit.* London: Alabaster & Passmore, 1859.

Stein, Robert. *A Basic Guide to Interpreting the Bible.* Grand Rapids: Baker, 1994.

Strickland, Carol. *The Annotated Mona Lisa: A Crash Course in Art History.* Kansas City: University Press, 1992.

Synan, Vinson. *The Century of the Holy Spirit.* Nashville: Thomas Nelson, 2001.

Thornsen, Donald A. D. *The Wesleyan Quadrilateral.* Indianapolis: Life & Light, 1990.

Tomlin, Graham. *Spiritual Fitness.* New York: Continuum, 2006.

Troeger, Thomas H. *Ten Strategies for Preaching in a Multimedia Culture.* Nashville: Abingdon, 1996.

Wiersbe, Warren W. *Preaching and Teaching with Imagination.* Grand Rapids: Baker, 1994.

Wesley, John. John Wesley to Dr. Rutherford, March 28, 1768. In *Letters,* edited by John Telford. London: Epworth, 1831.

Williams, J. Rodman. *Renewal Theology.* Grand Rapids: Zondervan, 1996.

Index

About the Author

Dr. James T. Flynn is originally from Pittsburgh, Pennsylvania, where he served in pastoral ministry for eighteen years. He helped to pioneer an interdenominational church there in 1976, serving as associate pastor as well as senior pastor and superintendent of the church's Christian day school. His education includes a Bachelor of Arts degree from Geneva College in Beaver Fall, Pennsylvania; a Master of Divinity degree from the Reformed Presbyterian Theological Seminary in Pittsburgh; and a Doctor of Ministry degree from Regent University in Virginia Beach, Virginia.

For the past eight years, Flynn has devoted his life to teaching and administration at Regent University in the School of Divinity with a focus on teaching practical theology. He has served as the administrative dean in the School of Divinity and was the founding dean of the Center for Professional Studies, which has since become the School of Undergraduate Studies. He is currently on the faculty of the School of Divinity as an associate professor of practical theology and the director of the school's Doctor of Ministry Program. He is active in his local church and in several para-church ministries, specializing in leadership training, discipleship, and nonprofit consulting. Flynn is the author of *A Well-Furnished Heart: Restoring the Spirit's Place in the Leadership Classroom* (2002) as well as numerous articles and workshops in the fields of preaching, distance education, pastoral theology, and Renewal-oriented theological education. He resides in Virginia Beach with his wife of thirty-three years, Monica. They have four grown children.

CPSIA information can be obtained at www.ICGtesting.com
Printed in the USA
BVOW08s0919080214

344297BV00003B/8/P